Prophecy in the Christian Era

Prophecy in the Christian Era

A study of Bob Dylan's work from 1961 to 1967, emphasizing his use of enigma to teach ethics, and comparing him to Dante Alighieri and other poets.

by Jenny Ledeen

December 1995

Peaceberry Press of Webster Groves, *St. Louis*

Table of Contents

Illustrations

Introduction

In lectures on the subject of "Poets Who Sing" I compare Bob Dylan to other singers, including Woody Guthrie, I talk about the evolution of American music, and I suggest that the efficacy of Dylan's work in the 1960s depended, to a great extent, on its musical component[1]; but in this essay I compare Dylan to Dante Alighieri and several other writers, and I pay scant attention to the subject of music. For this reason, I wish to point out in advance that some of the comparisons made in this text involve verse that was originally sung, not written. I am speaking now of verse composed over a thousand years ago in Old English, and of verse composed more than two thousand years ago in Hebrew. We do not know how these ancient texts were intoned, we do not know for certain who composed them, and we do not know how they influenced the historical moment in which they were produced. All that remains is the *words* of these texts; but this is just the point: words are the primary element through which prophecy is communicated.

It is easy to compare Dylan to Woody Guthrie, because we have audio recordings that enable us to confirm that Dylan consciously imitated Guthrie's composition and performance techniques, in 1961 and 1962, when he first began to perform in New York City. (He recreated Guthrie's sound almost miraculously–including the sound of Guthrie's accompanist's harmonica![2]) It is more difficult to show how Dylan has imitated Dante, since Dylan does not write verse that looks, or sounds, like Dante's. And the difference goes deeper than that Dante wrote in Italian and Dylan sings in English: Dante's monumental written works establish the highest standard of elegance and intelligence in Western poetics–especially his *Comedy*, which is an artificial memory system that stores information about Western history and culture; whereas Dylan sometimes imitates the diction of illiterate people, he concerns himself with the problems of poor and disenfranchised members of society, and he expresses dissent in such a way as to imply rejection of the West.

All the same, the likenesses between Dylan's work and Dante's are striking and significant. For example, Dante made himself the protagonist of his work, and so has Dylan; Dante addressed issues that were extremely controversial and obliged people to judge the morality of specific events of the day, and so has Dylan; Dante praised God in such a way as to suggest that God is manifest in the speech and conduct of gentle women, and so has Dylan; and Dante described visions of heaven and hell, and so has Dylan. I do not think that all these things can be said of any other poet[3]; but there is much more to be said about the likeness between Dante and Dylan.

I limit my discussion of Dylan's work to the first phase of his career, from the fall of 1961 until the fall of 1967–which is to say, from the time Dylan began to publish his compositions and win acclaim, to the time he stopped communicating with the public and fell silent for a full year. Furthermore, I limit my discussion to a few of Dylan's songs, a speech he gave in 1963, and one chapter from his book, *Tarantula*. In chapters 1 to 6 I review Dylan's work and the historical record concerning the impact he made on his generation during the 1960s, and I introduce comparisons between Dylan and other artists casually, as I proceed; but in chapters 7 and 8 I turn to the subject of enigma, and the comparisons, especially the comparison between Dante and Dylan, become all important.

In chapter 7 I compare the compositions that first brought Dante and Dylan fame, "To Every Chosen Soul and Gentle Heart" and "Blowin' in the Wind," which are both formal riddles. This is not the most obvious point of comparison between Dante's work and Dylan's; it is probably the most obscure one. I emphasize it because "To Every Chosen Soul" and "Blowin' in the Wind" concern human fate, and they teach ethics; and so far as I have been able to determine, this variety of riddle has not been identified before now, even though many books and articles have been written on the subject of enigma. In chapter 8 I name other examples of "ethical riddles."

A variety of poetic materials is printed in the appendix. The selections appear more or less according to the sequence in which they are named; but I gather Dylan's works together, then Dante's, then works by others. The translations of Dante's works are my own.[4] The sources used for other translations are named in footnotes. The last entry in the appendix is my response to Dante's riddle.

I would alert my reader that the first time I name Dylan's songs in this essay, I give the month and year of composition; but in almost every case the notation of the month is an approximation.

I thank my dear family, especially my mother and father, Clarence and Frieda Newberry, for their support, and for the way they went overboard for me and my children, again and again, during the years in which it was forbidden to write about Dylan, or to compare him to Dante, at Washington University. I thank Michel Rybalka, Richard Hazelton, Colbert Cartwright, Kenn Thomas, Randolph Pope, Mark Kornbluh, and Pinchas Giller, for helping me in this project. And I dedicate this essay to Bob Dylan.

Notes

1 "Poets Who Sing" was the title of a course I taught in 1986 and 1987, at Washington University.

2 Dylan's ability to reproduce Guthrie's sound is exemplified in "Talkin' World War Three Blues," which was released on *The Freewheelin' Bob Dylan* (1962). It sounds a lot like "Talkin' Dust Blues" by Guthrie, which was released on an album entitled, *Talkin' Dust Bowl* (Folkways, FA 2011) .

3 Years before Dylan was born Harry Dwight Sedgewick made the following remark about Dante: "Dante is a very great poet, but as a poet he has rivals, whereas as a prophet of righteousness he has no peer since the time of the Apostles." Harry Dwight Sedgewick, *Dante* (New Haven: Yale UP, 1918) 11.

4 My translations have been prepared from *Le Opere Di Dante, testo critico delta Societá Dantesca Italiana, a cura di* M. Barbi, E.G. Parodi, F. Pellegrini, E. Pistelli, P. Rajna, E. Rostagno, G. Vandelli, *col indice analitico dei nomi e delle cose di* Mario Casella (Firenze: R. Bemporad, 1921).

Chapter 1

"Where Were You In '62?"

In April 1962 Bob Dylan made up the words and music of "Blowin' in the Wind," the song that has been called the anthem of the peace movement. According to witnesses he brought his guitar and the lyrics of the song into a nightclub in Greenwhich Village one Monday afternoon, hoping to sing "Blowin' in the Wind" during an open-mic program scheduled for that evening.[1] He auditioned backstage for the master of ceremonies, who was his friend, Gil Turner. Turner loved the song; but he surprised Dylan by asking if he could sing "Blowin' in the Wind." Dylan agreed; and then he sat in the audience when his masterpiece was sung on stage for the first time. That incident was the beginning of the lionization of "Blowin' in the Wind," and a few hours later, when Turner sang "Blowin' in the Wind," some of his listeners, who had never heard the song before, sang along with the chorus! Things may not have gone exactly the way Dylan planned that day, but in retrospect it would seem that Monday, April 16, 1962, may be set down as the beginning of the peace movement.

Dylan's life at that time, and the world in which he moved, have been examined very carefully by a number of scholars, and a wealth of information about Dylan's activities during 1962 has been published; however, the relationship between "Blowin' in the Wind" and the rise of the peace movement has not been explained adequately. No historian seems to have noticed, for example, that "Blowin' in the Wind" circulated for over a year before it was heard on the radio, or that in this period it functioned very effectively as a confrontational device, and as a means of instruction on points of ethics of critical interest to members of the peace movement.

One reason why no one has addressed this subject before now may be that it concerns the attitudes and behavior of private citizens–especially adolescents and young adults, like Dylan himself, who was only twenty years old when he wrote "Blowin' in the Wind." Most accounts concerning the beginning of the peace movement focus on a number of other events, including the arrest and incarceration of Dr. Martin Luther King in

Birmingham, John Kennedy's decision to send American troops to Vietnam, and the Cuban missile crisis—all of which took place in 1962; and they proceed through analysis of the decisions and actions of official leaders of formal organizations. But the story of the peace movement really cannot properly be told through reference to these events or the actions of official leaders of formal organizations, alone; because the peace movement was religious in character as well as political, it was not organized, and it had no leader—except, perhaps, Bob Dylan, who usually communicated with the public by singing. In my opinion, the history of America in the '60s does not make sense, unless we recognize that Dylan communicated more effectively with his generation than any official leader did, and that his songs, especially "Blowin' in the Wind," influenced the attitudes and conduct of millions of people who might otherwise never have become involved with politics and dissent.

Wayne Hampton, the author of a book entitled, *Guerrilla Minstrels*, comes precisely to the point when he says, "The politicization of popular music was to be (Dylan's) major contribution to the generation of the 1960s,"[2] and when he goes on to say that Dylan advanced "a Christian-based moralism."[3] However, Hampton does not explore the relationship between "Blowin' in the Wind" and the peace movement; and even though he calls Dylan "the most important voice in popular protest in western civilization,"[4] he fails to explain what it is that sets Dylan apart from Joe Hill, Woody Guthrie, and John Lennon, whose works absorb his interest as much as Dylan's.

One historian who makes reference to Dylan as well as to official leaders, as he attempts to analyze the revolutionary political events of the 1960s, is Allen Matusow, author of *The Unraveling of America*. He calls Dylan, "the artist who first seized the power of rock and used it to change consciousness"[5]; but his only reference to "Blowin' in the Wind" concerns the commercial success of "Peter, Paul, and Mary's" recording of the song. He has nothing to say about how this song "changed consciousness" during the months in which it first circulated—before it was recorded, or broadcast on radio.

An important part of the story would be that the night "Blowin' in the Wind" was sung for the first time the audience included a number of musicians who recognized the virtue of the song and were immediately eager to sing it–including Pete Seeger, who was older than Dylan, and more famous both as a performer and as a political dissident.[6] Seeger sang "Blowin' in the Wind" regularly after that night, and before the end of summer hundreds of other performers, including Joan Baez, were singing "Blowin' in the Wind," too. The preference for this song that was shown by notable entertainers enabled many more people to hear it, before it began to be heard on radio, and during the time that elapsed before Dylan became well-known; but the popularity of "Blowin' in the Wind" was increased by means of the printed word, as well. Page 4 shows the May 1962 issue of a publication called *Broadside*, which bears the words and musical text of "Blowin' in the Wind." In this format "Blowin' in the Wind" passed from hand to hand among amateur folk music enthusiasts, some of whom began to sing it at civil rights demonstrations.

The appearance of "Blowin' in the Wind" on the cover of *Broadside* was not a chance occurrence; Dylan contributed regularly to *Broadside*, which announced to its readers that it existed in order to publish topical songs. Very little information about the production and distribution of *Broadside* has been recorded, but it is clear that *Broadside* was a low-budget enterprise. It offered no commercial advertising, it was typed on an ordinary typewriter, it was reproduced on a mimeograph machine, and it sold for 35 cents. Dylan published a song in the first and third editions of *Broadside*, before he composed "Blowin' in the Wind," which appeared in the sixth edition. After "Blowin' in the Wind" he published eighteen other songs in *Broadside* during the course of 1962, 1963, and 1964.

Broadside established precedents that would influence the character of the peace movement for years, because it was a noncommercial endeavor that looked to musicians for political leadership. Most important, *Broadside* provided Dylan a means of communication that would not censor him or slow down the distribution of his work. Dylan had signed a recording contract with Columbia Records in the autumn of 1961, and Columbia

4

PRICE -- 35¢

© 1962, by BROADSIDE

BROADSIDE # 6, LATE MAY 1962   BOX 193, CATHEDRAL STATION, NEW YORK 25, N.Y.

Blowin' in the Wind
by Bob Dylan

© 1962 by AUTHOR

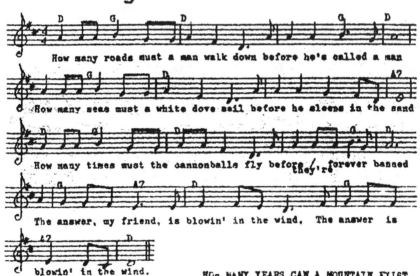

HOW MANY YEARS CAN A MOUNTAIN EXIST,
BEFORE IT'S WASHED IN THE SEA
HOW MANY YEARS CAN SOME PEOPLE EXIST, BEFORE THEY'RE ALLOWED TO BE FREE
HOW MANY TIMES CAN A MAN TURN HIS HEAD, AND PRETEND HE JUST DOESN'T SEE
    THE ANSWER, MY FRIEND, etc.

HOW MANY TIMES MUST A MAN LOOK UP, BEFORE HE CAN SEE THE SKY
HOW MANY EARS MUST ONE MAN HAVE, BEFORE HE CAN HEAR PEOPLE CRY
HOW MANY DEATHS WILL IT TAKE 'TIL HE KNOWS THAT TOO MANY PEOPLE HAVE DIED
    THE ANSWER, MY FRIEND, etc.

released his first album in March 1962[7]; however, Columbia did not produce recordings of his work quickly enough to suit Dylan, and he had reason to fear that some of the songs he recorded in their studios would never be released because of their political content. At the time "Talkin' John Birch Paranoid Blues," which mocked the John Birch Society, was a case in point: Columbia withheld it and *Broadside* published it. All of the songs Dylan published in *Broadside* were topical, and some of them–like "Masters of War," "A Hard Rain's A-Gonna Fall," and "The Lonesome Death of Hattie Carroll"–might be counted among his finest works of the period.

In September 1962 "Blowin' in the Wind" was also published in a quarterly magazine for folk music devotees called, *Sing Out!*, which had a much wider circulation than *Broadside*. In December 1962 a recording of "Blowin' in the Wind" by a male trio called, "The Chad Mitchell Trio," was released in an album.[8] Although this recording was not promoted on the radio, it is noteworthy because The Chad Mitchell Trio was a successful ensemble, they recorded other politically-sensitive songs, and they sang controversial material regularly in their concerts.

In the winter of 1962 the anti-war movement had barely begun to gather force, but the civil rights movement was beginning to crest. By the time a 45 rpm single of "Blowin' in the Wind" was released–which was in June 1963–tens of thousands of people already knew the words, and were accustomed to singing along with the chorus. And a few weeks later the participants in the largest and most spectacular civil rights demonstration of them all, the "March on Washington" of August 1963, sang it at the Lincoln Memorial. Dylan, Joan Baez, Pete Seeger, and "Peter, Paul and Mary," who recorded the 45 rpm single of "Blowin' in the Wind," actually stood on stage with Dr. King, when a throng of some 250,000 people sang "Blowin' in the Wind" together.

Peter, Paul and Mary's recording of "Blowin' in the Wind," which was produced by Warner Records, was the biggest hit Warner had ever had[9]; but statistics about the sales of their recording of "Blowin' in the Wind" tell us nothing about the phenomenon of real historic consequence–which is, that men and women who were *not* entertainers chose to sing this song, and in doing so made themselves advocates of the ideas it contains. I say "contains," rather than "expresses," because "Blowin' in the Wind" is an enigma: it invites us to find its meaning and define its contents. It makes no sense until we fit its clues together and reason over them; and even then its meaning must be chosen from two distinct possibilities—as is characteristic of the way true enigmata work. That is to say, the questions "Blowin' in the Wind" asks concerning human cruelty and indifference are answered by the idea of judgment before God at the end of time—that is why "Blowin' in the Wind" is still sung in American churches, synagogues, and schools, today, more than thirty years after it was written. It is important to add, however, that some people have assumed that the answer to "Blowin' in the Wind's" questions would be revolution.

During 1962 and 1963, as "Blowin' in the Wind" circulated by word-of-mouth and in print, it sowed the one idea that was essential to the peace movement, because the peace movement linked the civil rights movement and the antiwar movement, and transcended both of them—which is, that racism, militarism, and authoritarianism are interrelated, and are evil. It does not state this idea or explain it, but it does contain it, as well as the idea that one day human cruelty will be brought to an end. It does not say that the person who is singing knows how this will happen, or that he has seen God or heard God's voice; but ideas of that sort reside within this song—along with the idea that the singer speaks in God's stead.

Several people who have written about Dylan's work have made rather disparaging remarks about "Blowin' in the Wind," apparently because the naive quality of Dylan's expression, in this instance, persuaded them that anyone could write such a song. Actually, there are few poetic works that can properly be compared to "Blowin' in the Wind." "The Battle Hymn of the Republic" is like it in that "The Battle Hymn of the Republic" describes a vision of God and the day of God's judgment, and in that it is another example of a song that was chosen by the general community as a means of expressing the idea that human life should be respected, and that we should love one another; but "The Battle Hymn of the Republic" is explicit in mode, whereas "Blowin' in the Wind" is enigmatic. ("The Battle Hymn" is printed in the appendix beginning on page 239.[10])

Among riddles, I have found only one that is truly like "Blowin' in the Wind" in character–a riddle-sonnet written by Dante Alighieri, which begins with the words, "To Every Chosen Soul and Gentle Heart."[11] It is not like "Blowin' in the Wind" in form; but it is like "Blowin' in the Wind" in that it concerns a vision of the future and of God, and in that it contains an ethical precept that was of grave concern to a segment of the community at the time it was written–which is, that women are precious in God's sight. ("To Every Chosen Soul" is printed in the appendix on page 214.)

There are several differences between the way "To Every Chosen Soul" and "Blowin' in the Wind" work; but the only difference between them that is pertinent to this discussion of "Blowin' in the Wind's" influence on the peace movement is this: "To Every Chosen Soul" was made to be read, and "Blowin' in the Wind" was made to be sung. For a situation was created whenever "Blowin' in the Wind" was performed that enabled people to show that they were opposed to racism and militarism–all they had to do was to sing along. And just as important, this act of participation enabled them to see the faces and hear the voices of other men and women who were singing with them. It was this discovery of like-mindedness and this experience of communion that ignited the grassroots uprising called, "the peace movement."

Men and women of virtually every age, race, and religious persuasion participated in the peace movement; but the segment of the population that was represented most conspicuously in its ranks was made up of young people like Bob Dylan and Joan Baez, who were teenagers when they began to sing songs of political protest. The support of the civil rights movement by youth was indispensable to the success of that movement; furthermore, involvement in the civil rights movement "radicalized" young protesters, and opened their eyes to the racist aspect of American involvement in war in Vietnam. But no group, organization, or cause, owned the peace movement–although some scholars argue that an organization called Students for a Democratic Society was at the center of the antiwar movement. Todd Gitlin, who was president of S.D.S. in 1963, makes precisely this claim in his book, *The Sixties*; but it is interesting to read in Gitlin's account that it was when Bob Dylan made one brief appearance at an S.D.S. meeting that they knew that they were "at the center."[12]

Gitlin's interpretation of the events of the 1960s is particularly offensive in one regard–his remarks about the sexual conduct of members of S.D.S., which are summed up by him in these words: "The movement hung together on the head of a penis."[13] He continues for pages on this subject, saying at one point, "There (were) fewer women in the inner circle from the start"; and at another point, "The vulgar way to say it is that the clan was consolidated through the exchange of women."[14]   Gitlin admits that the total membership of S.D.S. was only eleven hundred people in the summer of 1963, and that there were not a dozen chapters[15]; but he never acknowledges, or shows that he understands, that membership of S.D.S. grew because of the popularity of the peace movement, not vice versa. He clings to his sexist interpretation of events, even though he identifies a women's organization that was a predecessor of the peace movement, and may have been the source of its name.   He merely says, in passing, that an organization called, Women Strike for Peace, mobilized over 50,000 women across the country, in November 1961, to protest against the testing of nuclear weapons.[16]

S.D.S. did not lead the peace movement, and it was not at the center of the movement, either. It would be more reasonable to say that Dylan led the peace movement, and that Dylan was at the movement's center. This is what his reputation as a prophet tells us about him! While he was still a youth, he began to write songs that teach ethics. One of the first songs of this sort that he wrote moved people to sing; and when they sang together a bond of love grew up between them. This extraordinary phenomenon happened years after Martin Buber wrote the following passage about the prophets of Israel; but what he said might apply to Dylan:

> (The prophets) never announced a God upon whom their hearers' striving for security reckoned. They always aimed to shatter all security and to proclaim in the opened abyss of the final insecurity the unwished for God who demands that His human creatures become real, and that they become human.[17]

Notes

The title of this chapter is printed inside quotation marks because it appeared as a rubric in the publicity for the movie, *American Graffiti*, which portrays teenage boys and girls who are graduating from highschool in the year 1962. The movie focuses on one character in particular–a young man who is about to leave home to prepare for undergraduate studies at a distinguished university in New England. The makers of *American Graffiti* assumed that their viewers would know that anyone who began studies at an ivy league school, in 1962, would be touched by the peace movement. (*American Graffiti* was directed by George Lucas [Universal-Lucasfilm Ltd., 1973].)

1　David Blue was with Dylan that day. His account of what happened is recorded in a book about the nightclub where "Blowin' in the Wind" was first performed. Robbie Woliver, *Bringing It All Back Home: Twenty-five Years of American Music at Folk City* (New York: Pantheon, 1986) 83-84.

2　Wayne Hampton, *Guerrilla Minstrels* (Knoxville: U of Tennessee P, 1986) 160.

3　Hampton 162.

4　Hampton 199.

5　Allen Matusow, *The Unraveling of America: A History of the Liberalism of the 1960s* (New York: Harper and Row, 1984) 294.

6　Seeger played with Guthrie in the 1940s, and he was a member of the "Almanac Singers" in the 1950s. He was called before the House of Representatives "Committee on Un-American Activities" in 1960, to answer questions about his politics and his loyalty.

7　*Bob Dylan,* is the title of the album, but it includes only one original composition–"Song to Woody."

8　Chad Mitchell Trio, *In Action*, Kapp Records, 1961.

9　Robert Shelton says almost 800,000 copies sold in the first eight days. Shelton also provides details that suggest that Dylan's manager and Peter, Paul and Mary made a deal behind Dylan's back to enable Peter, Paul and Mary to release a single of "Blowin' in the Wind," rather than Dylan. Robert Shelton, *No Direction Home: The Life and Music of Bob Dylan* (New York: Ballantine, 1986) 182, 3.

10　I mention "The Battle Hymn of the Republic" again in chapter 8, and give details there concerning authorship.

11　"To Every Chosen Soul and Gentle Heart" is the first poetic entry in the *New Life*. It was written in 1282, when Dante was seventeen years old. It is discussed in chapter 7.

12 Todd Gitlin, *The Sixties: Years of Hope, Days of Rage* (New York: Ballantine, 1986) 183.

13 Gitlin 108.

14 Gitlin 109.

15 Gitlin 109.

16 Gitlin 92.

17 Martin Buber, "Religion and Modern Thinking," *Eclipse of God*, trans. Maurice Friedman (New York: Harper, 1954) 97.

Chapter 2

The Nightingale's Code

Early in 1963 Dylan responded to the idea that he was a prophet in a song, with the words, "I know I ain't no prophet / And I ain't no prophet's son!"[1]; but from time to time he would write another song that hinted about Judgment Day the way "Blowin' in the Wind" did–by making reference to the wind, the rain, or other effects of a storm, including especially a deluge like the great flood described in the Bible.

The first time he came back to this meteorological "conceit" was in September 1962, when he wrote "A Hard Rain's A-Gonna Fall." He returned to it, again, in August 1963 with "When the Ship Comes In," in September 1963 with "The Times They Are A-Changin'," in February 1964 with "Chimes of Freedom," in October 1964 with "Gates of Eden," in December 1964 with "It's All Over Now, Baby Blue," in July 1965 with "Desolation Row," and in November 1965 with "Visions of Johanna." Dylan suddenly retired in the summer of 1966; but during the first year and a half of his retirement he continued to make up new songs, and among them was one more song that seemed to say that the end of the world was coming by referring to a storm. The date of composition of "All Along The Watchtower" has not been established, but it was recorded in November 1967. After that Dylan stopped communicating with the public altogether, for a while, and brought an end to the phase of his career in which his reputation as the prophet of the peace movement was established.

Between the fall of 1961 when he signed his first recording contract, and the fall of 1967 when he concluded his apocalypse, Dylan wrote dozens of songs that enhanced his reputation as a prophet; but "Blowin' in the Wind" and these nine other storm songs would probably be the best examples of prophecy from Dylan's compositions of that period, because of the way they worked in tandem to describe the coming of the Messiah, and heaven and hell.

Although these songs spoke darkly they shed light on numerous contemporary issues. Individually and in ensemble, they offered a complex critique of American society—which is a matter of utmost concern to the historical record, because the characteristic that distinguished the conduct of members of the peace movement was that they participated in political demonstrations on behalf of several social causes. In fact, four of these storm songs, "Blowin' in the Wind," "A Hard Rain's A-Gonna Fall," "When the Ship Comes In," and "The Times They Are A-Changin'," have repeatedly been mentioned or quoted by historians, in passing, when they discuss the civil rights movement and the antiwar movement. The other six songs, "Chimes of Freedom," "Gates of Eden," "It's All Over Now, Baby Blue," "Desolation Row," "Visions of Johanna," and "All Along the Watchtower," are more difficult than the first four, and they are not cited by historians; nevertheless, they had an influence on the evolution of the peace move-ment—especially the ones that Dylan played with rock and roll instrumentation ("Desolation Row" and "Visions of Johanna")—because after Dylan started playing with a rock and roll band he was able to reach a much younger, and much larger, audience.

I have one more reason for naming these ten songs as outstanding examples of prophecy, which has to do with the fact that they are all high-ly enigmatic—that is, when Dylan discovered the rhetorical means to address religious issues and political issues simultaneously, through enigma, he dis-covered one of the means used in magic cultures to make rain. I would assume that he did so instinctively, without thinking about rainmaking—as I would assume he crafted the music of these songs, which might be called "dance music," without thinking about dancing. Nevertheless, his discovery of this poetic device, which has been used since prehistoric times to make rain, was highly appropriate; for Dylan not only pretended to describe the Messiah's coming by describing an approaching storm, he pretended again and again to wish for that storm to begin. He even prayed for the Messiah to come in one song, "Mr. Tambourine Man," which he wrote in 1964. There the idea that the "tambourine man" will take him for a ride on his ship provides the best clue to the idea that he was addressing God, and was asking God to come (verse 2). There is no direct reference to the storm in "Mr. Tambourine Man," but Dylan hinted about the fate of the world by calling the world "evening's empire," and by saying that he wished to see himself beside the sea, at dawn, dancing, laughing, and ready to depart.

I will return to the subject of enigma. For now one observation about the genre should suffice: what makes riddles work is detail that does not make sense, or that runs counter to ordinary experience. In Dylan's storm songs it is what he implied about the way the storm will be related to society, above all, that is odd; furthermore, this is the essential prophetic content of these songs. For example, "Blowin' in the Wind" and "A Hard Rain's A-Gonna Fall" suggest that the storm will end cruelty and unkindness; "The Times They Are A-Changin'" suggests that people can help to bring the storm, but cannot stop it; "When the Ship Comes In" and "Chimes of Freedom" suggest that some people will be lifted up above the waters of the storm, while others will be swept away by them; "Gates of Eden" and "Visions of Johanna" suggest that some people will live happily in a garden after the storm, while others will be confined in a place of abject misery; and "It's All Over Now, Baby Blue," "Desolation Row," and "All Along the Watchtower" suggest, among other things, that the storm will take people by surprise.

Other enigmatic detail in the narratives sketched by these songs concerns the "ship" that will carry people who are saved to heaven. In "When The Ship Comes In" Dylan suggested that he and his friends will watch from the deck of this ship when the sea washes their enemies away (verse 8). He called it a "magic swirling ship" in "Mr. Tambourine Man" (verse 2); but in "Visions of Johanna" he used a more puzzling expression to describe a ship that has to do with one of the functions of ships. A ship hauls people and equipment for fishing, or a ship can haul fish back to land; so Dylan called the Messiah's ship a "fish truck" (verse 5). In "Gates of Eden" he suggested that there will be more than one ship to carry the saints to heaven, calling them "ships with tattooed sails" (verse 2). The idea that passage to another life might be like passage in a boat, over a river or sea, would seem to be universal; but Dylan's suggestion that the ships that carry souls to heaven will have something written, or drawn, or their sails may have been his innovation–certainly, his way of working with this idea was uniquely his own in "It's All Over Now, Baby Blue," where he pretended that the "empty-handed painter" was getting the ship ready by "drawing crazy patterns" on Baby Blue's "sheets"—which is another word for sails (verse 2). This was one of Dylan's more carefully hidden references to the ship, the storm, and the Messiah; but an equally difficult reference could be found in "Chimes of Freedom," where Dylan pretended to describe the moment of salvation and rescue as an event that had already happened, and said that he and his companions "ducked inside the doorway" to refer to their entry into the ship (verse 1). But the most obscure reference to the ship in all of Dylan's published songs of the period is the first reference he made to her, in "Blowin' in the Wind," where he compared her to a bird, and called her, *The White Dove*.[2]

Dylan worked with an unusual and ambiguous assortment of images to name the Messiah in these songs. In "Gates of Eden" he called him, "the cowboy angel" (verse 1) and "silver-studded phantom" (verse 5)[3]; in "It's All Over Now, Baby Blue" he called him, "the empty-handed painter" (verse 2) and "the vagabond" (verse 4); in "Desolation Row" he called him, "the Good Samaritan" (verse 3) and "the Phantom of the Opera" (verse 7); and in "Visions of Johanna" Dylan called Christ, "the fiddler" (verse 5).

The most common enigmatic references in these songs, and in Dylan's repertoire in general, concern the sea, the rain, and the element of water, per se. They include Dylan's subtlest images—beginning with two references to the sea that appear in "Blowin' in the Wind": he envisioned the "dove" sailing the seas in search of a place to rest; and he envisioned a "mountain" washing into the sea. There was not another word in this song, except in the chorus, to help Dylan's listeners understand that he had begun to sketch visions of a global deluge—but that was exactly what he was doing.

In "Hard Rain" Dylan made his meaning regarding the flood much clearer; however, the figure in this song that suggests most powerfully that water will cover the entire earth is profoundly enigmatic. It is near the conclusion, in the line which says, "I'll stand on the ocean until I start sinkin'." The wording might bring to mind the biblical anecdote concerning Jesus walking on water, and Peter sinking into it[4]; but Dylan's curious way of expressing himself in this case is not altogether different from the way he expressed himself in "Blowin' in the Wind," in the line, "How many years can a mountain exist before it is washed to the sea?" In both cases the listener is obliged to discover that the singer sees a flood in his mind's eye when he looks at dry land, and that for him the mountain will be "washed to the sea" in the same way that he will "start sinkin'" into the ocean—that is, the rising water will bring the sea up to them.

The influence of the English ballad, "Lord Randall," on "Hard Rain" is obvious, because Dylan borrowed the melody of "Lord Randall," and he imitated the dramatic situation presented in "Lord Randall" in his song—that is, ostensibly the song is a dialogue between a young man and his mother, concerning matters of life and death. But the self-portrait Dylan created in "Hard Rain" is nothing like the portrait of "Lord Randall," who came home to "lie down" and to die.[5] Dylan pretended that he was "going back out" (verse 5) and that he was going to "sing"; and when he said he would "walk to the depths of the deepest dark forest," he showed that he had read Dante's *Inferno*, and that he intended to do what Dante had done—that is, he would pretend to visit hell and to write about what he would see there.[6]

The only time Dylan explicitly pretended to describe the ship, the rescue of the saints, and the destruction of the damned, was in "When The Ship Comes In." In this song he scrambled the sequence of events, slightly, as he told his story: he described what will happen when the ship first appears in verses 1, 2, 3, and 4; he described what will happen when the ship arrives at heaven's shore in verses 5 and 6; and then he described what will happen when the ship departs from this world in verses 7 and 8. Although Dylan did not explicitly say so, here or anywhere else, the sea was all that separated heaven, as he envisioned it, from hell. It was a living part of a world in which everything was animated and happy (verses 1, 2, and 3); and it was also a monster that had broken its "chains" in the night to attack (verse 4). When Dylan pretended, in verses 7 and 8, that he and his companions will be able to see through the walls and into the bedrooms of people who "will be drowned in the tide," he was working with an idea he had already begun to elaborate in "Masters of War," and would continue to elaborate in "The

Times They Are A-Changin'," "It's All Over Now, Baby Blue," and "Desolation Row."

In "Masters of War," which Dylan wrote about six months before "When the Ship Comes In," he characterized his enemies and summoned them with the words, "You who hide behind walls!" and "You who hide behind desks!"; and he suggested that he could see through his enemies themselves, by comparing them to water that carries away sewage (verse 3). This would seem to have been the lowest comparison he could create–using water as his reference, that is–because it not only suggested that his enemies were filthy, it suggested that they had lost their proper form, and were no longer fully human.[7] "Masters of War" is not a riddle, and it does not make reference to the storm; but it is prophetic, because it is a formal curse: it names the enemy (verse 1); it invokes Jesus by name when it says that the enemy will "never" be forgiven (verse 6); and it expresses a wish that the enemy will "die" (verse 8).

"Masters of War" would be a fine example of the songs Dylan wrote, in addition to his storm-warning songs, that helped promote his reputation as a prophet; but "The Times They Are A-Changin'," which was Dylan's fourth storm song, proclaimed that the peace movement was a revolutionary movement in more explicit terms than anything he had written before, or anything he would write later. Its title, "The Times They Are A-Changin'," became one of the most frequently repeated catchphrases of the decade; however, journalists and historians used it to describe the present, whereas Dylan used it to describe the future, as well. He specified that he was talking to "writers and critics" (verse 2), "senators and congressmen" (verse 3), and "mothers and fathers" (verse 4); and what he told them was to leave young people alone, and to prepare to see destruction.

This was not the first time Dylan indicated that he was speaking on behalf of youth–he did so very subtly in the first line of "Blowin' in the Wind," and he did so most explicitly in "Masters of War"; but in "The Times They Are A-Changin'" he did not address militarism or racism. Working with the image of the "new road" to speak of the peace movement (verse 4), and pretending once again that he could see through things, and could speak to people inside buildings (verse 3), Dylan suggested three things about the movement: its members were gathered outdoors, they were young, and they were at war with their elders. He suggested that the authorities were indoors, that they were old, and that they were going to be defeated. When Dylan said that the "battle" was going to shake the "windows" and rattle the "walls" of the enemy, he equated the peace movement with the storm, and in effect he cursed cities and buildings, along with the people inside them.

"Chimes of Freedom" also mentions "walls" that will be destroyed at the end of time (verse 2), but the first reference in it to a structure, "We ducked inside the doorway thunder crashing" (verse 1), refers to the ship, not to a building; however, Dylan did not mention the ship, or the sea, in this song. He depicted the storm by speaking of the lightning and thunder, the "rain" (verse 2), the "hail" (verse 3), and a "cloud's white curtain" (verse 5)[8]; but to interpret his story the listener has to recognize that the events concerning the singer and his companions are told in reverse chronological sequence: verse 6 tells what happened first, "Starry-eyed and laughing...we were caught / ... / We listened...we watched...spellbound"; verse two tells what happened next, "In the city's melted furnace unexpectedly we watched / With faces hidden while the walls were tightening"; and verse one tells what happened last, "We ducked inside the doorway." If the listener turns past tense verbs to future tense, and reverses the sequence of the song's events, Dylan's prophecy emerges: the Messiah will come to claim his people before the storm hits; he will take them onto his ship; and as the world is destroyed he will take them to heaven.

"Chimes of Freedom" is less obviously political in character than "The Times They Are A-Changin'," and less obviously prophetic, because Dylan used the past tense in this song to describe what will happen in the future. It closely resembles "The Times They Are A-Changin'" in that it implies that the singer is a member of a company of people who will be saved. "When the Ship Comes In" makes this sort of statement, too; but after "Chimes of Freedom" Dylan pretended to describe the situation of the damned in four storm songs—"Gates of Eden," "It's All Over Now, Baby Blue," "Desolation

Row," and "Visions of Johanna." The ugly things he had to say about people in these songs, and problematic nature of the way these songs are constructed, make them difficult to contemplate—that is, they depict perversion and vanity, and they relate events in reverse chronological sequence. However, there is also humor in the way Dylan mocked his enemies, and in the way he envisioned the Messiah, in these songs.

"Gates of Eden" is the only song among these storm-warning-songs that hints that the vision it describes was seen in a dream, at night, during sleep; it is also the only one that seems to include references to Dylan's personal life. Verse 5 envisions him on stage, singing. Verse 8 envisions an empty "bed" that he said was "never" his. Verse 9 identifies a woman called, "my lover." The remark in that verse to the effect that she does not try to understand her "dreams" introduces the possibility that she dreamed the things the song describes—that is, that the song concerns the woman's dream, not the singer's. Dylan may have been hinting that he had met the woman he was going to marry; and, simultaneously, he may have been speaking allegorically in this reference to a woman of the dawn, in order to suggest that the day he described in this song is the "last day."

The content of the dream is revealed in verses 1, 3, 4, and 6; but the task of interpretation is made especially difficult by the fact that Dylan prefaced his narrative in verse 1 with an abstraction expressed in convoluted syntax, and then he entered the narrative abruptly—seemingly in the middle of forming a simile ("Of war and peace the truth just twists / Its curfew gull just glides / Upon four-legged forest clouds the cowboy angel rides..."). Furthermore, he interrupted his dream-narrative in verses 2, 5, 7, 8, and 9, to describe and comment on the world around him; and in those verses he used terms that blur the distinction between what was seen in the world and what was seen in the dream. For example, in verse 2 he said, "The lamppost stands with folded arms / Its iron claws attached / To curbs 'neath holes where babies wail." But in contrast to the ugly things he described in the world and in his vision of hell, he referred to heaven as a place with "trees" (verse 2), and he called it, "Eden." He also indicated that light could be seen there (verse 1), and laughter could be heard there (verse 4).

The only references to the storm in this song are extremely vague. There are no references to wind, rain, lightning, or flood, per se; but the first dramatic image in the song envisions a "gull" in flight, which implies the presence of an ocean, or a large river or lake, the second scene envisions "clouds," which implies the presence of moisture and the potential for rain, and the third scene envisions a "beach" and departing "ships," which distinctly implies the presence of the sea. All of these figures are clustered at the beginning of the song–which is to say, at the end of the story, at nightfall. In order to make sense of them the listener has to "see" all the song's images, and interpret all of its events; and this means that the listener has to know something about Dylan's other work, and the realm of ideas he tended to explore.

The song begins with a conclusion, which can be restated prosaically something like this: "The truth about war and peace will be revealed at the end of time"–that is, it expresses this thought enigmatically. It ends with a hypothesis that can be rephrased: "The truth may be revealed in dreams." Retold in normal chronological sequence, in the future tense, the dream narrative can be retold something like this: the Phantom and the "motorcycle-black-madonna-two-wheeled-gypsy-queen" will ride into the world; the "dwarf" in "grey flannel" will "scream" when he sees them; "Aladdin" and the "monks" will make a futile attempt to break out of hell; the "soldier," the "hunter," and the "dogs" will panic when they see the ships leaving them behind; then the cowboy angel will ride into paradise bearing light, a feast will begin "beneath the trees," and a bird will fly over the waters that will separate heaven from hell.

In "It's All Over Now, Baby Blue" Dylan pretended that the end of the world had come, and that the woman he was speaking to–"Baby Blue"–did not understand what had happened. He was speaking to her through the door of her house, and he could see her inside. He saw her strike a match in verse 4, apparently because the lights went out, for her, at about the time she heard him at the door. He saw the carpet being pulled out from under her in verse 3. He could read her mind as she continued to hesitate, wondering which way to go, and what to take with her, in verse 2. He told her to "grab" something that would "last," and he also insinuated that she was already dead, because he referred to her "orphan" in verse 1. In the third line of verse 1 he characterized this orphan by saying that he had a "gun," and that he was "crying".⁹ The fourth line, "Look out, the saints are coming through!" told the listener rather explicitly that this song was apocalyptic; but Dylan made only one reference to the storm–the enigmatic reference to the ship he made by saying the empty-handed painter was drawing patterns on Baby Blue's sheets.

There are several hints about the storm in "Desolation Row." Dylan pretended that he was one of the damned, and that he was inside a building talking to someone outside–which is to say, the dramatic situation presented in this song is similar to the dramatic situation in "It's All Over Now, Baby Blue," except that the role Dylan assumed in "Desolation Row" is the opposite role. He was playing a part like Baby Blue's, but he only seemed to be speaking to someone outside his door in verse 10; the rest of the time he seemed to be talking to himself about what was happening, and about what happened before the "doorknob broke." Someone called, "lady," was shut inside with him, which suggests that they were together when the world was suddenly transformed. The singer describes some of the sights and sounds of hell in verses 1, 2, 5, 6, and 8, and in the first half of verse 9. In the second half of verse 9 he describes heaven, mentioning laughing "calypso singers," "fisherman," "flowers," and "lovely mermaids" he glimpsed for a moment through the "windows of the sea"; but in verse 7 he indicates that his view of heaven–"across the street"–was permanently cut off, when cloud "curtains" were "nailed up," and the "Phantom" separated people he was going to leave behind from those he was taking to heaven. Dylan referred to water as a "window" again in verse 4, when he had the singer say that "Ophelia" was "beneath the window" wearing an "iron vest."¹⁰

In verse 3 the singer speaks about events he did not see, that unfolded when the storm hit and the Messiah "showed" himself. It may seem that another person is speaking in this verse; but the sardonic allusions to "Cain and Abel" and the "Hunchback of Notre Dame" indicate that the speaker is the same individual speaking in the other verses. Knowledge of the other "side" of the sea, and of the rescue that was carried out while he and "lady" were "making love," has come to him too late. He does not really understand, and he will never see heaven.

In "Visions of Johanna" Dylan pretended once again that he was in hell; this time he pretended he was inside a building with two other people: "Louise" and "Little Boy Lost." His song is a monologue; and as in previous songs he described what was happening to him and his companions, and what had happened to them, in a chaotic and surreal way. The first verse envisions the last event in his story: Little Boy Lost and Louise are in bed, and the singer stands near them. The second verse envisions scenes in hell outside the room where the singer, Louise, and Little Boy Lost are imprisoned. The third verse suggests that the singer is in Louise's embrace, and that Little Boy Lost stands with his face turned to the wall. The fourth verse seems to envision the Louvre and its patrons as a part of hell. And the fifth verse envisions the Messiah loading passengers aboard ship—which would be the first event of the story, if it were told chronologically.

The most important clues to this interpretation are the references to the "opposite loft" (verse 1), where there are lights and music, references to the fiddler and the fish truck (verse 5), references to the rain (verses 1 and 5), to electricity, i.e., lightning (verse 2), and to harmonicas, i.e., wind (verse 5). The idea that a cold rain will fall in hell, and that the damned will be naked, are ideas Dylan may have borrowed from Dante and the *Inferno*. In Dante's story the damned are naked and cold, and are exposed to bad weather[11]; whereas Dylan envisioned the damned as being indoors. Nevertheless, the line, "Louise held a handful of rain," can be taken to mean that she, Little Boy Lost, and the singer were naked, wet, and cold, like the damned in the *Inferno*; because in previous songs Dylan had hinted that the buildings that will be standing when the storm hits will be shaken and rattled ("The Times They Are A-Changin'"), and their walls will tighten ("Chimes of Freedom")—that is, it may be appropriate to think that the building in which the singer and his two companions are held is delapidated, and that rain is pouring in. Then it would be possible for Louise to just hold out her hand in order to fill it with rain.

In 1962 Dylan made up a song about a woman whose name was the diminutive of Louise–he called her, "Gypsy Lou."[12] The first verse presents the problem the song concerns:"She's a ramblin' woman with a ramblin' mind / Always leavin' somebody behind." The next six verses describe Gypsy Lou's travels, and the singer's pursuit, in a jocular manner; but the last lines of the last verse do not scan well, and the idea they express, that Gypsy Lou was jailed for breaking a boy's heart, though it is naive, brings emphasis to the thought that sexual immorality destroys people. Louise in"Visions of Johanna" resembles Gypsy Lou, because she is imprisoned, and because the sexual conduct attributed to her is immoral. The singer mocks his two roommates by calling her "delicate" (verse 2), and him"Little Boy Lost" (verse 3). This name, Little Boy Lost, seems to indicate that this is the "boy" who committed suicide in"Gypsy Lou."

The name "Johanna," in the title and refrain of "Visions of Johanna," has been interpreted as being a reference to Joan Baez[13]; but Baez could not have been Dylan's principal reference, because she did not see visions–or she did not say that she did. Joan of Arc suffered martyrdom on account of her claims about her visions; but Joan of Arc's visions cannot have been the visions Dylan referred to, because they compelled her to go to *war* in defense of a monarchy. The only interpretation of this name that fits an eschatological interpretation of "Visions of Johanna" would be that Dylan was referring to St. John the Divine. Johanna is closer in sound to the Hebrew name "Johanan," from which the Latin, "Johannes," and several variations (including John and Joan) are derived, than any other. It enabled Dylan to speak of the last book of the Bible, and to suggest that his song was apocalyptic, without using the word "Revelation" or the name "John."[14]

Dylan may have been on tour when he wrote "Visions of Johanna"; and he may have finished it before he was married, in late November, to Sara, the lady who would become the mother of his children. When he was not touring in late December he recorded "Visions of Johanna" with The Band calling it "Seems Like A Freeze Out." Then he recorded it a second time with Nashville musicians reflecting the idea that country music will play in heaven ("the opposite loft"), which is suggested in verse 2. He went to Nashville in February, just before he began his last tour, which went all the way around the world—that is, across the United States, then to Canada, Hawaii, Australia, Europe, Scandinavia, and the British Isles. He changed the last verse, slightly, so that his reference to the Messiah became clearer,[15] and he changed the song's title to the obvious choice—"Visions of Johanna."[16]

In March 1966 Robert Shelton interviewed Dylan, during the first segment of that rock and roll tour, as Dylan was flying from Lincoln, Nebraska, to Denver, Colorado.[17] He reports that Dylan was reading the galleys of *Tarantula*, which may indicate that Dylan brought that work to a conclusion before he retired; and Shelton says that Dylan talked about the movie that was going to be made during the last segment of the tour before him. The album on which "Visions of Johanna" appeared (*Blonde on Blonde*) was released on May 16, 1966, Dylan celebrated his twenty-fifth birthday on May 24, and he performed his last concert May 27. Then he went home with his wife to Woodstock. Later that summer Dylan's manager informed the press that he was canceling all of the concerts that were scheduled for Dylan for that fall and winter. He said that Dylan had fallen from his motorcycle and had broken his neck; but Dylan hinted in the pages of *Tarantula* that he was going to retire. He also made the following remarks to Shelton, in March, prior to his retirement:

> I could quit...People want to tear me apart, man. I don't take people up to the country now...I can be alone...I don't have anything to say to anybody...But it's hard for other people like that.[18]

Shelton reports that Robbie Robertson told him that when Dylan and The Band returned to the United States from their tour they, "didn't listen to music for a year."[19] That may mean that they didn't turn on the radio, listen to records, or go to concerts; but they did get together to play music. Their collaboration is documented by dozens of songs that were recorded on the clandestine "basement tapes," which told members of the peace movement's underground (the political "basement," so to speak) that Dylan was okay, and that he still had something to say. And after Dylan and The Band recorded these songs, Dylan worked with another ensemble to record an album entitled *John Wesley Harding*, which included the last storm-warning song he wrote before he began a more profound rest.

"All Along the Watchtower" begins with a conversation between two men—the "joker" and the "thief"—who are within a walled city; and it concludes with the singer's remarks about what is going on outside the city while this conversation is taking place. The joker complains about the world; but the thief warns him that the world is coming to an end. Their exchange resembles a conversation recorded in the Bible, between the two men who were crucified with Jesus; because in that story one man scoffed at Jesus, but the other recognized Jesus as the Messiah and humbly begged for life.[20]

The singer's remarks in the last verse characterize the city by saying its inhabitants are controlled by "princes" and are served by "women" and "barefoot servants"; and they conclude by suggesting that the city and its inhabitants are about to be destroyed. To be more precise, in the last verse Dylan employed four images. The "wild cat" that growls "outside," is an enigmatic reference to the sea and the storm, resembling the figure in "When the Ship Comes In" that says, in effect, that the storm and the sea will roar like a monster that has broken its chains. The "two riders" who approach the city were also sketched in "Gates of Eden," where Dylan called them the motorcycle-black-madonna-two-wheeled-gypsy-queen and her silver-studded phantom. They are just called "riders" here, so the listener might imagine them as riding on cycles or horses—or on clouds or wind. The fourth "image" is in the song's last line, "The wind began to howl." This phrase translated Dylan's enigmatic reference to the growl of the wild cat into explicit terms—the "howl" is the voice of the invisible *wind*—and it closed the cycle of songs that begins with questions about something that is "blowin' in the wind." The songs within this cycle suggest that the storm Dylan began to hint about in 1962 had drawn closer, had hit full force, and had devastated the world; and in January 1968, when "All Along the Watchtower" was released, the peace movement really *had* become a kind of storm, visiting several countries.

There is a legend in Welsh folklore, which says that twins were born at the beginning of the world, who were named "Llewellyn," which means "light," and "Dylan," which means "darkness."[21] This Dylan of Welsh lore leaped into the sea while he was still a boy; and he lived in the sea until the day he died. He was called, "son of the wave." Bob Dylan's work "reflects light," in that it teaches ethics through reference to the Judeo-Christian tradition; but "darkness" is a name that fit Dylan well, because from 1962 to 1967 he warned Americans that some of them were going to perish. Dylan hinted that the world was about to be destroyed, and that God was about to bring salvation–that is to say, he spoke as a prophet, not as a magician. In fact, Dylan's retirement and silence after autumn 1967 may be interpreted as a sign of humility and religiosity appropriate to a devout Jew. After six years of work (fall 1961 to fall 1967), perhaps Dylan believed that it would be a good idea to observe a special Sabbath. He may have bound himself to the peace movement, beginning in 1961 when he joined the founders of *Broadside*, with the idea that after six years of work he would rest for a year.

Notes

1 "Long Time Gone" has never been released on an official recording. It is printed in *Lyrics: 1962-1985* (New York: Alfred A. Knopf, 1985) 27. Here is verse 7:

> If I can help somebody with a word or song,
> If I can show somebody they are travelin' wrong.
> But I know I ain't no prophet an I ain't no prophet's son.
> I'm just a long time a-comin' an' I'll be a long time gone.

2 Dylan says, "The bird is here and you might want to enter it, but of course the door might be closed," in "Sign on the Cross" (*Lyrics* 306). This song was on the bootleg *Basement Tapes*, but it has never been released on an official recording.

3 According to Shelton, when people asked Dylan for his autograph in 1966 he signed, "The Phantom." Shelton 412.

4 Matthew 14: 25-32, begins: "During the fourth watch of the night Jesus went out to them, walking on the lake...." The translation I use here and elsewhere is, *The Holy Bible, The New International Version, Containing The Old Testament and The New Testament* (Grand Rapids, Michigan: Zondervan, 1978).

5 Lord Randall says, "I fain would lie doone," after he tells his mother that he has been poisoned.

6 Dante "stumbled on the side of a misty mountain," at the beginning of the *Inferno* (Canto I), and then followed the ghost of the poet Virgil to "the depths of the dark forest" (Canto II). Dante saw a "black branch with blood dripping," and "wicked birds of prey," too (Canto XIII).

7 There is a more elaborate example of this sort of figure in *Tarantula* on pages 121-122, in one of the book's "letters":

> ...you can't have me under your thumb anymore–not because
> i'm too squirmy, but because your hands are made out of
> water...when you wish to talk to me, let me know ahead of
> time...i'll have a bucket waiting.

8 In "Desolation Row," when he said, "Across the street they've nailed the curtains" (verse 7), he was referring to clouds, too.

9 Maybe Dylan compared the weeping of this person to a "fire in the sun," because the light of a fire is wasted in the sun, like tears that come too late.

10 Ophelia was the name of Prince Hamlet's fiancee. According to Shakespeare's rendering of the story, Hamlet wanted to sleep with Ophelia, and she refused him; but when he stopped courting her she committed suicide.

11 Dante said he saw an enormous throng of people, standing naked, outside

of hell, waiting to be carried across the River Styx (Canto III, 62-129). Inside of hell, he depicted gluttons beaten down by heavy rain, hail, and snow (Canto VI, 7-54).

12 "Gypsy Lou" has never been released on an official recording; but it appears in *Lyrics*, on page 26.

13 Anthony Scaduto assumes that Joan Baez was on Dylan's mind when he sang about "Johanna," because one chapter of his book is devoted to an interview he conducted with Baez, and it bears the title, "Visions of Johanna." Scaduto 191-210.

14 Nick de Somogyi would seem to agree with me, for he remarks that "Visions of Johanna" concerns the "Johannine end." Nick DeSomogyi, *Jokerman and Thieves: Bob Dylan and the Ballad Tradition* (Lancashire: Wanted Man, 1986) 21.

15 The change occurred at the end of stanza 5, which had said:
The fiddler now steps to the road
Everything's gone which was owed
He examines the nightingale's code
Still written on the fish truck that loads
My conscience explodes

The no-action-verb, "examines," was replaced by the action-verb, "writes," and Dylan told the listener what the fiddler writes. He eliminated the enigmatic reference to the "nightingale" (himself), which brought no action to the verse; and he added the word, "while," making the action described in the last line clearer.

16 "(Seems Like A) Freeze Out" may have referred to the exclusion of the damned from heaven, and to the ice and cold of hell. (Dante described the frozen depths of hell in the final cantos of the *Inferno*.)

17 Shelton describes this interview, and quotes liberally from it. Shelton 394-412.

18 Shelton 405,6.

19 Shelton 429.

20 The conversation between the two thieves and Jesus is recorded in Luke 23:32-43.

21 Charles Squire, *Celtic Myth and Legend, Poetry and Romance* (London: Gresham, 1910) 261.

Chapter 3

Prophet of the Peace Movement

When Dylan retired at the end of May 1966 the idea that he was the prophet of the peace movement had become a commonplace that was understood by millions of young adults and adolescents; but most "grown-ups" still did not know Dylan's name or the sound of his voice. On the other hand it would have been virtually impossible for anyone living in the United States at that time to escape having some knowledge of the peace movement, because by the spring of 1966 the peace movement had become a mass movement, it was the subject of daily commentary in the media, and it touched every community in America.

Whereas the movement first sprang to life on the East Coast, by mid-decade the community in which it assumed its most revolutionary and alluring aspect was on the West Coast, in the San Francisco Bay area, especially on the campus of the University of California at Berkeley, and in various parts of San Francisco—such as the neighborhood near the intersection of Haight and Ashbury Streets. Therefore, it would seem to be a point of interest to the historical record that Dylan performed more frequently in Northern California and around San Francisco, beginning in 1963, than in Greenwich Village.[1] He participated in the Monterey Folk Festival in May 1963, and then appeared with Joan Baez at Berkeley and other locations in Northern and Southern California in the fall of 1963. He gave his first solo concert on the West Coast at Berkeley in February 1964, and returned to the San Francisco area for a series of concerts in November and early December of that same year that included a concert at Berkeley. He performed repeatedly around San Francisco and at Berkeley, again, in 1965, and he returned to perform one more time in the San Francisco area in 1966, at the beginning of the world tour that preceded his retirement. However, no political historian has taken an interest in the subject of Dylan's relationship to the growth of the peace movement on the West Coast, in San Francisco, or at Berkeley.

In a way it cannot be said to be surprising that political historians do not comment about Dylan's work in San Francisco, because they do not comment about his work in Greenwich Village; but even Dylan's press, which is abundantly informative about Dylan's early years, loses track of Dylan, in a sense, in 1963, and begins to obscure the truth about his relationship to the peace movement. I do not mean to say that there was a lack of interest in Dylan on the part of the media in 1963, for the opposite is true. Even before Peter, Paul and Mary's recording of "Blowin' in the Wind" was aired on the radio for the first time, Dylan had become something of a celebrity—or that would seem to be the case, because he received four very attractive invitations to appear on television, between December 1962 and the end of June 1963.[2] But controversy over Dylan broke out in 1963, and much of what was written about Dylan that year, like much of what has been written about him since then, concerned suspicions about his character and his motives for singing the songs he sang.

Robert Shelton, Dylan's principle "biographer," enlarges on this subject; but he is a treacherous witness and interpreter. He reveals (between the lines) that he was involved in the publication of a story in *Newsweek* magazine, late in 1963, that suggested Dylan was a fraud, and that he did not write "Blowin' in the Wind," but bought the song from a high school student in New Jersey.[3] Furthermore, in his biography Shelton continually interjects innuendo to the effect that Dylan could not handle the success that came to him in 1963, that he surrounded himself with sycophants, and that he was "out of control" because of alcohol and drug abuse, the stresses of his career, and weaknesses in his personality.[4]

Dylan's first biographer, Anthony Scaduto, uses the expression "out of control" in his description of Dylan's behavior, too; but while Scaduto seems as eager to slander Dylan in this matter as Shelton, neither Scaduto nor Shelton describes conduct that would prove that Dylan was ever really out of control. According to Scaduto's account that expression was applied to Dylan by Eric von Schmidt, who became a member of Dylan's circle of acquaintances in Cambridge, Massachusetts, in 1961. Scaduto quotes von Schmidt at length to the effect that Dylan delighted his audiences by pretending, between feats of musical prowess, that he was about to stumble and fall—as if he were inebriated; but according to Scaduto, von Schmidt also said

that he drank gin and smoked "dope" with Dylan, before one of these performances in which Dylan played with uncanny brilliance.[5] If Scaduto's
motive for quoting von Schmidt was to incorporate eye-witness testimony
that Dylan got "stoned," Shelton surpassed him by testifying that Dylan
introduced him to "pot."[6]

Scaduto reports that Dylan drank the night the Emergency Civil
Liberties Committee presented the Thomas Paine Award to him in
December 1963.[7] Shelton suggests that Dylan began drinking earlier in the
day.[8] But both of them seem to emphacize that Dylan drank because they
want us to believe that Dylan's speech was inept.[9] They do not weigh
Dylan's words, or give him credit for insight concerning American foreign
policy and the assassination of President Kennedy, which had taken place
just three weeks earlier. (The full text of Dylan's remarks is printed in the
appendix, beginning on page 192). Dylan's words do not prove that he had
been drinking. They suggest that he spoke extemporaneously, and that he
held the same views that night as he did when he was on stage with his guitar and harmonica.

If Dylan had too much to drink, it is still remarkable that he said what
he said. He was explicit, not hateful; and his words were more politically
adroit than Shelton or Scaduto acknowledge, because he named people who
had recently visited Cuba, he called them his "friends," and he reasoned that
"no harm" would be done if people were allowed to travel freely between
the U.S. and Cuba. Dylan spoke directly to one of the issues that may have
been behind the murder of President Kennedy[10]; but Scaduto and Shelton
do not take notice. Scaduto quotes only parts of the speech, and he deletes
Dylan's last words, which say that he accepted the award "...on behalf of
those who went to Cuba."[11] Like Shelton, he obscures that Dylan recognized an opportunity to raise serious questions, and was courageous enough
to do so: Dylan was given a microphone; he saw the press and some of the
people he wanted to censure sitting before him; and he "let them have it."
A photo of Dylan and James Baldwin taken during the ECLC dinner is
printed on page 31.[12] Dylan looks sober and alert, because he spotted the
photographer–and Baldwin did not.

Shelton's book is the best resource available, at this time, for information about Dylan's early career and his relationship to the beginning of the peace movement; but while it is embellished with provocative details about Dylan's activities in 1961, 1962, and 1963, Shelton effectively closes the subject of Dylan's influence on the peace movement just at the point when Dylan was about to appear at Berkeley, solo, for the first time, in late February 1964. This is odd, because Shelton quotes the following remarks from the San Francisco *Chronicle*, which were published prior to that concert, as if he intended to tell more about the peace movement:

> To the generations who were raised on solid Judeo-Christian principles, on the rock of moral values of our fathers, on the idea that cleanliness is next to godliness, the deliberate sloppiness, the disdain for what we thought of as perfect by Dylan's generation is shocking. But we are wrong. Look where our generation has gotten....a hard core of reality connects the music of Dylan, the best of jazz, of contemporary poetry, painting, all the arts, in fact, with the social revolution that has resulted in CORE and SNCC, Dick Gregory, James Baldwin, and the rest.[13]

Shelton omits important facts about Dylan's work in 1964.[14] He suggests that Dylan performed poorly throughout the spring, summer, and fall of that year, and that Dylan was at his worst when he performed with Joan Baez at Forest Hills, in August of 1964.[15] And in his discussion of the Newport Folk Festival, which was one of Dylan's most important concerts of 1964, Shelton says that Dylan staggered on stage, turned his back on his audience, and sang between clenched teeth.[16] But the Newport Folk Festival was filmed that year, and the very segment of Dylan's performance Shelton singles out for abuse (Dylan's performance of "Mr. Tambourine Man") can be viewed in the movie *Festival*.[17] It proves that Shelton's report is inaccurate. As for the rest of Dylan's concerts in 1964—they were praised very enthusiastically by other witnesses (as I will show later in this chapter).

To correct Shelton I would point to listings of the songs Dylan sang at his concerts, which show that in 1964 Dylan emphasized politically-oriented material, and that he sang several of his storm songs at *every* concert appearance.[18] I would also emphasize that "Blowin' in the Wind" continued to circulate and to increase in popularity with the general public, in America and around the world, in 1964.[19] And I would focus attention on events at Berkeley, and around San Francisco, that suggest that Dylan's ideas were having an impact. For example, I would mention that Joan Baez performed Dylan's songs for student protesters at Berkeley, the day they conducted a vigil in Sproul Hall (the University's administration building) in November, and again the day they seized Sproul Hall in December.[20] I would also mention that several reports specify that group-singing took place at the massive convocations of the free speech movement, in September, October, November, and December, and that these reports say that thousands of students participated each time.[21] Shelton ignores the uprising at Berkeley, he wastes pages of his book on gossip about Dylan's private relationship with Baez, and he says very little about what Dylan did during all the weeks he was on the West Coast in the fall of 1964.[22]

The take-over of Sproul Hall in December 1964, by approximately one thousand students, who refused to leave and had to be removed by the Berkeley police, was the first incident of its kind at an American university. For that reason, and because it was followed by repeated, massive demonstrations, and by the growth of a highly-visible, politically-radical community, the 1964 insurrection at Berkeley has received more attention from historians than similar occurrences at other schools. W.J. Rorabaugh, the author of Berkeley At War, for example, makes note of Baez's presence on campus with students in December 1964, and that she sang "The Times They Are A-Changin'" for them immediately before they marched on Sproul Hall[23]; but he says nothing about Dylan's appearances at Berkeley, or in the Bay Area. Neither do the other historians I will cite in this chapter; but what is more surprising, all of them avoid using the words "peace movement," even though the peace movement would seem to be the proper subject of their respective works. They speak of "the civil rights movement," "the antiwar movement," "the new left," "the student movement," "the youth movement," and "the counter-culture"; but they forget the over-arching phenomenon that was the peace movement. Nevertheless, all of them illustrate their texts with photos of young men and women signing "peace," with one hand or with both hands—in fact, photos of young people shouting and making the peace sign, with their arms raised high over their heads, appear on the covers of the paperback editions of two of the books I am about to discuss—*The Unfinished Journey*, by William Chafe,[24] and *1968: A Student Generation in Revolt*, edited by Ronald Fraser.[25] (The photo of people making the peace sign reproduced on page 35 shows students singing inside Sproul Hall, in December 1964. The figure in the foreground is that of Mario Savio, who worked in Mississippi in 1963 to register black voters, and then reported about what he had seen to students and teachers at Berkeley, where he was enrolled as a graduate student.[26])

Scholars who leave the expression, "peace movement," out of their analyses of political events that took place in America during the 1960s are vastly in the majority; nevertheless, this deletion weakens their texts, and this abandonment of the words people used by preference causes a deep distortion in the historical record. Charles DeBenedetti uses the words, "peace movement," a few times in *An American Ordeal: The Antiwar Movement of the Vietnam Era*; but he and Charles Chatfield, assisting author, use "peace movement" exclusively as the equivalent of "antiwar movement,"[27] despite the fact that they provide a wealth of information about the relationship between the civil rights movement and the antiwar movement (especially from 1960 to 1964—which would be from the time members of the civil rights movement staged the first lunch counter sit-ins, until the "black power" movement became ascendant). It is to their credit, however, that DeBenedetti and Chatfield quote Stewart Meecham, a Quaker pacifist, on the subject:

> The reason that there is a new kind of peace movement today is not so much because people are frightened by the threat of nuclear destruction as that they are terrified at being lost as people. The deepest problem we face is not to escape physical destruction; but to regain a sense of the meaning and worth of our lives."[28]

DeBenedetti and Chatfield take care to explain that America has always had groups that have spoken out against militarism in general, as well as groups that have opposed particular military operations, tactics, or poli-

cies; and they manage to keep track of numerous factions as they report in great detail, and with eloquence, on this passage of American history. But their fascination with stories of all of the anti-war movement's would-be leaders and special interest groups leads them to a conclusion that is erroneous—that is, they report at various junctures that "the movement" was a "failure."[29] Many passages of *An American Ordeal* testify about the success of the peace movement—for example, these words appear in one of the concluding paragraphs of the book:

> Voluntarism in opposition to the war mushroomed, especially on the local level...All this citizen activity suggests that the movement in the broadest sense was not so peripheral to the American mainstream as its leaders feared. Its history on the national level reflected efforts in the American interior—in church meetings, college teach-ins, congressional offices, city street actions, curbside vigils, and divided families—where most Americans struggled among themselves over Vietnam.[30]

Elsewhere DeBenedetti and Chatfield reveal distrust and loathing for members of the movement they refer to as "the counterculture," "hippies," and "drug fiends." For example, they remark, "By mid-decade there was a perceptible loosening of mores, especially among young people"—and it is in this connection that they mention Dylan.[31]

DeBenedetti and Chatfield do not tell their readers, nor do any of the other scholars I quote in this chapter, that the word, "peace," was frequently used by political activists to greet one another, and in parting. "Peace" was a holy word for members of the peace movement: they did not define it or delimit it in any way. Even so, the expression, "peace movement," is more precise than any of the other expressions that are used to speak of the popular uprising in America in the 1960s, because it suggests that what was happening among participants was of a spiritual order—or that it had a spiritual dimension. To delete it undermines the capacity of those other expressions (civil rights movement, antiwar movement, new left, youth movement, student movement, protest movement, counterculture) to hold meaning. When historians delete the peace movement, *and* attempt to discuss Dylan casually, they compound serious problems.

Fraser's book, *1968*, reflects a collaborative effort, and it provides an original and highly-detailed analysis of political upheavals that took place within universities in several European countries, as well as in the United States, during the 1960s. It discusses events that transpired at Berkeley in 1964, at the University of Wisconsin in 1967, and at Columbia University in 1968; but it also discusses the resistance of French students to war in Algeria in 1959, the rebellion of Italian architecture students in Turin and Milan in 1963, and the growth of radical student organizations in Germany and Great Britain, in the early and mid-60s. The organization of this text features quotations from participants in radical political events (such as Mario Savio and Michael Rossman, who were students at Berkeley); but when Fraser, and the other writers working with him, try to fit Dylan into their narrative they quote no one, and they move too hastily—as the following passage shows:

> In neither West Germany nor Italy did the youth culture particularly affect university students; in the former probably because they were generally older than in other countries; in the latter because activists were influenced by a left-wing culture with its strong Resistance heritage and a certain moralism. In Germany it was not until the mid-1960s that protest songs about political issues and everyday life, influenced by the Bob Dylan of the early 1960s, became popular among teenagers, reflecting a radicalization that by then was taking place at other levels also. In Italy, student activists continued to wear suits, ties, and short hair until well into the second half of the decade.[32]

The book does not say how "the Bob Dylan of the early 1960s" influenced protest songs in Germany in the mid-60s, or what Dylan had to do with the abandonment of "suits, ties, and short hair," among students in Italy in the second half of the decade. The authors seem to have wished to say that the American peace movement influenced students in Germany and Italy, which is true, and that Dylan influenced young people in other countries, which is also true; but they do not quite make those connections.[33]

Fraser's text is readable and sympathetic—it is also valuable for a number of reasons; but it is somewhat misleading on certain points. One small matter is that Fraser and his associates were in a position to observe that matter is that Fraser and his associates were in a position to observe that most of the young people who started the "revolt" that reached its crescendo in 1968 were born during the second world war. They miss this point completely; instead, Fraser comments in his preface that the participants in the events of 1968 were born during the post-war "baby boom."[34] But Dylan, Baez, The Beatles, The Rolling Stones, The Byrds, The Grateful Dead, The Band, Jimi Hendrix, Aretha Franklin, Richie Havens, Joni Mitchell, Phil Ochs, Judy Collins, Eric Clapton, Donovan, Robert Moses, Bernice Johnson, Cordell Reagan, James Forman, Julian Bond, Todd Gitlin, Mario Savio, and almost the entire first wave of the movement, were *all* once "war babies."

A more important matter is that the American peace movement was not led by students, exclusively–not in 1962, or in 1968, or at any other time: it was partly led by musicians. If we use terminology that has a spiritual dimension, we might say it was inspired by poets who sing–like Bob Dylan. This perception is not altogether lacking in Fraser's book, *1968*; because appended to this book is a chronology that identifies important political events that took place between 1945 and 1975. The entries for 1961, 1962, and 1963, combined, all fit on one page; but the entries for 1964 fill an entire page. The items listed are certainly memorable, and all of them except one are discussed in the text; but heading the list of memorable events for 1964, unexplained, is: "Bob Dylan rockets to popularity."[35]

William Chafe makes his subject the history of "America Since World War II," so his discussion of the '60s is limited. He discusses events at Berkeley in 1964 in some detail; but he does not analyse uprisings at other schools with care, nor does he discuss subsequent events at Berkeley. His portrayal of the free speech movement is insightful; but it is near the conclusion of his text, within his discussion of the 1970s, that he comes closest to the essential truth about Berkeley and the rise of the peace movement. Unfortunately, he veers off course just when he gets to the heart of things, and then he brings up Dylan in a desultory manner:

> At its root, the social critic Paul Goodman observed, this vision was religious in nature. "I'd imagined that the worldwide student protest had to do with changing political and moral institutions,

that we had to deal with a religious crisis of the magnitude of the Reformation." Although such counterculture slogans as "make love not war" retained a link to politics, the counterculture frequently became totally personal and privatistic in emphasis, with liberation in dress style, sex, and attitudes toward respectability taking the place of activism in the public arena. Theoretically, building communes and "getting high" on interpersonal intimacy could have a political consequence. "You can have your cake and eat it too," Bob Dylan's lyrics said. But there was a tendency for these new cultural forms to become ends in themselves.[36]

The idea that the peace movement was like the Reformation is most compelling; but neither Chafe nor Goodman points out that the peace movement was like the Reformation because the Reformation was a revolutionary, popular uprising that tore nations apart, and that what was at stake in the Reformation, among other things, was the doctrine of God's love, and the idea of the sanctity of the conscience of the individual.[37] Drawing on Goodman's remarks, Chafe argues that young people made "sacraments" of music, sex, and drugs[38]; but this is unfair. The peace movement gave young people a new perspective on religious institutions, and it enabled many of them to shed sectarian bias; but that is precisely because the appeal the movement made to conscience and compassion was religious-in-kind.

It may be true that many young men and women who were part of the movement were irreligious, and perhaps the overwhelming majority of them *were* more interested in sex, drugs, and music, than in theology or religious observance; but that would not necessarily set them apart from youngsters of prior generations. It is their participation in civil rights demonstrations, antiwar demonstrations, "free speech" demonstrations, and the periferal activities involved in organized, passive resistance to racism, militarism, and authoritarianism, that must be explained by historians—and, perhaps, acknowledged as appropriate conduct for members of a free society.

Rorabaugh does not concern himself much with political events outside the San Francisco area; but he examines events that took place at Berkeley and in the San Francisco area, during the '60s, very carefully. He takes time to describe the community of Berkeley–separate from the University, that is–and to tell how events unfolded in Berkeley city politics, and in national politics, after 1968, when Ronald Reagan ordered in the National Guard to crush the peace movement in Berkeley.[39] Nevertheless, like Fraser and Chafe, Rorabaugh rushes his discussion of Dylan and spoils it:

> Folk music thrived because of new performers like Phil Ochs and the trio "Peter, Paul and Mary." More important was Bob Dylan, whose raw talent and dazzling performances captivated young America. Dylan's genius was matched by the power of Joan Baez's voice. A Chicana by heritage and a Quaker by conviction, Baez burned with a moral commitment to civil rights and peace. For a star, she had a rare devotion to being arrested. Dylan, she noted, never put his body on the line. Perhaps that failure explained his greater popularity, his nihilism expressed the spirit of the times better than did Baez's commitment. For much of the decade Baez lived near, and influenced, Berkeley.[40]

The words "raw talent" and "genius" are empty compliments, because Rorabaugh does not tell the reader about Dylan, his songs, or his "dazzling performances"; but his notion that Dylan's songs expressed "nihilism" is mistaken, and so is the thought that Dylan's unwillingness to participate in student demonstrations was timely and might account for his popularity. Dylan went to Greenwood, Mississippi, to perform for a voters' registration rally in July 1963, and to Tougalou College, in Jackson, Mississippi, to lend support to civil right workers there in February 1964. These appearances suggest that Dylan was idealistic (and courageous) better than singing at a student demonstration at Berkeley could have–since civil rights activists were sometimes beaten, or killed, in Greenwood and Jackson in those days.[41] As for Dylan's willingness, or unwillingness, to participate in demonstrations at Berkeley, Dylan was unwilling to attend school, so his support for the movement cannot be judged fairly by the fact that he did not participate in campus political activities. Dylan's influence was felt at Berkeley when he sang there; and it was felt at the rallys and sit-ins, inside and outside Sproul Hall, when his songs were sung–which is to say at *every* rally and sit-in during the days of the free speech movement. (Baez actually taught students how to sing and play guitar, using Dylan's songs as her material, inside Sproul Hall.[42])

Rorabaugh reports that he was at Stanford for a few years after 1965, but that he was still in high school in the spring of 1965, and did not spend much time at Berkeley until 1970–which may help to explain why he does not seem to have any idea about Dylan's appearances at Berkeley and at other places on the West Coast, between 1963 and 1966.[43] The next authority I will quote was in San Francisco at mid-decade; but he focuses his attention on Dylan and the rock and roll dance halls of San Francisco, and he does not mention Berkeley at all.

Craig Karpel, author of a booklet entitled, *The Tarantula In Me*, writes as a journalist, not as an academician, and he adopts a tone that is confidential, humorous, and sometimes bizarre; but he introduces several pertinent historical references in a way that yields important insights about the peace movement and Dylan.[44] On one level he presents a comparison of the dancing he witnessed in 1965 and 1966, to dancing that could be seen in Europe during socio-religious insurrections in the 14th century; and on another level he comments on American music, and on the existence of a coterie of wealthy white patrons, who helped popularize jazz and blues in the 1930s, in New York City. His object would seem to be to hint that primitive music and dancing have a revolutionary influence on society, and that Dylan could have started a revolution that would have brought America to halt, if he had continued playing rock and roll, instead of retiring, in 1966.

Karpel quotes extensively from the journals of J.F.C. Hecker, a nineteenth century physician,[45] and very briefly from *The Birth of Tragedy* by Friedrich Nietzsche,[46] concerning the "dance craze" that once spread through what is now Italy, France, Belgium, The Netherlands, and Germany. Both Hecker's and Nietzsche's remarks indicate that this epidemic was a cultural, political, and religious phenomenon–a spontaneous, popular uprising–and that it was not a physiological illness, even though it was called a "disease" in some accounts. Hecker notes that in Italy people said that the bite of the tarantula infected people with this dance mania; and in Karpel's opinion that legend furnished the title of Dylan's book, *Tarantula*.[47] Karpel suggests that Dylan named his novel *Tarantula* because he wanted to start an epidemic like the one Nietzsche and Hecker refer to, which was characterized by the fact that enormous crowds of men and women left everything behind them for days, weeks, and even months at a time, to join in wild dancing, and to follow bands of musicians from town to town. He also suggests that Dylan canceled the publication of *Tarantula*, and stopped touring, because he lost his nerve after his motorcycle accident.[48]

The value of the analogy Karpel draws does not depend, completely, on his interpretation of Dylan's motives. Karpel makes a valuable contribution to the historical record concerning the peace movement by exploring this comparison, and by focusing attention on what took place on dance floors in 1965 and 1966, rather than on what took place on the campuses of American universities; because the peace movement was never just a student movement, and anyone who tries to describe it by describing the political conduct of students, exclusively, will misrepresent it. However, Karpel does not mention the peace movement, he mocks Dylan's early work, and he embraces the misconception that Dylan "changed" when he began playing rock and roll.[49] He is also difficult to quote, because even though he is lucid when talking about music and literature, when he speaks about Dylan, dancing, and the movement, he raves (or pretends to rave):

> Why did Bob Dylan determine to suppress *Tarantula*? Why did
> he never tour America with The Band after his controversion to
> electricity around the time of the first San Francisco ballroom
> rock dances? Had he once been stung with the intuition that he
> was the cosmic vesicle of that venomous intoxicant behind
> which we would, despite ourselves, begin the Dance again, be
> haunted by visions, our fancies, yes conjuring up spirits, immers
> ing us in a stream of blood? Had he thought he had discovered
> the tarantula in him that would discover the tarantula in you and
> me, the hidden autonomous synthesizer of Orange Sunshine,
> magical mega-mikes of it, the hallucinogenic neural sweat of the
> Dance? Did he (unwarily) fall off that bike out of 1966 into the
> soft silk-lined burrow of a large hairy running spider...and did
> it...belch, "I am the American pseudo-Tarantula behind whose
> bite no man has boogied the full tilt and lived to tell the tale!"

and did Dylan, next thing, wake in a hospital room and, like a soldier coming-to in a medevac copter trying to wiggle his foot to see if it is still there, try to wiggle the tarantula in him to see if it was still there, and find to his nausea that where it should have been there was only an eight-pronged numbness?" (No page numbers are given.)

Karpel is mistaken when he says that Dylan did not tour America with The Band after his "controversion to electricity" and the first ballroom dances in San Francisco. In fact, Dylan performed with The Band all across the country during the fall and winter of 1965, and during the beginning of 1966; and he gave one of his last performances in North America with The Band in the San Francisco area, prior to the overseas part of his world tour and his retirement.[50] The virtue of this passage lies in the fact that Karpel found a way to testify about the nature of the dancing, leaping, and visionary experiences of some of the people who loved to dance to the music called "rock and roll." His phrases, "haunted by visions," "conjuring up spirits," and "immersing us in a stream of blood," and his choice of words, in general, in this passage are drawn from his quotation of Hecker. Here is a portion of Karpel's text:

> (Dr. Hecker) correlates the onset of the "tarantella" with that of the St. John's Dance and the St. Vitus' Dance, which were brought on, not by tarantulophobia, but by the "wild revels" of St. John's Day, in the summer of 1374:
>
> > "The effects of the Black Death had not yet subsided, and the graves of millions of its victims were scarcely closed, when a strange delusion arose in Germany... It was called the Dance of St. John, or of St. Vitus, on account of the bacchantic leaps by which it was characterized, and which gave to those affected, while performing their wild dance ...all the appearance of persons possessed....
> >
> > "So early as the year 1374, assemblages of men and women were seen at Aix-la-Chapelle who had come out of Germany...They formed circles hand in hand, and appearing to have lost all control over their senses, continued dancing, regardless of the by-standers, for hours together in wild delirium, until at length they fell to the ground in a state of

exhaustion....

"While dancing they neither saw nor heard, being insensible to external impression through the senses, but were haunted by visions, their fancies conjuring up spirits whose names they shrieked out; and some of them afterward asserted that they felt as if they had been immersed in a stream of blood, which obliged them to leap so high. Others, during the paroxysm, saw the heavens open and the Saviour enthroned with the Virgin Mary, according as the religious notions of the age were strangely and variously reflected in their imaginations....

"...this demoniacal disease had spread from Aix-la-Chapelle, where it appeared in July, over the neighboring Netherlands. In Leige, Utrecht, Tongres, and many other towns of Belgium the dancers appeared with garlands in their hair. In Leige the priests had recourse to exorcisms, and endeavored, by every means in their power, to allay an evil which threatened so much danger to themselves: for the possessed assembling in multitudes, frequently poured forth imprecations against them, and menaced their destruction."

Opposite this passage are photos of two paintings, one entitled, *Bacchus,* and the other entitled, *St. John.* In these paintings we see virtually identical, full-figure likenesses of a beardless, long-haired, semi-nude, young male, who is seated, with one leg bent and resting on the knee of the other leg. Leonardo da Vinci is said to have painted the *Bacchus*; and the *St. John* is said to have been painted by a member of Leonardo's school.[51] In a note that appears below the reproductions Karpel reminds the reader that St. John's Dance was still fresh in people's minds when these paintings were made; and he asks, "Why did the painter associate St. John with Bacchus?" The best clues he provides to the answer he seems to want are in his quotations of Hecker and Nietzsche—that is, Hecker says the dance mania broke out on St. John's Day, it was called St. John's Dance, and it was characterized by "bacchantic leaps"; and Nietzsche says the St. John's Dancers resembled the "bacchic chorus of the Greeks."[52] Here is the passage by Nietzsche that Karpel quotes (he acknowledges that Ralph Gleason quoted this same passage in 1966, in an article describing the music and the conduct of young people in San Francisco[53]):

> Orgiastic movements of a society leave their traces in music. Dionysiac stirrings arise either through the influence of those narcotic potions of which all primitive races speak in their hymns—or through the powerful approach of spring, which penetrates with joy the whole frame of nature. So stirred, the individual forgets himself completely. It is the same Dionysiac power which in medieval Germany drove ever-increasing crowds of people singing, and dancing from place to place; we recognize in these St. John's and St. Vitus' dancers the bacchic chorus of the Greeks, who had their precursors in Asia Minor and as far back as Babylon and the orgiastic Sacae. There are people who, either from a lack of experience or out of sheer stupidity, turn away from such phenomena, and strong in the sense of their own sanity, label them either mockingly or pityingly "endemic" disease. These benighted souls have no idea how cadaverous and ghostly their "sanity" appears as the intense throng of Dionysiac revelers sweeps past them.[54]

Neither Hecker nor Nietzsche commented about political ideas or events that may have been associated with the phenomenon they were describing; and neither of them speculated that the dancing may have had something to do with song, or that words set to music may have been the vehicle of revolutionary communication. But neither Hecker nor Nietzsche had an example like San Francisco, under the influence of Bob Dylan and the peace movement, before him; furthermore, neither Hecker nor Nietzsche was interested in the example of St. John, or the subject of prophesy, per se. Nietzsche seems to have been more interested in the physical, orgiastic aspect of the "contagion" than in its political significance; but Hecker remarked briefly about the impact of dancing on the social order, and on the Church, in 1374. His remarks continue with the following paragraphs, which are especially interesting because they hint about the repression of the dancing through "exorcism," and because they provide more details about the spread of a revolutionary musical "disease":

> Some of the affected had...declared, when under the influ-

ence of priestly forms of exorcism, that if the demons had been allowed only a few weeks more time, they would have entered the bodies of the nobility and princes, and through these have destroyed the clergy. Assertions of this sort, which those possessed uttered while in a state which may be compared with that of magnetic sleep, obtained general belief, and passed from mouth to mouth with wonderful additions. The priesthood were, on this account, so much the more zealous in their endeavors to anticipate every excitement of the people, as if the existing order of things could have been seriously threatened by such incoherent ravings...

A few months after this dancing malady had made its appearance at Aix-la-Chapelle, it broke out at Cologne where the number of those possessed amounted to more than 500, and about the same time at Metz, the streets of which place are said to have been filled with 1100 dancers. Peasants left their plows, mechanics their workshops, housewives their domestic duties, to join the wild revels, and this rich commercial city became the scene of the most ruinous disorder. Secret desires were excited, and but too often found opportunities for wild enjoyment, and numerous beggars, stimulated by vice and misery availed themselves of this new complaint to gain a temporary livelihood. Girls and boys quitted their parents, and servants their masters, to amuse themselves at the dances of the possessed, and greedily imbibed the poison of mental infection...

Gangs of idle vagabonds, who understood how to imitate the...convulsions of those really infected, roved from place to place seeking maintenance and adventures...spreading this disgusting spasmodic disease like a plague; for in maladies of this kind the susceptible are infected as easily by the appearance as by the reality...It was found necessary to drive away these mischievous guests...equally inaccessible to the exorcisms of the priests and the remedies of the physicians. It was not...until after four months that the Rhenish cities were able to suppress these impostors.

Neither Hecker nor Nietzsche could have imagined an institution like Berkeley, the series of rebellions that occurred there (the "free speech movement," the "filthy speech movement," "stop the draft week," etc.), or an organization like the "Black Panthers," which was founded in the Bay area by students at Oakland's community college; but Karpel had all these things and the fullness of the peace movement before him, and he knew that Dylan was called the prophet of the peace movement. He purposely excludes discussion of the larger cultural context in which the dancing took place, calling San Francisco, "Baghdad-by-the-Bay"; and he pretends that rock and roll and LSD were all that he, Dylan, and the rest of the young men and women in San Francisco cared about in 1965 and 1966 (which sounds like what Chafe says about members of the "counterculture" in 1969 and 1970).

Karpel's sensitivity to American racism and militarism, and his knowledge of radical politics, are revealed in various ways, as he develops the idea that there is a historical parallel between events that occurred in the 1960s and events that occurred in the 1370s. But Karpel's interpretation of events of the '60s, and of Dylan's motives, is weakened by his vagueness and wildness, and by the fact that he associates visions of Jesus and Mary with rock and roll, dancing, and LSD, but ignores the verbal content of Dylan's songs completely, and makes no reference to the compositions in which Dylan hinted about the end of the world. He is wrong to say that the revolutionary component of Dylan's music was the "4/4 African back-beat" of rock and roll, and to virtually obliterate the fact that Dylan's songs had words; but since he does, it is rather absurd that he should insist that one word, "tarantula," was important, and this book was important, to a hypothetical plan Dylan hypothetically abandoned in July 1966.

Greater clarity and sobriety can be found in a brief statement about Dylan made by an anonymous undergraduate student, whose words were first quoted in the *Sunday New York Times* in December 1965:

> We're concerned about things like the threat of nuclear war, the civil rights movement, and the spreading blight of dishonesty, conformism, and hypocrisy in the United States, especially in Washington; and Bob Dylan is the only American writer dealing with these subjects in a way that makes any sense to us. And, at the same time, as modern poetry, we feel that his songs have a high literary quality. As far as we're concerned, in fact, any one

of his songs, like "A Hard Rain's A-Gonna Fall," is more interesting, both in a literary and a social sense than an entire volume
of Pulitzer Prize verse by someone like Robert Lowell.[55]

Unfortunately, this student's testimony cannot be trusted entirely,
because he, or she, did not mention dancing or rock and roll. The student
called Dylan a "writer," praised "Hard Rain," and said that Dylan was "dealing with" subjects like the threat of nuclear war and the civil rights
movement; but in December 1965 Dylan was playing rock and roll on tour
with The Band, and none of the songs he was performing or recording
spoke unequivocally to the issues of racism or militarism. As for "Hard
Rain," it had been included in Dylan's concerts regularly from September
1962 through May 1965; but after the Newport Folk Festival of 1965 he did
not sing it, or any of his early songs, on stage, anymore.

Newport 1965 was the occasion of Dylan's rock and roll surprise-
attack on the folk music establishment, which was his most famous
revolutionary act. The student quoted in the *Times* should have known, if he
admired Dylan so much, that Dylan defied the authorities at Newport by
bringing an electric guitar and a rock and roll band on stage; because there
was dissension within the audience at Newport and at subsequent concerts,
when some of Dylan's admirers took offense at the spectacle of Dylan playing rock and roll,[56] and there was an uproar in the media—that is, on pop
music radio stations and in the entertainment sections of newspapers like the
New York Times, and magazines like *Newsweek,* and also in *Broadside* and similar, limited-circulation papers.

Dylan "made news" in several ways: things were written about him
and his work—as might be the case with any singer or writer of verse; but so
far as the peace movement is concerned, what may matter more is that
Dylan inspired others to express dissent and to sing songs of their own composition. Both processes began in 1961, after Dylan won his first recording
contract, was written up and photographed by the *New York Times,* and
began to participate in *Broadside.* By 1965 new publications that published
dissent had appeared in many communities; but the most important medium for Dylan and the movement, by then, was radio. Dylan's music was
broadcast very frequently in 1965, on conventional pop radio stations.

Perhaps it would be fair to say that one song or another by Dylan was played every hour, every day, on pop stations from coast to coast, in renditions by Dylan or by others; but in addition, like underground newspapers in the early '60s, alternative radio stations that were responsive to the movement proliferated after Dylan produced his first rock and roll album and came on stage with a rock and roll band. Non-commercial FM radio stations on college campuses, and pirate radio broadcasts from ships, to England and Europe, turned the world "on" to the movement and '60s style rock and roll. By 1968 commercial FM radio stations appeared in cities all across the United States. They took over the function of promoting radical music, much as the commercial enterprise, *Rolling Stone*, took over the function of printing news about radical music from *Broadside*.[57]

In light of Karpel's recollections about "dance mania," Chafe's comments that suggest that young people made a "sacrament" of rock and roll, and Alan Matusow's remark that Dylan "seized the power of rock and roll and used it to change consciousness,"[58] the most important fact about the controversy that exploded at Newport would seem to be that the majority of the young women and men who purchased record albums *liked* Dylan's new songs, and admired Dylan for insisting on playing rock and roll. The least important point may be that Dylan was making plans to retire, and he knew that he would never play at the Newport Folk Festival again.

Dylan prepared his fans for his first rock and roll stage appearance by releasing albums that featured rock and roll months before he brought a band on stage. He dropped hints about *Tarantula,* and about his movies, in advance, too; but he did not prepare the public for his retirement. Dylan probably planned his rock and roll breakthrough and his retirement, simultaneously, well in advance; but I draw that impression, in part, from passages of *Tarantula,* and from the fact that Dylan made two films–*Don't Look Back* and *Eat the Document,* which portray him in his final appearances as a solo artist, and in his final appearances with The Band. Those documents were not in circulation in late July 1966, when Dylan's manager reported to the press that Dylan had been hurt in a motorcycle accident.[59]

The idea of filming Dylan's last appearances as a solo artist in

England, in 1965, has been attributed to Sara Dylan, who knew D.A. Pennebaker, the filmmaker.[60] Pennebaker shot and edited *Don't Loot Back*, but the second film, which documents Dylan's return to England with a rock and roll band, was Dylan's idea, and he intended to edit it with Pennebaker.[61] *The Document* was to be broadcast on ABC-TV, but that plan was abandoned. Instead, with Pennebaker's help Dylan made a film called *Eat the Document*, which was shown a few times in 1970 and 1971. Pennebaker's patience, his unobtrusive camera, his editing in the first film, and Dylan's editing in the second, created two portraits of a young poet. There are no other films like these in all the world—especially since they concern Dylan, who was at the center of a seismic chain of events.

No printed document about Dylan reveals so much about his work on stage, and his comportment off stage, as *Don't Look Back* and *Eat the Document*; and since they were made in England, rather than in the United States, it was possible to portray Dylan without portraying the peace movement. In the United States that would not have been possible—but the peace movement did enter these films, because they are about Dylan and his songs, and because in *Eat the Document* the peace movement "walked on stage," so to speak, in the form of a young man someone spotted on the street in London, as he waited for the theatre doors to open for Dylan's concert. Anonymous, he answered questions that were posed to him by an unidentified interviewer. A camera and microphone were pointed at him, which may explain why he did not recognize that the voice of the person who was questioning him was Dylan's voice. (Dylan is not shown, but I presume that he was wearing a disguise.[62]) The youth was blond and long-haired. He was dressed in knee-length, oriental bloomers, a coat, and sandals, but he had no umbrella; and when he spoke it was in the accent of an American midwesterner. He was asked to explain himself, and he began to do so; but before he could finish a sentence, he was pressed to explain his appearance as well, and why he wanted to see Bob Dylan. Then he must have guessed that the interview was a joke, because he suddenly smiled, and the scene ends.

This brief segment of *Eat the Document* is just one of a number of scenes that prove that Dylan was interested in the world around him, and full of affection for people[63]; it is just one of several scenes in which Dylan's admirers speak (some people who did not see to know Dylan speak, too, and some who seem to have disliked him); but it is the only scene in either of the two movies in which an American is interviewed–other than Dylan himself. This fan looks like he may have been nineteen or twenty years old, and a runaway (or "dropout") like tens of thousands of young people who came to San Francisco in 1965, 1966, and 1967, to join the "generation of love." He was mannerly, forthright, and good-humored, and he did not seem to have been physically or mentally intoxicated; but he was alone, and that made him stand out distinctly. Assuming that Dylan selected this footage from all the reels of film taken in approximately one week of shooting (*Eat the Document* is less than an hour long), the appearance of the "lone hippie" must be pondered as a statement of some kind: it is proof that the contagion that had to do with politics, religion, youth, sex, drugs, long hair, and rock and roll, had crossed the Atlantic by the middle of May 1966. Maybe the reason Dylan chose to film *Eat the Document* in color was to celebrate the spread of this "epidemic." (*Don't Look Back* was in black and white.) But the film is about Dylan, and only indirectly about the American peace movement; so the use of color would seem to suggest that Dylan was *content* and full of vitality–not tortured, frightened, or strung out.

The portrait of the peace movement that I would recommend, above all, is rendered by the words of participants in the political confrontations that took place between April 1962 and November 1967. Since Berkeley was the scene of the first large-scale student demonstrations it seems fitting to quote a student from there. The following passage appears in Ronald Fraser's book, in his discussion of the spontaneous first sit-in:

> ...on October 1, university police tried to arrest a student who was working a table for the Congress of Racial Equality (CORE), several hundred others spontaneously sat down and prevented the police car from taking him away. "I was the first one to sit down–along with two hundred other people who say they were the first," recalled Michael Rossman, a mathematics graduate student. "And everyone's telling the truth. It was an act of spontaneous initiative." Then Savio

climbed onto the car. "He spoke, but not as a leader giving directions," Rossman continued. "He said it was wrong, we mustn't let the police take Jack (Weinberg) away. We don't know what to do—let's talk about it. That was the first speech and that was the nature of the leadership—to give voice to the common consciousness."

The group, which swelled from two hundred to a peak of more than three thousand, sat around the car for thirty hours, talking about...free speech in a democratic society, "I was twenty-four, almost twenty-five, and this was the first time I'd really heard a democratic public discussion in America," Rossman continued. "No one could even say it, because the words themselves had been so abused—'democracy,' 'Congress.' It was like going to church for years, then watching God walk on Earth. You just realized, that's the meaning inside those dry terms. Here it is...among us...so we were literally enraptured from that point on."[64]

A second quotation from the lips of a participant describes events that occurred one year earlier, during "freedom summer" in Jackson, Mississippi. The student who is quoted was Steve Fraser of the University of Wisconsin, and the students mentioned were Karen Duncanwood of San Francisco State, and Mario Savio of Berkeley—who was the first to speak the day of the spontaneous sit-in, when he climbed on the police car, as described above. This passage, and the next one, appear in Fraser's book:

Savio's clearest memory revolves around the announcement early in the week that three young workers had disappeared. The three young men—Andrew Goodman, Michael Schwerner, and James Chaney—were later found dead: the whites had been shot; the black, Chaney, beaten to death. Announcing the disappearance, (Robert) Moses called upon the volunteers to think carefully about their decision...

In Jackson, Savio was assaulted in broad daylight...by a group of white men armed with metal pipes. The church where Duncanwood taught...was bombed by the local police; and when she and other white students tried to worship in a white church one Sunday they were evicted by men wearing brass knuckles. But a sense of personal and collective power also characterized the campaign. Fraser was present at a meeting...when the local police chief, accompanied by officers and dogs, tried to break it up.

"They did the standard number, they were there to scare the hell out of us, threatening to bust up the meeting. On previous occasions they might have succeeded but someone—it might have been me, I don't know, I was almost moved to tears by it—someone began to sing. We continued the meeting by singing. And we outbluffed them. They retreated, went away. It was joyous, ecstatic. We became something different as a community that night."[65]

A final quotation from a participant concerns events at the University of Wisconsin in 1967. Between the fall of 1964 and the fall of 1967 the antiwar movement had become much more powerful and much angrier. Militarism and authoritarianism became burning issues—as racism had been from the start. The protest described here was against recruiting by Dow Chemical on the campus at Madison (Dow was the manufacturer of Napalm, which was used by the American military to destroy jungles in Vietnam):

...On 16 October (1967) SDS members handed out leaflets; the following day they led several hundred people into the University's "Commerce" building, where the Dow recruiter was scheduled to hold interviews. The campus police were called to move them. Paul Buhle, a graduate student member of SDS recalled, "To a man, to a woman, we said, 'We're not going to leave. You can't scare us.'" The campus police then called in the city police of Madison. Heavily armed, dressed in riot gear, they assembled outside the building. With little warning they moved into the building's lobby where the protesters stood massed in tight ranks.

"The police tried to push their way in, and were pushed back," recounted Buhle. There was a moment, he claimed, of terror. "The police were pushing in, and we were pushing back, you were picked up off your feet and couldn't control your own movement, and you thought, 'Oh shit, I'm going to die.' or, 'I'm going to lose my glasses.' Whatever. 'Something will happen. I can't control it. I can't control it.' Then the police smashed in the doors and began to drag students out of the building through the glass. Between the glass and the clubs of the police, student blood was soon spattered all over. At first the students absorbed the blows, but then began to move. "The police allowed us to escape out of a rear door," Buhle recalled, "But instead of running away, which maybe they thought we would do, we circled around to the front of the building. By the time we got there, there were a thousand students there." The crowd, many of whom never considered themselves radical, was furious at the beatings they witnessed. "The second the cops started clubbing heads, the entire situation changed dramatically—emotionally, psychologically, politically, sociologically," says Buhle. "Very suddenly, fraternity boys, athletes, all sorts of normal people who were just going to classes, people who were a little ambivalent about the war but who would never go to a demonstration, were unbelievably outraged and were eager to wade into the crowd and sock the jaw of a cop."

The police began to tear gas the students, but the clouds of stinging gas only made the crowd angrier. "Tear gas was pretty easy to deal with...You take your jacket off, pick it up and throw it back at them." As the crowd grew larger and began to outnumber the police, students challenged them: shouting, throwing rocks..." "There was," says Buhle, "a strange aura of excitement. There was in that terrifying moment an aura of tremendous romantic upsurge. I wouldn't call it erotic, but somehow you were in a new relation with all kinds of people immediately around you, men and women. It was an epiphanic moment. And it was so exciting that you lost your fear. You had this feeling that you had to go back. Maybe because you were so angry about the war, maybe because you would have missed the most important, exciting moment in your life if you didn't."[66]

A documentary movie called *War at Home*, which is about the evolution of the peace movement at the University of Wisconsin, includes footage of events described in the above passage; and behind the title and credits of this film Bob Dylan's voice can be heard singing "When the Ship

Comes In."[67] Furthermore, one line from this song, "The whole wide world is watchin'," was chanted by antiwar protesters in Chicago, in 1968, outside the building where the Democratic Convention was taking place.[68] These uses of "When the Ship Comes In," alone, would seem to prove that Dylan was a kind of prophet, because Dylan wrote this particular song during the summer of 1963.

By mid-summer of 1966, when Dylan's manager announced that he was canceling all of Dylan's engagements, the movement had gathered enormous strength among young people who were part of the general community, as well as among college and university students. But the way I use the term "peace movement" may require clarification: the peace movement was not issues or events, per se, even though it has often been described through reference to issues and events; the peace movement was the young men and women who recognized the issues and helped define them, who created the events, and sacrificed other commitments and other relationships to lend themselves to a new community called the "peace movement," which was a community of love.

In a sense Dylan was like everybody else who got involved. He has acknowledged that he was inspired by things other people were doing.[69] But Dylan had the ability to "make waves" like no one else; and he contributed the ingredient that gave birth to the movement in the first place by making common cause against racism, militarism, and authoritarianism.[70] Dylan made his every appearance in public, between 1961 and 1966, a political happening, because he sang controversial material, and he did and said controversial things; and when he and his admirers looked about them at his concerts, beginning in April 1962, they could *see* the movement, and *feel* its growth and vitality. At the outset of his career Dylan needed *Broadside,* and other singers, to reach his audience, because he was new and his name was unknown, and because his work could be censored by the recording company that held his work; but by the end of 1963 it would have been more difficult for Columbia Records or anyone else to censor Dylan. He had begun to reach enormous audiences, in person, from coast to coast. Happily, it is possible to reconstruct what Dylan did with these opportunities to communicate directly with people who came out to hear him.

According to the information that is available about what Dylan sang, begining in 1961 he used every concert appearance to promote ethically-oriented, politically-controversial material. Up to July 1965 every concert included explicit attacks on racism, and explicit attacks on militarism, plus several of the songs that rendered his vision of the end of the world[71]; but in 1964 Dylan had begun to introduce songs that formed a middle-ground between his early explicit songs and his more ambiguous rock and roll masterpieces of 1965 and 1966. "Mr. Tambourine Man" is the best example, but "Gates of Eden," "It's Alright, Ma (I'm Only Bleeding)," "Chimes of Freedom," and other songs, might be mentioned here.

The songs I am speaking of are "middle-ground" because none of them rendered Dylan's vision of the end of the world unequivocally, and none of them addressed the issues of racism or militarism unequivocally. These are things they have in common with his rock and roll songs; but Dylan played them solo, with an acoustic guitar and harmonica to accompany himself, which is something they have in common with the songs he composed in 1961, 1962, and 1963. They were middle-ground in another sense, too; because Dylan continued to sing these songs after he made his rock and roll breakthrough at Newport in 1965, whereas he would not sing his earlier songs anymore—that is, after Newport he would sing nothing he had written in 1961, 1962, or 1963!

Dylan seems to have enjoyed playing rock and roll. If that were not true, he could hardly have produced his rock and roll songs and taken them on the road successfully in 1965 and 1966; but Dylan used rock and roll—he worked with it—to communicate. He learned to play jigs, reels, and countrified ballads and waltzes, when he mastered Guthrie's musical vocabulary, for the same reason—these forms served him; but rock and roll served him best, in 1965, because in addition to all its inherent virtues, it was the best way to communicate with kids.

Dylan's biographers point out that he formed his first rock and roll band when he was fifteen, that he played publicly for teenagers in Hibbing during his high school years, and that Columbia Records released Dylan's first rock and roll single in 1962.[72] He was attacked unfairly for playing rock and roll in 1965, but no one has attacked Dylan because he sang about heaven and hell; underneath it all, though, it was not the *sounds* Dylan made, but *the things he said,* that were most profoundly disturbing. There is proof that this is so in the fact that rock and roll was around for years before Dylan played it, but before Dylan came along, people were not prompted by the words of rock and roll songs to talk about *ideas.*

Dylan's concerts gave him an opportunity to communicate with thousands of members of the peace movement face-to-face, in a setting that excluded grown-ups and confrontation; so the selection of songs he made for his concerts (beginning especially in early 1964, after his second visit to Mississippi, after his attack on the liberal establishment at the Emergency Civil Liberties Committee award dinner, after his coast-to-coast tour with Joan Baez, after the March on Washington, after three TV appearances that identified him as a writer of protest songs, after he walked off the set of the *Ed Sullivan Show*—in short, after he had established himself in political circles as a radical figure) must be regarded as the indicator of highest value to an assessment of the truth about his influence on the peace movement. His performance record shows that he continued to give the apocalyptic warning he had given in 1962, and he reiterated this warning in a combination of old and new songs, so that there could be no doubt that he considered the content of the older songs and the newer songs to be in agreement. When he stopped singing his earliest works in July 1965, he knew, because he enjoyed a unique perspective from the stage, that his songs had had an effect—that they had, in fact, shaken things up considerably. He continued to deliver a warning, and to attack vice, trusting that he would find listeners who would enjoy the challenge of enigma, and the rhythms and harmonies of the world's loudest and least "polite" music—rock and roll.

Dylan expected people to seek his meaning; and it would seem that millions of young men and women did that, and thought that they understood Dylan—or loved him without thinking they understood him entirely. Todd Gitlin indicates that listening to Dylan's records was the standard form of socializing for his circle of acquaintances during the sixties[73]; Phil Ochs, a singer who helped popularize Dylan's songs in the early sixties, is quoted as having said, "Dylan got inside people's minds"[74]; and Allen Matusow names several of Dylan's rock and roll hits and says, "...in 1965 millions of radios and record players were daily pounding Dylan's message, subliminally or otherwise, into the skulls of a generation."[75] What is strange, in light of such remarks and their abundance, is the fact that the epithet, "prophet of the peace movement," which was associated with Dylan's name for several years, has apparently never been recorded in any book, article, or movie, before now. But this is not to say that the word "prophet" has not been used in association with Dylan's name in print—for it has, many times.[76]

Shelton reports (quoting someone else) that by August 1963 certain "Messiah-makers" had convinced themselves that Dylan was, "a prophet for their cause."[77] The witness in this case was Carla Rotolo, and she was referring in particular to Irwin Silber, the editor of *Sing Out!*, who was very powerfully moved by Dylan; but Rotolo was wrong to call Silber a "Messiah-maker." Silber saw Dylan as an outstanding talent—that is a matter of record[78]; and it is also a matter of record that he was intolerant of Dylan's deviations from topical composition, and unable to bear rock and roll.[79] But no one made Dylan a prophet; and no one, but Dylan, himself, created the impression that he was somehow Christlike.

People who compared Dylan to Christ did so, perhaps, because he delivered a fatal warning about eternal life; and he reiterated this warning in public, from April 1962 until the end of May 1966. Dylan did not participate in student demonstrations, as Joan Baez has pointed out; but he disturbed the peace on behalf of the peace movement with his songs, and by setting an example in his expression of dissent for others to follow. Playing rock and roll, in itself, was an important means of expressing dissent, because rock and roll is revolutionary music, *sui generis*. Karpel suggests that it was the "4/4 time," or the "black backbeat," of Dylan's rock and roll songs that excited his admirers' enthusiasm for his work in 1965 and 1966; but he neglects to mention the mass, volume, and complexity of the music, the color of the spectacle rock and roll ensembles present on stage, the capacity of rock and roll to express ideas and feelings, and the revolutionary history of the music.

Dylan did not withdraw his support for the peace movement when he wrote difficult songs and printed verse in 1964, or when he began to play rock and roll at concerts in 1965. Just the opposite would be true: he intensified his involvement with the movement; he mingled with members of the movement, especially musicians, all over the U.S. and abroad; and his critique of American society became increasingly radical. He distanced himself from Greenwich Village, Shelton, the Rotolo's, Silber, and company, in 1964; but before the year was out he had composed two of his rock and roll masterpieces, "Subterranean Homesick Blues" and "Maggie's Farm."

Rock and roll was the perfect medium for Dylan. He was "swimming" in his natural element in the sea of sound created by the electronically-amplified instruments played in his rock and roll bands: drums, bass, guitar, electric keyboards, and harmonica. The loud, complex sound of rock and roll is essential to its character and its effects; but it is worth noting that Dylan did not play in dance halls, and that some of the songs he played with rock and roll ensembles were not in 4/4 time. For example, "Highway 61 Revisited" was sung in 4/4 time, but "Desolation Row" and "Visions of Johanna" were not.

Before I conclude this chapter I would like to recommend the work of one political historian who is not mentioned above–David Caute, the author of *The Year of the Barricades: A Journey Through 1968*.[80] Caute does not pay much attention to Dylan, to music, or to the religious aspect of the peace movement; but he informs his reader in fine detail about many issues, personalities, and events of the '60s, in the U.S. and eight other countries (including Japan and Mexico), and as he weaves a very complex account together he respectfully communicates the idea that the young protesters of the '60s were inspired by principle.

Caute uses the words "peace movement" twice in his book, but apparently only by accident: once, in passing, when he mentions "the upside down Y symbol of the peace movement"[81]; and once when quoting someone else.[82] The terms he prefers are "new left" and "counterculture." He does not keep his usage of these two epithets perfectly straight; but that hardly matters, because Caute manages to explain enough about the character of the movement for the truth to shine through—which is, that it was essentially non-doctrinaire and anti-dogmatic, and that when it functioned well it was truly democratic. He shows that its members sometimes acted in unison, understanding one another perfectly—not as a mob, but as a chorus. I would add, and I think Caute would accept as a summary note, that "sit-ins," "teach-ins," "love-ins," "be-ins," music festivals, "alternative" radio stations, and thousands of co-operative ventures in community service, were the products of the peace movement, and that, while some individuals and groups attempted to destroy draft records, most of the men and women who participated in the events of the peace movement, in America, never attempted to destroy anything, and did not conspire to overturn the U.S. government.

Caute mentions that some members of the American religious community, like the Berrigan brothers, entered the movement and defended it[83]; but he does not explicitly acknowledge that religious principles were at stake in the tumult that looked like "politics" in the '60s. But dissent *is* an inalienable right; and freedom of speech *is* a religious principle. I would add to what Caute says that members of the peace movement were prepared to be clubbed, gassed, incarcerated, or ostracized from their families, for participating in political demonstrations in opposition to racism and militarism, because they believed that they were doing what God wanted them to do.

Some men and women who admired Dylan during the '60s may protest that I exaggerate the religious aspect of Dylan's message; some may even deny that Dylan was singing about the Messiah, and heaven and hell, in his visionary songs. I would answer that what Dylan had to say can only be fully grasped if the listener understands that he was invoking the Judeo-Christian tradition. I cannot say whether Dylan believed in Jesus or not; but Dylan's compositions make allusion to the Bible and to Christianity—the ideational system that is virtually synonymous with the West. That is why it was possible for Dylan to make himself understood through enigma; and that is why it was possible for him to influence the conduct of so many people. Dylan may be the greatest teacher of the Judeo-Christian tradition his generation, born during World War II, has produced, because he taught that there is a relationship between racism, militarism, and authoritarianism, and he exposed that relationship. After all is said and done, it is Dylan's success as a teacher of ethics that sets him apart, and makes it reasonable to compare him to Dante Alighieri.

The historical record does not say, clearly, that Dante made an impact on politics in his day, and it seems certain that he did not cause a "social revolution"—as Stewart Meecham called the peace movement; but Dylan *did*. He never said he wanted to see the government of the U.S. overthrown—in fact, he had a huge flag mounted on the stage behind him when he played on tour in the spring of 1966, and he wore a tailored shirt and "mod" suit when he played before the flag. According to hints within the lyrics of his songs he wanted everyone to play music and sing songs—which is to say, he wanted something "not of this world."

Notes

1 Apparently no one has published a complete listing of all of Dylan's concerts prior to his retirement. Michael Krogsgaard's catalog of Dylan tapes is a useful reference text. It includes dates and locations, the names of the songs Dylan performed, the names of the musicians who played with Dylan, and other details, for all the concert recordings in his collection. In addition, it provides the dates and locations for a number of Dylan's concerts that are not represented in Krogsgaard's collection; nevertheless, it would seem that all Krogsgaard's listings, for 1961 through 1966, name only about half of Dylan's formal concerts. Michael Krogsgaard, *Positively Bob Dylan* (Ann Arbor, Michigan: Pop Culture, Inc. 1991).

2 Dylan's first television engagement was in England, in December 1962, in a play that was written for the BBC (he sang "Blowin' in the Wind" and a song called "Ballad of the Gliding Swan"); the second was within a special program about American folk music, which was broadcast on ABC-TV in late May 1963; the third was to have been his featured appearance on the *Ed Sullivan Show* in May 1963; and the fourth was in a program about the civil rights movement called, *Freedom Songs*, which was produced by Arthur Barron. (Dylan traveled with Barron to Greenwood, Mississipi, for the filming of one segment of *Freedom Songs*, in early July 1963; and the show was broadcast a few weeks later, just before the March on Washington.) After July 1963 Dylan rarely accepted invitations to appear on TV; but in late February 1964 Dylan appeared on the *Steve Allen Show*, which let his admirers know that he was in California.

3 Shelton does not explain his role in the publication of this article coherently or candidly. He insinuates that the writer for *Newsweek* was rudely turned away by Dylan's manager when she wanted an interview with Dylan for a cover story, and that when she continued to seek information about Dylan, she and her associates at *Newsweek* dug up the truth. But Shelton also lets it be known that he personally told this reporter (Andrea Svedberg) about Dylan's family, and the story that Dylan did not write "Blowin' in the Wind." Furthermore, he names a reporter in Duluth (Walter Eldot), who confirmed information about Dylan's background for *Newsweek*, and interviewed Dylan's father; and he lets it be known that he spoke to that reporter about Dylan's background, prior to the publication of the *Newsweek* article, too. Shelton even tips us off to the fact that he read the *Newsweek* article prior to its publication. What I find most remarkable is that Shelton says that an economics professor in New Jersey, named Harry Levin, told him the rumor that Dylan was not the author of "Blowin' in the Wind." Shelton could have refuted the rumor that Dylan bought the song, but he chose to repeat it. (Incidentally,

he reports that Suze Rotolo's mother married a "New Jersey teacher"; but he does not name this man, or the school where he taught.) Shelton 53-54,145-146,184-185, 213-215, 220.

    4 Shelton's use of the phrase, "out of control," occurs on pages 286 and 293.

    5 Anthony Scaduto, *Bob Dylan: An Intimate Biography* (New York: Grosset and Dunlap, 1971) 88, 129-132. (Scaduto also says that Suze Rotolo told him she would push drinks on Dylan before his performances, and that Joan Baez told him she would put Valium into Dylan's drinks, "to help him relax.")

    6 Shelton 387.

    7 Scaduto 161.

    8 Shelton 222.

    9 Scaduto calls it, "disastrous"; Shelton calls it, Dylan's "Bay of Pigs."

    10 Kenn Thomas and Bob Heyer discuss Dylan's speech to the E.C.L.C., and the meaning of his remarks about people who visited Cuba, suggesting that Dylan was the target of "dirty tricks" by a right-wing political group. "Only a Pawn," *Steamshovel Press,* No. 9 (St. Louis, 1993) 12.

    11 Scaduto 162, 3.

    12 Stephen Pickering published this photo in *Praxis: One,* but he does not name the photographer.

    13 Shelton 283,4. (Gleason's article appeared in the San Francisco *Chronicle,* on Februry 24, 1964.)

    14 For example, he says, "From Woodstock (Dylan) traveled to two major concerts in 1964"; but he names two concert appearances on the *East* Coast, deleting all reference to the series of concerts Dylan gave on the *West* Coast in November, and early December, 1964. Shelton 300.

    15 Shelton uses these words to describe Dylan's performance with Baez: "...struggling on one wing, never quite able to leave the ground"; "His voice was harsh, badly projected..."; "Dylan's disorder..." Shelton 300.

    16 Shelton 293.

    17 Dylan is shown singing one verse of "Mr. Tambourine Man." The song had not yet been released on a recording (*Bringing It All Back Home* came out in March 1965), and Dylan sang it with care, inclining his body toward his listeners, pronouncing every word and phrase with what might be called "feeling." He was dressed in a suit (no tie). *Festival* was produced and directed by Murray Lerner (1967).

    18 Here are listings from three concerts:

New York City, Town Hall, June 1964:
    "The Times They Are A-Changin'" 1963
    "Girl of the North Country" 1963
    "Who Killed Davey Moore?" 1963
    "Talking John Birch Paranoid Blues" 1962
    "To Ramona" 1964
    "Ballad of Hollis Brown" 1962
    "Chimes of Freedom" 1964
    "I Don't Believe You (She Acts Like We Have Never Met)" 1964
    "It's Alright, Ma (I'm Only Bleeding)" 1964
    "Mr. Tambourine Man" 1964
    "Talking World III Blues" 1963
    "A Hard Rain's A-Gonna Fall" 1962
    "Don't Think Twice, It's All Right" 1962
    "Only A Pawn In Their Game" 1963
    "It Ain't Me, Babe" 1964
    "The Lonesome Death of Hattie Carroll" 1963
    "All I Really Want to Do" 1964

New York, Philharmonic Hall, October 1964:
    "The Times They Are A-Changin'" 1963
    "Spanish Harlem Incident" 1964
    "Talking John Birch Paranoid Blues" 1962
    "To Ramona" 1964
    "Who Killed Davey Moore?" 1963
    "Gates of Eden" 1964
    "If You Gotta Go, Go Now" 1964
    "It's Alright, Ma (I'm Only Bleeding)" 1964
    "I Don't Believe You (She Acts Like We Have Never Met)" 1964
    "Mr. Tambourine Man" 1964
    "A Hard Rain's A-Gonna Fall" 1962
    "Talking World III Blues" 1963
    "Don't Think Twice, It's All Right" 1962
    "The Lonesome Death of Hattie Carroll" 1963
    "Mama, You've Been On My Mind" 1964
    "Silver Dagger" (J. Baez singing) traditional
    "With God On Our Side" 1962
    "It Ain't Me, Babe" 1964

"All I Really Want to Do"1964

Berkeley, U. of California, November 1964:
    "The Times They Are A-Changin'" 1963
    "Talking John Birch Paranoid Blues" 1962
    "To Ramona" 1964
    "Gates of Eden" 1964
    "If You Gotta Go, Go Now" 1964
    "It's Alright, Ma (I'm Only Bleeding)" 1964
    "Mr. Tambourine Man" 1964
    "A Hard Rain's A-Gonna Fall" 1962
    "Talking World III Blues" 1963
    "Don't Think Twice, It's All Right" 1962
    (This listing is incomplete.)

19 The "Chad Mitchell Trio" recorded "Blowin' in the Wind" in 1962, "Peter Paul and Mary" recorded "Blowin' in the Wind" in 1963, and according to Shelton, dozens of artists and ensembles recorded it in 1964. Shelton 187.

20 Max Heirich says that students at Berkeley asked Baez to come to Sproul Plaza to sing at a rally in November, and that their intention was to attract people who might stay and participate in the march to Sproul Hall, and vigil, which were to follow. It may have been Baez's idea to march with the students and sit-in with them, and to return in December–Heirich does not say. Max Heirich, *The Spiral of Conflict: Berkeley 1964* (New York: Columbia U P, 1971) 250-253.

21 The statement published by the University of California on the subject of the 1964 insurrection at Berkeley, written by Verne Stadtman, mentions the singing and Joan Baez's participation. Stadtman confirms that tens of thousands of people participated in the rallies, marches, and sit-ins in October, November, and December. The number of people gathered around the police car that came to take away a student in October 1964 has been estimated most often. Witnesses agree that between 2,000 and 4,000 people gathered on that occasion. Stadtman adds the information that 500 armed policemen were brought to the scene to control the students. Verne Stadtman, *The University of California: A Centennial Publication of the University of California* (New York: McGraw Hill, 1970) 448-452.

22 The way Shelton portrays Dylan's relationship with Baez emphasizes that Baez owned a piano, a sports car, and a house above the sea. Shelton 203-209.

23 W. J. Rorabaugh, *Berkeley At War: The 1960s* (New York and Oxford: Oxford UP, 1989) 32,3.

24 The image on the cover of Chafe's book is a photo-collage that makes a

particularly ugly statement about the 1960s; and young people making the peace sign are nowhere near the center of this composition. William A. Chafe, *The Unfinished Journey: America Since World War II* (NewYork and Oxford: Oxford UP, 1986).

25   The cover of Fraser's book shows the forms of young peace activists, thrusting their arms high in the air, and making the peace sign; on the spine of the book the hand of one of these protesters is shown close-up, making the peace sign. Ronald Fraser, editor, *1968: A Student Generation In Revolt: An International Oral History* (NewYork: Pantheon Books,1988).

26   I will have more to say about Savio in this chapter. Max Heirich published this photo in *The Spiral of Conflict*, and he names Don Kechely as the photographer.

27   The following passage shows this tendency to equate the peace movement with the antiwar movement, *exclusively:*

> By 1960 the American peace movement had been reconstituted. It had grown rapidly on the issue of atmospheric testing, but it had not effectively popularized its larger agenda of disarmament and a negotiated end to the cold war. Indeed, the politics of persuasion and advocacy of its liberal wing had yielded disappointment and frustration. Perhaps the time was not ripe...there was no longer any expectation for an immediate breakthrough on the government level or through the political process. The momentum of the movement shifted a bit to the radical pacifist wing, with its emphasis on individual acts of moral protest.The experimentation of southern black protest suggested that such actions could have a collective impact—that "at the very moment when the system appears impregnable to the realist, it often turns out to be vulnerable to the quixotic." Throughout the 1960s that hope would increasingly infuse the peace movement and its antiwar successor.

DeBenedetti wrote most of the book; Chatfield completed it. Charles DeBenedetti, author, and Charles Chatfield, assisting author. *An American Ordeal: The Antiwar Movement of the Vietnam Era* (Syracuse, NewYork: Syracuse U P, 1990) 51 .

28   DeBenedetti and Chatfield 73.

29   DeBenedetti and Chatfield 63-64,149, and 355.

30   DeBenedetti and Chatfield 405.

31   Here is the quote in full:

> By mid-decade there was a general loosening of mores, especially among young people. Reflecting a pervasive mood and fed by atten-

dant fads, a vaguely definable youth subculture began to emerge. Its leitmotif was experimentation, its symbols "grass" and rock. Musically it ranged from Joan Baez through Bob Dylan to the Grateful Dead... DeBenedetti and Chatfield 135.

32 Fraser 87.

33 Dylan did not perform in Italy or Germany during the '60s. He performed in France one time (May 1966). But books and articles about Dylan, and anthologies of his songs and written verse, in translation, began to appear in all these countries in the early '70s.

34 Fraser 2.

35 Fraser 379.

36 Chafe 410. The quotation is drawn from Paul Goodman, *The New Reformation: Notes of a Neolithic Conservative* (New York: Random House, 1971) 20-23.

37 Article XX of the *Augsberg Confession,* which was delivered to Emperor Charles V in 1530, states the protestant position clearly:

> ...Hence there was a very great need to treat of, and renew, this doctrine of faith in Christ, to the end that anxious consciences should not be without consolation, but that they might know that grace and forgiveness of sins and justification are apprehended by faith in Christ.

38 Chafe 326,7.

39 Rorabaugh describes what happened to the town of Berkeley, in May 1969, in considerable detail. He points out that the University was not touched. Rorabaugh 160-171.

40 Rorabaugh 127.

41 Dylan was part of a group that traveled from New York City to Greenwood, Mississippi, to participate in a voter registration rally, and to film the event for WNEW-TV in New York; but the day Dylan spent with Cordell Regan and Bernice Johnson in Atlanta, in February 1964, and his visit with Robert Moses and Dorie Larner in Jackson, a few days later, were private expressions of Dylan's desire to lend support to the civil rights movement.

42 When Dylan and Baez appeared together in 1963 she was at the zenith of her career as an interpreter of old folk songs; but one year later, after having sung Dylan's songs at every concert, and after having brought Dylan on stage with her before audiences from coast to coast, she was called the "peace queen." (Incidentally, Baez left the students in Sproul Hall before the police arrived.)

43 Rorabaugh misuses the term "folk music" in this passage, and he misrepresents the facts about Dylan's place in the history of the peace movement:

> In early 1964 mainstream culture under went an unprecedented, frontal

attack, when the youthful postwar generation discovered The Beatles. In the fifties Elvis Presley had led the first rock and roll boom; this second, Beatles-led boom was greater...Folk music all but disappeared; by 1965 Dylan played folk rock with amplification.

Rorabaugh 120. (Rorabaugh may be right to compare The Beatles to Elvis Presley; but they did not "attack" mainstream culture in "early 1964." Dylan did! The Beatles rapport with the peace movement began after they met Dylan. All four Beatles made published statements acknowledging indebtedness to Dylan; and Elvis recorded two songs by Dylan.)

44 Craig Karpel, *The Tarantula In Me* (San Francisco: Klone, 1973). This piece was originally published in the Village *Voice* in 1972.

45 J.F.C. Hecker, *The Epidemics of the Middle Ages*. Translated by B.G. Babington (London: Sydenham Society, 1844).

46 Friedrich Nietzsche, *The Birth of Tragedy Out of the Spirit of Music*, Translated by Walter Kaufman (New York: Vintage, 1967) 54.

47 Other sources for the title occur to me. For example, in the spring of 1965 students at Berkeley began publishing a mimeographed newssheet called *SPIDER*, which stood for "Sex, Politics, International communism, Drugs, Extremism, and Rock and roll." A photo of the editor selling *SPIDER* from a table on a sidewalk at Berkeley is printed in Rorabaugh's book. What makes this photo stand out is the replica of a huge, shaggy, black spider, dangling from a string, above the head of this young man and his table. *SPIDER* might have given Dylan the idea of calling his book *Tarantula*–and it would have been a positive connotation, supporting Karpel's idea that Dylan was referring to himself as the tarantula; but the primary connotation of the title would still seem to be that Dylan's enemy is the tarantula–like the "deadly tarantula" Harry Belafonte sang about in his 1950s hit, "Day-O."

48 Karpel does not question the veracity of Grossman's report that Dylan had a motorcycle accident–he questions Dylan's motives for not getting back on stage! But he really should be skeptical about the report that Dylan broke his neck. People who saw Dylan reported that he seemed well, and within a few weeks of reporting that Dylan had broken his neck, Grossman reported that Dylan was unscarred and ready to perform again (Shelton 428). In other words, the official report, "Dylan's badly hurt," was contradicted by the report that went through the underground: "Dylan's okay."

49 Karpel labels Dylan's early work, and the influence of Guthrie and his circle, as "white"; but he shows by this that he is not well-informed about the origins of the music Guthrie played. American popular music is *not white*.

50 Dylan's last concerts in North America took place in the following cities: March 3 - Miami Beach, Florida; March 11 - St. Louis, Missouri; March 12 - Lincoln, Nebraska; March 13 - Denver, Colorado; March 19 - Los Angeles, California; March 20 - Santa Monica, California; March 24 - Seattle, Washington; and March 26 - Vancouver, British Columbia, Canada. April was spent in the Orient, and May was spent in Europe, Scandinavia, and Great Britain.

51 Cesare da Sesto is believed to have painted the *St. John*. The same figure and pose would have served very well to depict David as a young man. Presumably, if Bacchus was compared to John the Baptist, it was because in the worship of Bacchus (and Dionysos) people celebrated the mystery of eternal life and resurrection.

52 Nietzsche had more to say about Dionysos:

> Under the charm of the Dionysian not only is the union between man and man reaffirmed, but nature which has become alienated, hostile or subjected, celebrates once more her reconciliation with her lost son: man.

The words, *"verlorene Sohn,"* were used here by Nietzsche; and they were used by Luther used to translate Jesus's story of the "prodigal son." Nietzsche, *Birth of Tragedy*, 54.

53 Gleason was present when Dylan sang for the first time in California, at the Monterey Folk Festival, in March 1963. He became a fan, gradually, as he took time to listen with care to Dylan's compositions. Gleason was not a political radical or an adolescent, but he promoted Dylan repeatedly.

54 Nietzsche, *Birth of Tragedy*, 55. Elsewhere Nietzsche declared, "God is dead." It is Nietzsche I am thinking of, in particular, when I speak of the "Christian era," rather than the "post-modern era."

55 Thomas Meehan, "Public Writer #1," *New York Times (Sunday) Magazine*, December 12, 1965, 44,5.

56 Joe Boyd, the production manager at Newport in 1965, has described the audience's response:

> I'm out there on the stage before (Dylan) comes out, setting up all the amps to exactly the right levels, and Rothchild's out at the mixing board, right in the middle of the audience, where it would be today at a concert, getting everything cranked up. And when the first note of "Maggie's Farm" hit–I mean, by today's standards it's not very loud, but by the standards of those days it was the loudest thing that anybody had ever heard.
> The volume. That was the thing, the volume. It wasn't just the music, it wasn't just the fact that he came out and played with an electric band, it was the fact–and this, I suppose is what this whole thing is leading up to–care was taken to get Paul Rothchild to mix the sound. As a result, you

didn't have some square sound guy fumbling around, you had powerfully, ballsy-mixed expertly done rock-n-roll.

...When they came out the first hit of the guitar was like PPPAARRR! a wall of sound, you know, hitting the audience with tremendous power. It really knocked people back on their seats. As soon as I had gotten the stage set, I ran around to the press enclosure which was the front section, and stood sort of at the door and watched at the side of the stage...

Then somebody pulled at my elbow and said, "You'd better go backstage, they want to talk to you." So I went backstage and there I was confronted by Seeger and Lomax and, I think, Theodore Bikel or somebody, saying, "It's too loud! You've got to turn it down! It's far too loud! We can't have it like this! It's *unbearably* loud!" And they were really upset. Very, very upset. I said, "I don't control the sound, the sound is out there in the middle of the audience." And so Lomax said, "How do you get there? Tell me how to get there, I'll go out there!" I said, "Well, Alan, you walk right to the back—it's only about a half a mile—and then you walk around to the center thing, show your badge, and just come down the center aisle." And he said, "There must be a quicker way." So I said, "Well, you can climb over the fence"—I was looking at his girth, you know—and he said, "Now look, you go out there, you can get there, I know you know how to get there! Go out there and tell them that the Board *orders* them to turn the sound down!"

I said, "OK." So I went out—there was a place where anyone could climb on top of a box and get over the fence from backstage. By this time I think it was the beginning of the second number, and there were Grossman, Newirth, Yarrow, and Rothchild, all sitting at the sound desk, grinning, very very pleased with themselves—and meanwhile the audience was going nuts!

...There were arguments between people sitting next to each other! Some were booing, some were cheering. It was very very hard to tell. There was a ROAR of noise. I mean, it was definitely shocking. I relayed Lomax's message and Peter Yarrow said, "Tell Alan Lomax...that the Board of the festival are adequately represented on the sound console and that we have things fully under control and we think that the sound is at the correct level."

So I went back, climbed over the fence, and by this time all I could see of Pete Seeger was the back of him disappearing down the road past the car park. I was confronted by Lomax and Bikel again, frothing at the mouth, and I relayed Yarrow's message and they just cursed and gnashed their teeth. By this time the thing was almost over. Yarrow followed me back—I think he'd had a conversation with Dylan earlier in which he said, "You can't just do three numbers. You've got to come on and do some acoustic stuff afterwards." 'Cause Dylan had been scheduled for 40 minutes, certainly half an hour. People had not come all that way to see 20 minutes of Bob Dylan, or 15...So Yarrow was all poised to go up on stage, and suddenly they'd finished.

There was a HUGE roar from the crowd..you know. "More!" and "BOO!" sound very similar if you have a whole crowd going "More!" and "BOO!"–you couldn't really tell what was happening, I think it was evenly divided between approbation and condemnation from the crowd. Well, this roar went on for quite some time, and Yarrow then went on stage and rather embarrassingly began to do his impression of a sort of Las Vegas compere–"C'mon folks, let's hear it for Bob Dylan, see if we can get him back out here!" No Bob Dylan. Bob Dylan was hiding in a tent. Grossman didn't want to get involved. He wasn't going to bully Dylan about it. Anyway, finally Dylan stumbled back on stage with an acoustic guitar and he went into "Mr. Tambourine Man."...

"Newport '65: Joe Boyd interviewed by Jonathan Morley" in *Wanted Man: In Search of Bob Dylan*, edited by John Bauldie (New York: Citadel Press, 1991) 57-66.

57 Ron Elz, alias "Johnny Rabbit," one of the founders of KSHE-St. Louis, was interviewed by Steve DeBellis in a provocative article describing the breakthrough of alternative music on FM, in 1967 and after. Elz and his associates used the freedom they had at KSHE to design exciting musical programming. He says they specifically sought and played albums by new groups, and urged new groups to visit St. Louis. *St. Louis Inquirer*, vol 7, No 7, Nov 1992, 12-15.

58 I quote Matusow above, on page 3.

59 Dylan was taken to a hospital, and he wore a neck brace after he left the hospital; but no one saw the accident, and no one has reported seeing any sign of injury in Dylan–except that he wore a neck brace.

60 Shelton indicates that Pennabaker and Sara met a year prior to the filming of *Don't Look Back*. Shelton 343.

61 Shelton 417.

62 Dylan wears a disguise–a thick black moustache–in one scene of *Eat the Document*. He is shown in the company of a friend, "clowning around," in a hotel room or apartment in Paris. (In the moustache he pretended he was a villain.) He appears in disguise in one scene of *Renaldo and Clara*, seated with friends in a delicatessen or cafe, wearing a hat and sunglasses; and apparently he held the camera in some scenes, including one segment in which Alan Ginsberg interviews people

on the street.

63 Apparently Dylan enjoyed having a chance to mingle with people, without being recognized. He is shown in the countryside and in cities, sightseeing; but it is the scenes of Dylan singing and playing music with his friends, on stage and off-stage, that provide the most touching effects in *Eat the Document* (not least of all because he is shown singing pieces, off-stage, which might otherwise never have been recorded).

64 Fraser 89,90.

65 Fraser 50,1.

66 Fraser 153,4.

67 *War At Home* was produced by Glenn Silber and Barry Alexander Brown (1986).

68 Shelton 239.

69 Dylan was quoted in the *National Guardian* (August 22, 1963): There's a feeling in the air. More people are willing to say, "To hell with my security, I want my rights!" I want to help them, if I can.

70 Dr. Martin Luther King embraced a position somewhat like Dylan's after mid-decade; but in 1961 he did not. Chafe reports that in 1967 King spoke the following words to his staff:

The black revolution is much more than a struggle for the rights of Negroes. It is forcing America to face all its interrelated flaws–racism, poverty, militarism, and materialism...It reveals systemic rather than superficial flaws and suggests that radical reconstruction of society itself is the real issue to be faced. (Chafe 365.)

Women Strike for Peace supported both the "ban the bomb" movement and the civil rights movement; but no individual from Women Strike for Peace can be said to have been the leader of the peace movement.

71 Dylan's concert at Royal Albert Hall, on May 9, 1965, shows what I mean as well as any other would. I selected this concert because it was filmed, and excerpts are included in *Don't Look Back*. Dylan sang:

> "The Times They Are A-Changin'"
> "To Ramona"
> "Gates of Eden"
> "If You Gotta Go, Go Now"
> "It's Alright, Ma (I'm Only Bleeding)"
> "Love Minus Zero/No Limit"
> "Mr. Tambourine Man"
> "Talking World War III Blues"
> "Don't Think Twice, It's All Right"

"With God On Our Side"
"She Belongs To Me"
"It Ain't Me, Babe"
"The Lonesome Death of Hattie Carroll"
"All I Really Want To Do"
"It's All Over Now, Baby Blue"

"With God On Our Side" and "Talkin' World War III Blues" are antiwar songs; "The Lonesome Death of Hattie Carroll" may be called a civil rights song–it concerns racism *and* the abuse of women; "The Times They Are A-Changin'," "Gates of Eden," "It's Alright, Ma (I'm Only Bleeding)," and "It's All Over Now, Baby Blue" concern Dylan's vision of the end of the world–and in a sense, so does "Mr. Tambourine Man."

72 "Mixed Up Confusion" was released in December 1962. Apparently Dylan did not jam regularly with rockers until the fall of 1964. Shelton records important information about Dylan's move back into rock and roll when he says Dylan was excited by the success of "The Byrds" with "Mr. Tambourine Man" (Shelton 355,6); but he does not explore the subject of jam sessions Dylan may have been part of in the fall and winter of 1964, or in the spring of 1965.

73 Gitlin also says that listening to Dylan constituted a "collective ritual." Gitlin 200-203.

74 Ochs was being interviewed by Gordon Friesen for *Broadside* #63 (October 1965). Ochs also said: "I can just picture (kids) all over the country listening to Dylan again and again and again, trying to figure out what he's saying"; and, "It's a form of hypnosis."

75 Matusow 295.

76 Quoting others, Shelton uses the word "prophet" to refer to Dylan several times (for example on pages 213, 296, and 339); but he does not use this word to describe Dylan, except in hyphenated form ("social-prophet" and "prophet-seer," page 305). David Pichaske calls Dylan a "prophet," in the title of an article about Dylan's work through 1980, and he says people study Dylan's work as if it were "the new law and the prophets"; but Pichaske does not mention the relationship between the apocalyptic songs I discuss here. David Pichaske, "The Prophet and the Prisoner: Bob Dylan and the American Dream," Part One, *Telegraph*, spring 1987. Two other scholars who have written about Dylan's work in such a way as to support the idea that Dylan is some sort of prophet are Stephen Pickering and George Montiero, who are quoted below in chapters 4 and 7.

77 Shelton 213. (Shelton also quotes her as saying that Dylan made the "mistake" of getting "caught up in the vortex of being the Messiah." Shelton 150.)

78 Silber promoted Dylan in *Sing Out!* in the fall of 1962, by publishing his photo on the cover of the magazine and a rave review of his work inside it. In the fall of 1964 he began to attack him; but even then he called Dylan a "genius" ("An Open Letter to Bob Dylan" *Sing Out!*, November 1964).

79 Silber published an apology to Dylan in *The Guardian* (October, 1968). Here is an excerpt:

> Many of us who did not fully understand the dynamics of the political changes...in America...felt deserted by a poet who—we had come to believe—cared. And Dylan did desert—not us, but an outmoded style of values which had become unequal to the task of reclaiming America. "This land is not your land," Dylan told us in 1965. But some of us raised on the songs of Guthrie and Seeger...inheritors of a superficial Marxism, based on diluted Leninism and rationalized Stalinism, were not ready to accept the revolutionary implications of Dylan's statements. Because if we accepted them...we would have to act on them.

80 David Caute, *The Year of the Barricades: A Journey Through 1968.* (New York: Harper and Row, 1988).

81 Caute 139.

82 Allen Samson, District Atorney, March 1970, "Milwaukee 14" trial: "I'm more violently antiwar than anyone in this courtroom, but I don't burn draft records. It's bad for the Peace Movement." Caute 141.

83 Caute 27, and 139, 40.

Chapter 4

"this is my last letter"

Tarantula was by far the longest and most complex poetic work by Dylan that was published in the '60s, and it may be the only book he has written. He has sometimes called *Tarantula* a "novel"[1]; but it would be more reasonable to say it is an "anti-novel," since for the most part it is made up of broken sentences and broken anecdotes, and it does not tell a story. *Tarantula* does, however, render a detailed portrait of an individual and the society in which this person lives, which are familiar characteristics of novels.

The publisher's introductory note to the authorized edition says that *Tarantula* was written when Dylan was twenty-three.[2] But Dylan informed the public that he was writing a book in May 1963, a few days before his twenty-second birthday. He was being interviewed by Studs Terkel, on tape, for Terkel's radio show, and he mentioned that his book described his first week in New York City.[3] According to the narrative composed by Anthony Scaduto, it would seem that this book became *Tarantula*. Scaduto specifically says that Dylan worked on "*Tarantula*" at Joan Baez's home later in 1963, and he quotes Baez's remarks about the way Dylan worked, and about the segment of the book she read—which she said evoked Dylan's childhood in Hibbing.[4] But that project was abandoned, or it was transformed; because Dylan did not tell his readers anything explicit about his past in *Tarantula*.

Scaduto reports that Dylan carried his typewriter with him during his road trip across America in February 1964[5]; and one scene in *Don't Look Back* shows Dylan typing, with his back turned to a group of people, in a hotel room in London. (A photo of Dylan with his typewriter in his arms, taken in that same hotel room, appears on page 76.[6]) Dylan's use of a typewriter while he was on the road is indicative of writing habits that would have enabled him to finish *Tarantula* in 1965, in addition to his other activities. Final editing of the text may have been completed during the spring of 1966; but that date is a matter of interest only because *Tarantula* did not appear in the fall of 1966 when Macmillan had said it would, and Dylan has been blamed because it did not.[7] The detail of greatest historical

importance about the publication of *Tarantula* really does not concern the authorized edition; because the galley proofs of *Tarantula* got into the hands of Dylan's admirers before they had been edited and approved by Dylan, and many thousands of copies were made from these liberated galleys.

The coy remarks of "The Publisher" in the preface of *Tarantula* were written five years after this debacle. (They have been retained in the paperback edition of *Tarantula* that St. Martin's Press released in 1994—so has the typesetting and the numbering of pages.) Macmillan did not apologize; but it would seem that they were virtually confessing that they did not ask Dylan's permission to circulate galleys of *Tarantula*, and that they enabled the book to get out, even though Dylan had not said it was ready:

> We weren't quite sure what to make of the book—except money....
>
> We worked out a design for the book...and we set it up. We also made up some buttons and shopping bags with a picture of Bob and the word *Tarantula*. We wanted to call everyone's attention to the fact that the book was being published. We wanted to help *Life* and *Look* and The New York *Times* and *Time* and *Newsweek* and all the rest who were talking about Bob....
>
> There were also a few sets of galleys that had gone around to different people who were being given a preview of the book. These advance review galleys are made of every book....[8]

Macmillan's preface does not say that Dylan was angry, or disappointed, when he learned that his work was being passed around. It says he told them that he wanted to make changes in the book, and that he had a motorcycle accident; and it implies that Dylan was late with final editing.

No one has directly challenged Macmillan's explanation concerning the long postponement of their publication of *Tarantula*, and no one has shown much interest in the subject of the circulation of the bootleg edition of the book. But the surrepticious publication of *Tarantula* may have been a phenomenon that is without parallel in history; for *Tarantula* was not banned and would not have been censored if Macmillan had released it in 1966, nevertheless, it was published internationally, without the support of the publishing industry, and without the consent of the author.

Stephen Pickering describes the copy of the bootleg of *Tarantula* he owns in *Praxis: One*; he also reprints a dedication, a prologue, and an epilogue, that appear in the bootleg, but were deleted from the final edition.[9] He remarks that the bootleg has "1965" written inside the cover, and that "minor word changes" were made throughout the text before it was printed by Macmillan. Robert Shelton provides no facts or figures about the distribution of the bootleg of *Tarantula*; but he supplies very important information when he says that Dylan had the galleys of *Tarantula* in his hands when they talked in March 1966, and that Dylan said he was going to read them that night.[10] Assuming that Dylan did work on *Tarantula* after he talked to Shelton, he may well have finished final editing of the galleys before he left the continent for Hawaii and Australia. Shelton also says that Dylan complained to him that, "*Tarantula* has already been publicized and written about...You know, I just don't like the obvious." Had Shelton published this interview in 1966, Dylan would not have been accused of making Macmillan wait for his manuscript; but Shelton's interview was not published until 1986, and then it appeared toward the end of a text that repeats the idea that Dylan was "out of control" during the years in which *Tarantula* was written.

In an article published in the *New York Times* in 1971, Robert Christgau refers to the distribution of the bootleg of *Tarantula* as if it were a contemptible subject when he remarks that *Tarantula* was "hawked on the street and under the counter over the past few years by hip rip-off artists"; but he also ridicules *Tarantula* in his review and says, "Dylan is not a poet."[11] In contrast, Craig Karpel, whose discussion of the meaning of the title, *Tarantula,* was published in 1972 in the *Village Voice*, seems to take delight in saying that bootleg copies of *Tarantula*, "appeared piled next to underground-FM-bookstore cash registers."[12] This is an apt phrase; but it assumes that the reader knows that Dylan influenced politics, that the FM radio band carried music and news of interest to members of the peace movement, and that certain bookstores (especially bookstores around universities) carried books, newspapers, magazines, and posters, of interest to the peace movement. It also supports the contention that some people made profits from the sale of the bootleg of *Tarantula*. Dylan's admirers and the "rip off artists" were at work abroad, too, it seems; because Alain Rémond, author of a book about Dylan that was published in France in 1971, says that copies of Dylan's "phantom-novel" could be found in several bookstores in Paris, before Macmillan's authorized edition was released.[13]

Elia Katz goes to the heart of the matter in an article reprinted in *Praxis: One*, that was originally published in Great Britain in 1969, when he calls *Tarantula*, "the first post-printing press novel," and explains that *Tarantula* circulated in "xeroxes and xeroxes of xeroxes" and passed "like drugs from hand to hand among longhairs."[14] Unfortunately, Katz does not mention the peace movement, or its issues and events, in explicit terms. He says, "…there are those who feel *(Tarantula)* to be a 'Revolutionary' work of art…"; but he makes fun of this idea.[15] He suggests that Dylan may have been complicitous with the circulation of *Tarantula* through the underground[16]; but he does not attempt to explain why the people he characterizes as "longhairs" were interested in the book. In the last sentence of his review, however, Katz says, "It is almost a certainty that *Tarantula* will sooner or later be Scripture to the children of America…."[17] There is nothing, whatsoever, in Katz's review that would help the reader understand why anyone would compare *Tarantula* to Scripture, nevertheless, the remark reflects Katz's awareness that some of Dylan's admirers were avid to read *Tarantula* because they believed that Dylan's works teach religious principles.

The first section of *Tarantula* is printed in the appendix, beginning on page 194. It is, in effect, "chapter 1"; but Dylan only provided a title: "Guns, the Falcon's Mouthbook, and Gashcat Unpunished." *Tarantula* has 47 of these sections, or chapters, bearing titles. "Guns, the Falcon's Mouthbook, and Gashcat Unpunished" is much longer than most of the other sections of *Tarantula;* but it is fairly typical in that a word-stream that looks like prose begins it and runs through it, and in that this stream is interrupted by prose passages that look like bits of free verse, or like brief epistles. In some chapters prose dominates, and the stream is brief or nonexistent; but in most chapters the stream creates the impression that words and phrases gushed out of Dylan unordered, and that, unstopped, they might have poured out indefinitely. The prose inserts create stops, which alter the visual appearance and tone of the text. While the stream is characterized by abundance of language and the absence of elements that create coherent sentences or paragraphs, the inserted prose passages are characterized by the sparceness and clarity of their language. They offer the reader a chance to "come up for air," so to speak, from the stream; but the action these passages present is bizarre, and they do not provide much of a break from the rigors involved in interpreting Dylan.

The reader is plunged into the depths of enigma with Dylan's first word: "aretha." The remarks of several reviewers indicate that they understand that Dylan was referring to Aretha Franklin; but his words may also be interpreted as having been addressed to God. The first descriptive phrase partially fit Aretha Franklin ("aretha crystal jukebox queen of hymn"), because Franklin's voice could be heard on jukeboxes in the mid-60s, and because she learned her art as a gospel singer—which is to say, as a singer of "hymns"—before she became famous as a secular artist.[18] But the fit of the words "crystal" and "queen" is uncertain; and the next phrase is extremely problematic: "& him diffused in drunk transfusion wound." The pronoun, "him," in this phrase might be understood to refer to Dylan, whose photo is on the dust-jacket of the book; but the prophetic songs Dylan wrote in 1964 and 1965 make reference to the Messiah in puzzling ways, and their example supports the idea that "him diffused in drunk transfusion wound" refers to Christ. If Dylan meant to say that Jesus is with aretha, or that aretha is Jesus's sovereign, he must have been speaking allegorically, pretending for the moment that God is a woman and a singer like Aretha Franklin, who happens to be about the same age as Dylan.

There is not one sentence in the following 137 pages of *Tarantula* that explicitly confirms the idea that Jesus is meant by, "him diffused in drunk transfusion wound," and there is no passage in the book that proves that Dylan was addressing God, or speaking about God, when he used the name aretha; furthermore, none of Dylan's reviewers suggest that Dylan was referring to God when he talked about aretha. But support for this "divine" interpretation may be drawn indirectly from Stephen Pickering, who has shown insight into the mystical nature of Dylan's work in articles where he is not discussing *Tarantula*. For example, in "Bob Dylan and the Book of Splendour" Pickering suggests that Dylan's songs have been influenced by a mystical work called the *Zohar*[19]; and he explains that the author of that work, who was a contemporary of Dante Alighieri, speaks about the "presence of God" by using the feminine epithet, "*Shekhinah.*"[20] (A passage from the *Zohar,* entitled, "Creation of Man," is printed on the appendix, beginning on page 219.[21])

Pickering's remarks in that particular article, and in his other works on the subject of Dylan's mysticism, make difficult reading, because Pickering quotes from the works of so many authorities that he sometimes seems to forget Dylan and the reader. There are also inherent weaknesses in the comparisons Pickering tries to establish between Dylan and the sages he names. Dylan is an entertainer. He was a kind of spiritual leader during the era of the peace movement, but he makes money by singing and writing songs. The men to whom Pickering would compare him did not address their words to the world at large, and none of them were regarded as leaders outside the Jewish community.[22] Dylan was very young when he became famous, he addressed the young in his songs, and he criticized secular powers aggressively; but the men to whom Pickering would compare him were adults, and they addressed adults. None of them were openly on the attack against the establishment, the way Dylan was; and certainly Moses de Leon, who wrote during Inquisitional times, was not. Another weakness in Pickering's argumentation is that he says that Dylan "changed" at some point; but he cannot make up his mind about the timing of this change, and he does not admit that he is hypothesizing.[23]

Pickering is convincing at numerous points where he discusses Dylan's mysticism and Dylan's craft. For example, in an article entitled "*John Wesley Harding*: The Prospect of Immortality," where he discusses relationships he sees between Jewish mysticism, psychoanalysis, surrealism, existentialism, and the lyrics of some of Dylan's songs, Pickering quotes André Breton and Antonin Artaud, and in doing so makes several points that are of interest to discussion of *Tarantula*. Rather than quote Pickering in full, I have selected the following passages from several pages of discussion:

...in so far as Dylan's Judaic "symbolism" and early surrealism are concerned, it is possible (perhaps imperative) to examine the concepts (of) Andre Bréton, the leading spokesman of surrealism, who...acknowledges the influence of Jung and Buber upon surrealism.

Surrealism, according to Bréton (in his 1924, *"Le manifeste du surréalism"*) is unrepressed thought, thought which is "dictated in the absence of all control exerted by reason, and outside all aesthetic or moral preoccupations." And, Bréton later writes, "Surrealism believes in the "omnipotence of the dream, and in the disinterested play of thought. It leads to the permanent destruction of all other psychic mechanisms, and to its substitution for them."

...(Bréton) is echoed by Antonin Artaud. In his "Letter to the Buddhist Schools," Artaud says, "We suffer from a corruption, the corruption of Reason." And in an editorial written by J.A. Boiffard, P. Éluard, and R. Vitrac for *La revolution surréaliste* (1925), it is maintained that, "...the dream alone entrusts to man all his right to freedom..."

...According to Bréton (in *Le second manifeste du surréalism* (1929), "There is every reason to believe that there exists a certain point in the mind at which life and death, real and imaginary, past and future, communicable and incommunicable, cease to be perceived in terms of contradiction. Surrealist activity would be searched in vain for a motive other than the hope to determine this point." Later, in the same statement, Bréton cites Freud in noting that at the level of the unconscious, there is an "absence of contradiction, a timelessness."[24]

Unfortunately, in this article Pickering goes on to say that Dylan is not a surrealist, but a Jewish mystic. This exclusionary conclusion is in error, and it obliterates the fact that Dylan made himself understood by people who did not identify themselves as Jews. In his review of *Tarantula* Pickering makes no reference to the *Zohar* or to surrealism[25]; but *Tarantula* would be the outstanding example of a surrealist composition among Dylan's works, and it is the only piece in which Dylan seems, at times, to communicate ecstatically. Maybe the reason Pickering does not see this is because he does not see that Dylan may have been speaking of God, as well as of a woman, when he used the name, aretha.

This name, the first challenge of the book proper, is also the book's hardest puzzle, and most evocative, and "surreal," image; but it is intrinsically appealing. Virtually every reviewer comments about aretha, and they all think that they understand Dylan in this case; but no one who has reviewed *Tarantula* has taken up the challenge of saying what Tarantula means, even though this word, or name, is the title of the book. In part their silence is to be expected. The word, tarantula, does not appear in the book, the image evoked by this word is ordinarily deemed to be repulsive, and the meaning of the title, *Tarantula*, is almost as difficult to find as the meaning of the first word, aretha–which evokes a particular woman, who is geninely beautiful. The name, aretha, comes up repeatedly in the first chapter, and then in passages of five other chapters,[26] nevertheless, both these names, Tarantula and aretha, must be interpreted by anyone who would fully make sense of either of them, or of the book. If I understand Dylan correctly, they are the key words of the text.

The photo of Dylan by Jerrold Schatzberg that is shown on the dustjacket of the hardback edition of *Tarantula*, and on the cover of the original paperback edition, may assist interpretation; but this image introduces more enigmatic detail, as well.[27] (It is reproduced on page 84.) It shows Dylan's face close up, in black and white; but half of his face is shadowed, while the other half is brightly illuminated. An image has also been produced from the negative of this photo. The image in natural light values appears on the front of the dustjacket, and the image in negative light values appears on the back. Macmillan used this photo and others from the same sitting, to promote *Tarantula* in 1966, and again in 1971. The image on the dustjacket has the name, "Tarantula," and the name, "Bob Dylan," printed side-by-side–that is, these two names appear on the front and back of the dustjacket, on the spine of the book, and on the title page. Since these words are printed directly on

Dylan's likeness, the reader would seem to have no choice but to conclude that the name *Tarantula* refers to Dylan, as well as to the book.

In this photo Dylan was beardless, slender, fair, and unsmiling, and he was dressed in black and white attire, as might be appropriate to a funeral or wedding. Two features of his appearance may suggest that he was a "nonconformist": his hair was rather long and touseled; and he wore no necktie, even though his shirt collar was tailored to be worn with a tie. The way the light shone on Dylan from a horizontal position may be a reference to the "evening of the world," or the "dawn of redemption"; but above all the "hatchet lighting" creates the impression that Dylan has two sides, or aspects, to his being. The presentation of this image in negative light values on the back of the book may mean that the book recounts that something happened to Dylan, or it may mean that something was about to happen to him–or to the world; but it also redoubles the impression that Dylan has more than one side, and introduces the impression that he has *no back*.

If I understand Dylan correctly, he called his book, *Tarantula,* and had the word, *Tarantula,* printed on his photo as a kind of warning about what is to be found in the book. He compared himself to a spider, because he is a creature, and more like a spider than like God; and he compared himself to the venomous tarantula, because he carried a burden of anger and words like poison for the society he was addressing. Other meanings that attach to the use of this epithet (such as the possibility that Dylan was "spidery" because he was thin, or the possibility Karpel suggested, that Dylan called himself, Tarantula, because he wanted to make everybody dance) may be valid, but would be of secondary importance[28]; because *Tarantula* concerns salvation, and is essentially about good and evil.

On the subject of the book's difficulty Katz says, "The novel is a denseness"; and, "...it often appears dictatorial in the way the phrases demand so much attention without the reward of comprehensibility."[29] He continues with other remarks that revile *Tarantula*. For example, he says of the book, "...rage and distrust (seem) to frame it." Then he strikes harder, "Grotesquery, degeneracy, and mental anarchy are what the book concerns and what it is."[30]

At the beginning of his essay Katz refers to *Tarantula* as something "precious" and as a "privilege to read," and when he speaks of its being smuggled across borders and across the sea, he rightly emphacizes that its history as contraband is "context which helps to illuminate and explicate its content"[31]; but as Katz continues writing he seems to change his mind, and to completely forget about the context in which *Tarantula* was written. He does not mention the peace movement or any of the issues addressed by the movement, even though the peace movement became an international, revolutionary, youth movement during the years in which *Tarantula* circulated "in xeroxes and xeroxes of xeroxes":

> ...(Dylan) is mean to everyone, poking them all out of shape and making bitter fun. Very much like William Burroughs, except that Dylan hasn't got the defining obsessions of Burroughs...

> ...Dylan creates a single crystal focus for the book–himself. As with Burroughs, the essential fact is not the world (not its sense or senselessness or anything, really, about the world at all), but the mind's response to the world, its rejection of it, and its creation, finally, of other worlds...

> ...There is very little understanding or kindness in *Tarantula*, as there was little in (Dylan's) previous songs.[32]

The way Katz compares Dylan to William Burroughs is revealing about *Tarantula's* effect on him: he does not like the book, he distrusts Dylan, and ultimately his purpose in writing is to warn people against *Tarantula*. But the first time Burroughs's name was associated with Dylan's work, it was Dylan who made the comparison. He was being interviewed by a reporter from the Los Angeles *Free Press* in September 1965, and he only mentioned Burroughs in passing; but his words reveal something about him, as well as something about *Tarantula*. Here is the portion of the interview in which the subject of the book comes up (the elipses are copied from the original):

> Robbins: You have a book coming out. What about it? The title?

> Dylan: Tentatively, *Bob Dylan Off the Record*. But they

tell me there are already books out with that "Off the Record" title. The book can't really be titled, that's the kind of book it is. I'm also going to write the reviews for it.

Robbins: Why write a book instead of lyrics?

Dylan: I've written some songs which are kind of far out, a long continuation of verses, stuff like that–but I haven't really gotten into writing a completely free song. Hey, you dig–something like cut-ups? I mean, like William Burroughs?

Robbins: Yeah. There's a cat in Paris who published a book with no pagination. It comes in a box and you throw it up in the air and, however it lands, you read it like that.

Dylan: Yeah, that's where it's at...OK, I wrote the book because there's a lot of stuff in there I can't possibly sing...all the collages. I can't sing it because it gets too long, or it goes too far out...the audience would just get totally lost. Something that has no rhyme, all cut up, no nothing, except something happening which is words.

Robbins: You wrote the book to say something?

Dylan: Yeah, but certainly not any kind of profound statement. The book don't begin or end.

Robbins: But you had something to say. And you wanted to say it to somebody.

Dylan: Yeah, I said it to myself. Only I'm lucky, because I could put it into a book. Now somebody else is going to be allowed to see what I said to myself.[33]

Dylan's remarks prepare people for the sort of reading experience they will discover in *Tarantula*–especially the expressions, "cut-ups" and "all cut up," and, "I said it to myself...now somebody else is going to be allowed to see what I said to myself." Katz's remark, that Dylan does not have "Burroughs's defining obsessions," teaches nothing. It shows that he despises Burroughs; but perhaps Katz should say that Burroughs wrote about heroin addiction and about an addict's way of life–if that is what he means to say.

Dylan's mention of Burroughs's name may be taken as being evidence that his "defining obsessions" are justice and the defense of free speech. He has mentioned Burroughs's name favorably to the press on other occasions, too[34]; and over the course of his career he has praised a number of writers and entertainers who were once censored, or blacklisted, because they were critics of American society.[35] Woody Guthrie, who Dylan called his "first idol," would be the outstanding example of an entertainer Dylan admired and imitated, who had been blacklisted and branded a "communist." Guthrie had been a passionate and effective champion of the poor during the "dust bowl era," but he was not under attack anymore in 1965; whereas, when Dylan spoke Burroughs's name to Paul Robbins for the *Free Press* in 1965, Burroughs was under fire, and the novel that made him famous, *Naked Lunch*, was widely banned.[36]

Dylan's praise of Lenny Bruce and Allen Ginsberg would be more readily comparable to his defense of Burroughs, because both Bruce and Ginsberg were members of the beat generation in the '50s, they were heroin users, and like Burroughs, they portrayed American society as repressive, hypocritical, corrupt, and violent.[37] When Dylan named these men as artists he admired, he invited people to compare him to them; and in *Tarantula*, where Dylan did not explicitly name them, he pretended to speak for them.[38] He did so pointedly when he made an allusion to heroin, on page 48, in one of the little letters inserted into the poetic stream. It begins, "okay, so I shoot dope once in a while. big deal. what's it got to do with you?"[39]

Dylan's motive for including these words in *Tarantula* may have been to exhibit a predilection for heroin, or to poke at laws and attitudes in America that make the use, possession, or sale of this substance a crime; but the book does not mention heroin, and it is not really about drugs, drug laws, or drug use. On the other hand, this reference to "dope," like the reference to "amphetamine" in "Just Like a Woman" (1964),[40] is an integral part of Dylan's characterization of a doomed society. Not only do several passages in the book contain hints about alcohol or heroin abuse, Dylan also seemed to hint about medical confinement for detoxification.[41] If these passages are interpreted to mean that Dylan's life was burdened by the influence of stupifying chemicals, that might be a matter of intrinsic interest to the text, since the word-stream is wild, and may seem to be something that flowed from someone who was "beside himself," or "intoxicated"—or both. But when Dylan composed *Tarantula's* stream-of-consciousness passages his mind and soul may have been free of hatred, and his body may have been free of alcohol, pot, speed, nicotine, and heroin; in which case, the state of mind he recreated in the word-stream of *Tarantula* might best be described as ecstatic.

Katz says Dylan is "mean to everyone, poking them all out of shape"; and, "...rage is directed at everyone in the book except Aretha Franklin." Actually, Dylan was *not* "being mean" to anyone, since he was telling the truth, as it was interpreted by his generation (the peace movement); and when he used the name, aretha, he may have been speaking of the ineffable—as he did when he used epithets like, "tambourine man," "empty-handed painter," "silver-studded phantom," and "cowboy angel," to speak of the Messiah. The name, aretha, is more difficult, because it is a personal name for a female, and it is a very unusual name that is well-known only because of Aretha Franklin and her singing; but Dylan was not "making an exception of Aretha Franklin"—she *is* exceptional. He paid homage to her when he chose the name, aretha; but aretha is not the only name Dylan used when he called out to God, and talked about God. Seven passages in the first chapter seem to refer to God, and Dylan only used the name, aretha, in four of them. Dylan also called God, "great particular eldorado," "ye battered personal god," "bossman of the hobos," "Great Romantic," and "daisy mae"; and apparently Dylan saw God in his mother, his wife, himself, and others—not only in Aretha Franklin.

The first two of these seven praise-passages appear in the opening "paragraph" of the book:

> aretha/ crystal jukebox queen of hymn & him diffused in
> drunk transfusion wound would heed sweet soundwave
> crippled & cry salute to oh great particular el dorado reel &

ye battered personal god but she cannot she the leader of whom when ye follow, she cannot she has no back she cannot...

...aretha with no goals, eternally single & one step soft of heaven/ let it be understood that she owns this melody along with her emotional diplomats & her earth & her musical secrets

The next reference to God names God, "bossman of the hobos." It is near the opening of the second passage of the stream. It also hints about the peace movement ("spiritual gypsy davy camp") and about Dylan—who was a kind of bossman of hobos:

...hallaluyah & bossman of the hobos cometh & ordaining the spiritual gypsy davy camp now being infiltrated by foreign dictator, the fink FBI & the interrogating unknown failures of peacetime as holy & silver & blessed with the texture of kaleidoscope & the sandal girl...

At the conclusion of this same passage Dylan spoke about aretha's body, about the motion of her body, about her disposition, and about her songs, using words that lend themselves to the idea that he was speaking about a woman. The last phrase, "dont you know no happy songs," may also refer to Dylan; but there is very little in this passage to help the reader understand that Dylan was speaking of God. The indispensible clue to his meaning is the phrase, "watch her tame the sea horse," because "sea horse" is a term that may be substituted for "ship," and this would suggest that he was envisioning the sea when he talked about "aretha's religious thighs and movement":

...into aretha's religious thighs & movement find ye your nymph of no conscience & bombing out your young sensitive dignity just to see once & for all if there are holes & music in the universe & watch her tame the sea horse/ aretha, pegged by choir boys & other pearls of mamas as too gloomy a much of witchy & dont you know no happy songs

About halfway through the chapter (in the fifth passage of the stream) Dylan cried out to "Great Romantic"; and this time his words would not apply to any mortal:

...fingering eternity come down and save your lambs & butchers & strike the rose with its rightful patsy odor...& gramps scarecrow's got the tiny little wren & see for yourself while saving him too/ look down oh Great Romantic, you who can predict from every position, you who know that everybody's not a Job or a Nero nor a J.C. Penney...look down & seize your gambler's passion, make high wire experts into heroes, presidents into con men. turn the eventual

Dylan used the name, aretha, in direct address, again, at the end of the chapter. He seems to have been talking about Aretha Franklin and about himself at the beginning of this passage, and about himself and his wife at the end; but he was also praying:

...so sing aretha...sing mainstream into orbit! sing the cowbells home! sing misty...sing for the barber & when youre found guilty of not owning a cavalry & not helping the dancer with laryngitis...misleading valentino's pirates to the indians or perhaps not lending a hand to the deaf pacifist in his sailor suit...it then must be time for you to rest and learn new songs...forgiving nothing for you have done nothing & make love to the noble scrubwoman

The last passage that refers to God is not part of the stream. It is the little letter that concludes this chapter. Dylan seemed to be speaking to his wife, and to be hinting to her about his retirement; but if his words are read as a prayer, he was talking to God about *Tarantula* when he said, "I will nail my words to this paper":

what a drag it gets to be. writing
for this chosen few. writing for anyone cpt you. you, daisy mae, who are
not even of the masses...funny thing,
tho, is that youre not even dead yet...
i will nail my words to this paper,
an fly them on to you. an forget about
them...thank you for the time.
youre kind.
love an kisses
your double

Silly Eyes (in airplane trouble)

In a way it is not fair to suggest that "Guns, the Falcon's Mouthbook & Gashcat Unpunished" is a representative chapter of *Tarantula*, because it begins and ends with words inspired by love; but Dylan also condemned his enemies in this chapter in a manner that shows that his critique of American society was more radical than that of any other member of the peace movement. Shelton, Christgau, Katz, and others, say that he is incomprehensible. Pickering is close to the truth when he says that Dylan was depicting hell[42]; but in my opinion, Dylan was depicting the people he would have us believe were bound for hell. As I see it, his little book is a prayer to God to come, and it is a curse. The following passage is the third segment of the stream in "Guns, the Falcon's Mouthbook, and Gashcat Unpunished." It shows that Dylan attacked females in *Tarantula*, as well as males:

> the hospital grave being advertised & given away in whims & journals the housewife sits on. finding herself financed, ruptured but never censored in & also never flushing herself/ she denies her corpse the courage to crawl—close his own door, the ability to die of bank robbery & now catches the heels of old stars making scary movies on her dirt & her face & not everybody can dig her now. she is private property...bazookas in the nest & weapons of ice & of weatherproof flinch & they twitter, make scars & kill babies among lady shame good looks & her constant foe, tom sawyer of the breakfast cereal cursing all females paying no attention to this toilet massacre to be hereafter called LONZO & must walk the streets of life forever with lazy people having nothing to do but fight over women...everybody knows by now that wars are caused by money & greed & charity organizations/ the housewife is not here. she is running for congress

Dylan is on the attack throughout most of *Tarantula*; but he does not attack everyone. He attacks certain people, and he defends others—just as he did in his songs. One positive portrait (of someone named "jenny") appears much later in the book, in a chapter entitled "Flunking the Propaganda Course":

> strange men with belly trouble & their pin up girls: zelda

rat–crooked betty & volcano the leg–here they come–theyre popped out & theyve been seen crying in the chapel–their friend, who says that everybody cries alot–he's the congressional one & carries the snapshots–his name is Tapanga Red–known in L.A. as Wipe 'M Out–he coughs alot–anyway they walk in–it's very early & they ask for black mongrels apiece–jenny says "why not roll 'm?""theyre cops!" says a little boy who just climbed a mountain & who's learned how to smell in the circus–jenny retires to the pinball machine–steam getting thicker–zelda rat asks for second black mongrel–please make it hot–one of the men, he dangles a watch in front of her face "it's late–zeld babe–it's late" & zelda's face turns into a measle & she says "i'm allergic"–a ringing sound & she say "oh look–that girl over there is getting free balls"–trying to get jenny's attention, one of the men, he asks "anything bothering you?" jenny replies "yes–whatever happened to Orval Faubus?" & the man quickly drops the subject–his eye swollen he pushes one of the hot mongrels down poor zelda's dress–asks now does she wanna nother one–everybody breaks into stitches excpt someone who's talking to a window and jenny, who's busy racking up balls...the man who looks like an adam's apple–I think he belongs to crooked betty–he goes thru his stool–volcano–she wraps him in the national insider–everybody reads him–jenny tilts the machine–the man's dead–just then the congressional one, he pulls out a luger he says a kraut give to him during the war which is a goddamn lie, & begins to shoot up the barbecue beef signs...the radio plays the star spangled banner–next day, a young arsonist, with a turtle on his head & his hands on his hips & his backbone slipping, sees me walking the donkey on the east side–"saw you with jenny last nite–anything happening there?" i say "oh my God, how can you ask such a thing? dont you know there are starving kids in china?" he say "yes, but that was last nite–today's a new day" & i say "yeah–well that's too bad–i still aint gonna tell you nothing about jenny" he calls me an idiot & i say "here take my donkey if it'll make you feel any

better–i'm on my way to the movies anyway" it is five minutes to rush hour–a strange transaction of goods takes place
on third avenue–the supermarket explodes from malnutrition–God bless malnutrition[43]

Gabrielle Goodchilde has remarked that "*Tarantula* works best where
the combination is funny."[44] She may have meant to say that prose anecdotes like this one are easier to understand than the word-stream; but
Dylan's outstanding accomplishment in *Tarantula* is the word-stream, where
he praised God, as he elaborated a curse that fit American society unmis-
takably.

Dylan did not hint about the Messiah's ship in *Tarantula*; but he hinted about lost ships and the storm repeatedly, and he explicitly damned his
enemies to hell by referring to a flood–for example, at the very beginning
of the book (almost immediately after the dedication to aretha and the first
prose insert):

> ...nay and may the boatmen in bathrobes be banished forev-
> er & anointed into the shelves of alive hell, the unimaginative
> sleep, repetition without change...

Several lines below this, in the same passage, he called people "neptune's unused clients," and "fishlike buffoons." In the fifth stream-passage of
chapter 1, apropos of nothing in particular, he said, "it usually starts to rain
for a while." In the last stream-passage of this same chapter, he provided
fragments of an anecdote concerning the storm, which the reader must find
and interpret. First, near the opening he named six people who form a com-
posite caricature of American society:

> ...Gus & Peg & Judy the Wrench & Nadine with worms in
> her fruit & Bernice Bearface blowing her brains on Butch &
> theyre all enthused over locker rooms & vegetables...

Then near the end of this passage he alluded to the storm and the
destruction of these people:

> ...sometimes a tornado destroys the drugstores & floods
> bring polio & leaving Gus & Peg twisted in the volleyball net
> & Butch hiding in madison square garden...Bearface dead
> from a flying piece of grass!

On pages 32-33 Dylan scattered another anecdote concerning bad weather:

> ...both go off & get a bus schedule & she saying all the time "steady big fella! steady!" while on the other side of the street this mailman who looks like shirley temple & who's carrying a lollypop stops & looks at a cloud & just then the sky he gets kinda pissed & decides to throw his weight around a little & bloop a tulip falls dead–the mailman starts talking to a parking meter & foxeyes, he say "it sure wasnt like this in abilene" & its a hurricane & a bus reading baltimore leaves them in a total mess...

In another chapter ("Advice to Tiger's Brother," page 43) another fragmented anecdote begins like this:

> ...you are in the rainstorm now where your cousins seek raw glory near the bridge & the lumberjacks tell you of exploring the red sea...

Another reference to the storm appears on page 55:

> it sounds like john lee hooker coming & oh Lordy louder than a train...the punch-drunk sailor with a scar beneath his nose suddenly slaps and kicks little sally & makes her let go of the bottom of his dungarees & you know he knows something's happening & it aint the ordinary kind of sound that you can see so clearly & carrrrashhhh...a bridge girder all lonesome & gone & the trumpets play what theyve always been taught to play in time of emergency

On page 57, near the conclusion of this chapter, he added one more detail to describe the destruction of the world: "one day, the day of the Tambourines, the astronaut Mickey McMickey will remove a thumb from his mouth–say "go to hell."

Most of Dylan's hints about the storm and flood are extremely vague. For example, Dylan made indirect reference to the storm by mentioning ships lost at sea. He named the *Titanic* on pages 18 and 64, and the "Lucy Tunia"–which would be the *Lucitania*–on page 74. He inserted the phrase "empty ships on the desert," on page 23; and he said, "the ship is lost," on page 81. I have already noted his most obscure reference to a doomed ship, which appears on page 3, where he hinted about the power of the sea by praising "aretha's religious thighs and movement," and said, "watch her tame the sea horse." He worked with this sort of comparison again on page 103, when he mentioned "ship commanders riding stallions into the howling Gulf of Mexico."

Dylan joked about the flood and about end of the world on page 42, in an anecdote about "Phombus Pucker," where he said, "all of a sudden a wave's commotion washed him and his name right into the ocean." Dylan joked about death, about the end of the world, about being married, about being "chosen," and about being interpreted, on page 20, when he pretended that he slept "on a hook," and on page 97, when he pretended that a "hook" was coming in his window that would haul him up to heaven. He suggested that Malcolm X has been saved, on page 101, when he said, "Malcolm X (is) forgotten like a caught fish."

He opened a chapter entitled "Black Nite Crash" with his most beautiful reference to the sea and the flood: "aretha in the blue dunes" (page 71). Five pages later he seems to have been remembering this image when he said, "there is no aretha on the desert." (He repeated this phrase a few lines later, "there is no aretha on the desert," to draw attention to it.) But Dylan's most difficult and shocking references to the flood depend for their effect on the reader's knowledge of Rimbaud's "Drunken Boat." Rimbaud also envisioned a flood that destroys the world, but in his poem "redskins" torture and kill men who work along the river when the flood begins.[45] On page 70, Dylan merely mentioned "johnny drumming wind–an indian, passing through on his way to St. Louis,"[46] and on page 91 he said, "forget about those hollywood people telling you what to do–theyre all gonna get killed by the indians."

Dylan's references to the storm and to aretha are very brief, and they are placed at fairly wide intervals. Most of the book characterizes and mocks American society and the West; and in a sense, the entire book portrays Dylan. I will return to the subject of the way Dylan has portrayed himself in chapter 6; but it is pertinent to mention here that Dylan's loathing of the society in which he found himself is the most prominent feature of his self-portrait in *Tarantula*, and that his self-portrait is partly fictional. Dylan's revulsion is expressed very effectively by references that seem to concern the physical symptoms of alcohol abuse—or perhaps, heroin abuse. For example, on page 17 he mentioned "vomiting into the flowers," and on page 80 he mentioned "sliding on vomit." He seems to have seen the world from the perspective of someone who had fallen to the floor, or the gutter, when he said, "dogs wave their tails goodby at you," on page 43, and when he described "Orion" (who I assume is a dog), on page 75: "looking evil & he wipes you off and keeps you clean." (He also used these phrases to speak of Orion: "licking his flesh"; and, "shades of fire hydrants.") More hideous are phrases in which Dylan seemed almost to quote Burroughs's remarks about heroin addiction: on page 17, "you will sit sick with coldness in an unenchanted closet"; and on page 53, "getting some glass in the veins." These phrases have a second sense, however; because, like Dante, Dylan described hell as a place of confinement and cold.

The most remarkable signs of revulsion that Dylan presented in *Tarantula* are two passages in which he explicitly spoke about his own death. Both passages could be taken to mean that Dylan was considering suicide; but that would be a mistake. The first of these passages is on page 74. It begins with words that suggest that Dylan felt alienated and lonely; but it concludes with words that suggest that he wanted to see the end of the world, and that he expected to live again after he dies:

> —on the side of the highway—where nobody can stop—where he can cause no trouble—where the show must go on—He wishes to die in the midst of cathedral bells—He wishes to die when the tornadoes strike the roofs and the stools "so much for death" he will say when he dies

In the second passage, on page 98, Dylan pretended he could see his own body lying dead. He complained about the way he had been "jumped" and "murdered"; but the most telling image is in the first verse, where he referred to himself as a "streetcar" (i.e., he carried other people):

> here lies bob dylan
> murdered
> from behind
> by trembling flesh
> who after being refused by Lazarus,

jumped on him
for solitude
but was amazed to discover
that he was already
a streetcar &
that was exactly the end
of bob dylan

he now lies in Mrs. Actually's
beauty parlor
God rest his soul
& his rudeness
two brothers& a naked mama's boy
who looks like Jesus Christ
can now share the remains
of his sickness
& his phone numbers
there is no strength
to give away—
everybody now
can just have it back

here lies bob dylan
demolished by Vienna politeness—
which will now claim to have invented him
the cool people can
now write Fugues about him
& Cupid can now kick over his kerosene lamp—
bob dylan—killed by a discarded Oedipus
who turned
around
to investigate a ghost
& discovered that
the ghost too
was more than one person

According to the information we can piece together today, Dylan was about to marry when he finished writing *Tarantula* and submitted it to

Macmillan; and he was about to turn 25, and to retire, when he finished final editing of the text. Therefore, his references to his death may be read as a kind of joke: Bob Dylan, "prophet of the peace movement" and "spokesman of his generation," was "dying" in the sense that he was growing up. When Dylan's manager told the press that Dylan was hurt in a motorcycle accident, perhaps he was just taking the gag one step farther.

In this connection I would point out that the bootleg edition of Dylan's book had its own title, *Tarantula Meets Rex Paste*, which could have been taken as a hint about Dylan's death—if the name, "Rex Paste," refers to God, and the name, "Tarantula," refers to Dylan. But this would also have been a suitable title for a book named *Tarantula* before final editing—if "Tarantula" is the book and "Rex Paste" is Dylan. This interpretation is very attractive, because Dylan could, at some point, have taken what he had written, cut it up, and pasted it back together again. This would seem to agree with what Dylan said in his interview for the *Free Press* with Robbins—where he referred to his work as "cut ups." It also agrees with the following comment Dylan included in an open letter he published in *Broadside*, in January 1964:

> my novel is goin' noplace.
> absolutely noplace.
> like it don't even tell a story
> its about a million scenes long,
> and it takes place on about a billion scraps of
> paper...certainly I can't make nothin' out of it.[47]

However, while Dylan invited the reader to think that he did not know what he was doing in writing *Tarantula*, he was surely dissembling. The disclaimers, "I cant make nothin' out of it," "goin' noplace," and "don't even tell a story," hide the truth—which would seem to be that, by the time Dylan sent this letter to *Broadside*, he had stopped writing an autobiography, and had begun to write *Tarantula* as we know it.

In the opening lines of *Tarantula* Dylan called his book a "melody"—perhaps in imitation of Dante, who referred to the *Divine Comedy* as a "song."[48] Both poets drew attention to something that is actually lacking and cannot be added to their texts: musical intonation. Both of them were intimating that their use of language is highly personal, and that their words praise God. Dante's poetic manner is "golden" (to borrow a term C.S. Lewis used to describe Spencer's verse[49]), whereas Dylan's poetic manner in *Tarantula* is "absurd"; but Dylan is not the first poet of the West who has chosen to speak about God through the use of techniques that are designed to provoke laughter and a sense of malaise—the German poet, Rilke, and the French poet, Jarry, and others, have done so very effectively.[50] However, Dylan's language usage in the word-stream of *Tarantula* departs more radically from standard usage than that of Rilke or Jarry (or James Joyce, or William Burroughs). It gives expression in an almost miraculous way to the idea that we live in a world in which "everything is broken"—as the philosopher, Gabriel Marcel, might have said[51]—because Dylan managed to teach *ideas* through shattered syntax.

It was characteristic of Dylan, in his visionary, prophetic songs of the '60s to attack racism, militarism, and authoritarianism, simultaneously, and to suggest that evil permeates American society. In *Tarantula* he had the appropriate medium to refine his attack, and elaborate it in great detail. He dumped contempt on Western culture in general, he even mocked the food we eat, the roofs over our heads, and the cloths we wear, and he seems to have wished to see most of us dead and damned for eternity. But he put his photo on the cover of his book, and had the name, *"Tarantula,"* printed beside his name, on that photo, to show that he is the author of this book, and that he, too, is a westerner, a man, blue-eyed and white-skinned.

Karpel, who argues that Dylan wanted to make everybody dance, also says that Dylan lost his nerve after his motorcycle accident. He intimates that Dylan might have started "the revolution"—if he had allowed Macmillan to publish *Tarantula* in 1966, and if he had continued touring with The Band. But Karpel does not discuss the contents of *Tarantula* (except to say that it "begins and ends with aretha"). Actually a kind of revolution *did* take place in America while Dylan toured; furthermore, *Tarantula was* published, without Dylan's consent or Macmillan's. But *Tarantula* did not cause the revolution that briefly came to life during the days of the peace movement.

Tarantula is a revolutionary work of art in that it attacks western civilization, and it is also revolutionary in that it praises God with a woman's name; but it was not revolutionary in the same sense as "Blowin' in the Wind." "Blowin' in the Wind" drew people together, it put words of protest into the mouths of millions of people, and it created a spectacle that was revolutionary. The peace movement sprang to life when "Blowin' in the Wind" was first sung. But *Tarantula* is typically consumed in silence, in privacy, indoors[52]; and by the time Macmillan published the authorized edition of *Tarantula* the whole world could see that the peace movement had disbanded.

Notes

The title of this chapter is borrowed from the first line of the letter found in "False Eyelash in Maria's Transmission" (the 46th section, or chapter, of *Tarantula*). This letter is not addressed to anyone in particular, but it is signed, "water boy," which would be Dylan.

1   Dylan published a long letter in *Broadside* (January 1964), using the word "novel" to speak of *Tarantula*. I quote the relevant passage on page 99.

2   Macmillan added three pages of introductory remarks to *Tarantula*. They begin, "This is Bob Dylan's first book"; and they end, "It is the way he wrote it when he was twenty-three. So now you know." Bob Dylan, *Tarantula* (New York: Macmillan, 1971) v-viii.

3   Dylan sang seven songs, and he talked at length in response to Terkel's questions. Krogsgaard includes a tape of the show in his listings. It was broadcast on WFMT in Chicago, in May 1963.

4   Baez indicated that Dylan wrote copiously. She quoted Dylan as saying that he was writing about his childhood, but she described an anecdote that is not in *Tarantula*. Anthony Scaduto, *Bob Dylan* (New York: Grosset & Dunlap, 1971) 208, 9.

5   Scaduto 164. (Shelton describes the trip too, but he does not mention the typewriter.)

6   Krogsgaard published this photo, but he does not know who composed it. D.A. Pennabaker, who appears among the people behind Dylan, may have set up a tripod and camera for a timed exposure. Krogsgaard 38.

7   For example, Gabriel Goodchilde wrote the following remarks, "After the accident it became less and less possible for him to rewrite the book. By 1968 he was repudiating the project." She does not say where, when, or how Dylan repudiated *Tarantula*. He did not "rewrite" it, and he probably finished final editing in March of 1966. Gabriel Goodchilde, "Tarantula," in *Conclusions on the Wall*, edited by Elizabeth Thompson (Manchester, England: Wanted Man, 1980) 52.

8   *Tarantula* viii.

9   Pickering reprints the review of *Tarantula* written by Elia Katz in *Praxis: One*, and he adds the following editorial note:

> It is a soft-bound book, stapled, 8 1/2" by 11", blue cover with no writing of any kind. The title page: TARANTULA MEETS REX PASTE, and when one turns the page, the dedicatory lines and a poem called "Looking Forward to Menopause." On page 85 (the last page) is the epilogue. The book, with

no author mentioned anywhere, is somewhat shorter than the final, published book. Minor word variations throughout the volume, some deleted sentences from the published version are here. It is marked, on the inside, "1965." The copy I have was given to David Crosby, who in turn gave it to a friend of the Grateful Dead, who in turn gave it to me. Mr. Crosby received it while in New York, June 1970.

The dedication:
>
>dedicated
>to the folks back home
>who wouldn't be able
>   to understand it
>   &
>to T-Bone Slim

The prologue:
>Saint Viscious
>   kept
>within another's bounds
>   to paw the yard
>   ignoring the hounds
>the warmth of the barn
>   draped
>with furry thoughts,
>while the sleigh
>   in the attic
>   holding empty boots
>   await imagination
>   and his horse
>   the scabbard wails
>   as Beauty pales
>   and stands outside
>   locked doors

–Cuchlain O'Brien

The epilogue:
>and as he especially enjoyed dark things, when, in the bare room with closed shutters, high and blue, sourly humid, he read his endlessly med-

itated novel full of heavy orchreous skies and drenched forests, of flesh flowers–opened wide in the sidereal woods–dizziness, crumblings, flights and pity!–alone and lying on pieces of unbleached cloth and violently anticipating

a sail!

-Arthur Rimbaud

Stephen Pickering, editor, *Praxis: One* (Berkeley, California: No Limit, 1971) 123. Pickering has also published one passage from the bootleg that was subsequently deleted from the final edition. See note 26 for the text of this deleted piece.

10 Shelton 410.

11 Robert Christgau, *New York Times Book Review*, June 27, 1971.

12 Karpel's essay is discussed and quoted in chapter 3.

13 Alain Rémond, *les chemins de bob dylan* (Paris: Epi, 1971) 59. On the same page Rémond publishes these remarks borrowed from Jann Wenner:

The story of this phantom novel is informative. People in the publishing industry, impressed by Dylan's success, asked him if by chance he might not like to write a novel. Dylan grabbed the opportunity and signed a contract with the publishing house that offered the most loot–he only asked himself why later. He wrote the book in nothing flat, and sent it to the editor. Everybody raved, "He's another James Joyce..." Then he saw the galleys; and he said to himself, "Lord! Did I write that? I could never publish that..." He insisted on making some changes. He sent a second manuscript; and the same scenario followed: upon reading the galleys he said he could not publish the book. He tried to begin again. Then there was the accident...and the project was dropped.

14 Elia Katz, "*Tarantula*: A Perspective." Pickering, *Praxis: One*, 119. (In an introductory note Pickering says Katz's review first appeared in Great Britain in 1969, but he does not name the publication.)

15 Katz 118. Katz refers to the idea that *Tarantula* might have been "suppressed for reasons of politics," part of "the sociology of *Tarantula's* existence"; and he calls this, "...entertaining, like the fact of Beethoven's deafness and the gold G - clefs over the gates of Elvis Presley's estate."

16 Katz 119. Katz says, "...maybe Dylan himself sent the first five copies out into the public sea...as an experiment in publishing..."

17 Katz 123. His sentence ends, "...by then Dylan will have forgotten he wrote it."

18 Aretha Franklin was signed by John Hammond to record for Columbia Records when she was 18 years old. That same year, 1961, Hammond also signed

and recorded Dylan. Franklin was more successful with a different recording company a few years later.

19 Pickering, "Bob Dylan and the Book of Splendor," *Praxis: One*, 64-70. Pickering does not really describe the *Zohar*, or the tradition out of which its ideas and language eminate. A brief, but fairly detailed discussion of the *Zohar*, by Gershom Scholem, may be found in the *Encyclopedia Judaica* (New York: Macmillan, 1971). Scholem's books are indispensable sources of information about the *Zohar*, Kabbalah, and Jewish mysticism.

20 Pickering introduces the term, "*Shekhinah*," early in his essay, and he mentions these alternate expressions: "the Presence of God," "the Bride," and "the Queen." He also repeats the following words from the *Zohar*:

> "Why weep ye? Is he not the son of the King? Is it not meant that he should take leave of you and live in the place of his father?"; and, "Is it not the highest glory for them when the Queen (the divine presence) comes down into the midst of them to lead them into the place of the King, to enjoy the delights thereof for evermore?"

Stephen Pickering, "*John Wesley Harding*: The Prospect of Immortality," in *Praxis: One*, 109. Pickering mentions several songs in which he says Dylan is talking about the *Shekhinah*; but he does not include "Sad-Eyed Lady of the Lowlands," which may be the outstanding example of what he means to show.

21 I use Gershom Scholem's translation of "Creation of Man" from *Zohar: The Book of Splendor*. Selected and edited by Gershom Scholem (New York: Schocken, 1949) 31-37.

22 Pickering explicitly compares Dylan to S.Z. Setzer, Abraham Isaac Kook, Baal Shem Tov, Barukh of Mezbizh, Yitzhak Luria, Avraham Abulafia, Moses Cordovero, Rav Schneur Zalman, Rav Arele Roth, and Rav Nachman of Bratzlav. He identifies Moses de Leon as the author of the *Zohar*, but he never directly compares Dylan to him (nor does he compare Dylan to writers of Scripture).

23 In 1971 Pickering argued that Dylan "changed" as a result of his "motorcycle accident"; years later he said that Dylan changed in 1964.

24 Pickering, "*John Wesley Harding*: The Prospect of Immortality," *Praxis: One*, 101-106. Within this same article, Pickering mentions *Tarantula* in connection with *Blonde on Blonde*, the "Basement Tapes," and *John Wesley Harding*, as he speaks of "Dylan's utilization of dreams." He does not provide examples to clarify what he means:

> From *Tarantula* through *Blonde on Blonde*, within the April 1967 Woodstock session and ... *John Wesley Harding*, Dylan's utilitzation of dreams, in the Talmudic origins, presents archetypes which recognize man's dream-based consciousness.

(Pickering does not say why he dates the *Basement Tapes* session as April 1967.)

25 Pickering opens his review by quoting Jung; but he does not cite passages of *Tarantula* that illustrate why he does so. Pickering, "*Tarantula*: A Question of Interpretation," *Dylan: A Commemoration*, 41.

26 The name, aretha, appears in "Guns, the Falcon's Mouthbook, and Gashcat Unpunished," "Prelude to a Flatpick," "Black Nite Crash," "Electric Black Nite Crash," "Seems Like a Black Nite Crash," and "Al Aaraaf and the Forcing Company." The word, tarantula, only appears in the bootleg, in the title of a passage that was subsequently deleted from the authorized edition. Pickering published this deleted passage in *TBZB*. I suspect that "Flunking the Propaganda Course" replaced it in the final edition; but Pickering says "Tarantula/One Leg At A Time" appears between "Mouthful of Loving Choke" and "Forty Links of Chain," in the bootleg, and "Flunking the Propaganda Course" appears a few chapters later in Macmillan's version:

"Tarantula/One Leg At A Time"

Rockbottom, the pop demonologist & Lady Whiplash, his faithless well-wisher/she runs a hairloom shop on the upper west side & tosses coins in fountains for a living/they come rolling thru town in a package of camels, on the lookout for evil spirits. "we're here!" says Rock & throws his thesaurus into the air "this must be the holy city" Lady she doesnt hear him, she's poking at a wino with her fungo bat & licking his left ear "got any spare change?" Grandma Grapevine climbs by and Lady freezes—says "you can't fool me old lady, youre just a boycott in drag—now take off those leaves & let's see where you're really at"/"shut up, Whip" says Rock, "hey lady, you seen any evil spirits around?" Grape she nod & whisper in a distinctly bulgarian dialect "the jewish boy, Zimmerman, i seen him walking his spider on the Pan Am building & what are you gonna do about it, creep?" Rock he's steady as a dead man, "well i been lookin' for something to figure out an i guess this'll do/where's my bag, jellyroll?" Lady Whip she don't budge till she hear her rightful title/Grandma Grapevine just keep walkin'—her pet streetcleaner on a chrome leash, "see ya, don't take no buffalo chips honey" & she's gone in a puff of smoke? Whip she's just comin' around. "tell me somethin' Rock, if you know so much—how come we gotta go around tellin' everybody?" "shut up Whip & hand over the bag" & he puts his eye thru her needle. she duffles the bag up & lets him have it. the Good Humor man slips by whistling Let's Go Get Stoned in the sound of bells. Rock is stricken with backhanded nostalgia, "can we ride in yr truck mister—Whip here'll dig the cold, she's part eskimo" Good Humor, a negro wearing dark glasses/keeps on truckin'—says over his shoulder holster "Racist dog! quit makin' fun of people dumber than you!" & whap! slugs him with a fudgcicle/wonder what he meant by that thinks Rock and Whip say "i think some spider just crawled into yr bag & he's pretty hairy"

27 Pickering says that Jerrold Schatzberg took this photo and several others, in Paris, in May 1966. He is mistaken about that. Mr. Schatzberg has reported to me that he took this photograph of Dylan in his studio, in New York, in December 1965.

28 Since the fingers of two hands can resemble the legs of a spider, and since Dylan works with his fingers as a guitar player, to *weave* melodies by manipulating the strings of his guitar, he might be compared to a spider. Pickering has published a diagram of two hands in which the fingers have Hebrew letters written on them, in the introduction to *Bob Dylan Approximately*; but he does not discuss *Tarantula* in that text, or explain the diagram. Stephen Pickering, *Bob Dylan Approximately* (New York: David McKay, 1975) 18.

29 Katz 119.

30 Katz 120.

31 Katz 118.

32 Katz 120.

33 Paul J. Robbins, "Bob Dylan as Bob Dylan," Los Angeles *Free Press*, September 17 and 24, 1965. (Pickering has reprinted this interview in *Dylan: A Commemoration.*)

34 The following remarks were spoken to Shelton in the interview of March 1966, mentioned above in this chapter. They show, again, that Dylan was determined to praise Burroughs, but that his admiration was not unbounded:

I know two saintly people. I know just two holy people. Allen Ginsberg is one. The other, for lack of a better term, I just want to call "this person named Sara." What I mean by "holy" is crossing all the boundaries of time and usefulness…William Burroughs is a poet…But if we're talking now in terms of writers I think can be called poets, then Allen must by the best….

…I want to keep (Sara) out of this. I don't want to call her "a girl." I know it's very corny, but the only thing I can think of is, more or less, "madonnalike." (Shelton 400.)

35 John Henry Faulk would be an important example. He was a news commentator who was fired from CBS, in 1956, and blacklisted. He worked with Arthur Barron and Dylan on *Freedom Songs* in July 1963, and he was the toastmaster in December 1963, for the E.C.L.C. dinner, when Dylan was given   the Tom Paine Award. Shelton indicates that Dylan wrote a song inspired by Faulk in 1962. Apparently the song was "Talkin' John Birch Paranoid Blues" (Shelton 172, 173,

190, 202, and 222).

(On page 57 of *Tarantula*, Jerry Lee Lewis is recommended for the #1 position on Dylan's blacklist.)

36 William Burroughs, *Naked Lunch* (London: Olympia Press, 1959).

37 Dylan mentioned "lenny bruce" in "Some Other Kinds of Songs" (1964), and he named him and quoted him in "11 Outlined Epithets" (1964); furthermore, in a song called, "Lenny Bruce" (1981), he indicated that he met Bruce on one occasion. Dylan mentioned Allen Ginsberg in "Some Other Kinds of Songs" and in the notes for *Bringing It All Back Home*. Ginsberg appears in one scene in *Don't Look Back*, and in several scenes in *Renaldo and Clara* (1976).

38 Dylan paid tribute to "lenny" in a chapter of *Tarantula* called, "Guitars Kissing and the Contemporary Fix" (pages 52 to 57); but he did not use Bruce's full name in *Tarantula*. His most memorable line about Bruce is: "lenny i'm sure is already in a resentful heaven" (page 57). But the most revealing thing Dylan has said about Bruce was his first remark in the opening lines of that chapter: "lenny speaks of Jesus, brave." Maybe it was from Lenny Bruce that Dylan learned to "speak of Jesus" in his art (it was not from Guthrie's example, Robert Johnson's, Little Richard's, or Allen Ginsberg's). Bruce's humor sometimes involved making fun of Jews and Judaism, and it often involved exposing religious hypocrisy in Christians. Dylan called Bruce, "the brother that y'never had" (in "Lenny Bruce").

39 Here is the passage in full:

> ok. so i shoot dope once in a
> while. big deal. what's it got
> to do with you? i'm telling you
> mervin, if you dont lay off me,
> i'm gonna rip you off some more
> where that scar is, y'hear? like
> i'm getting mad. next time you
> call me that name in a public
> cafeteria, i'm just gonna haul
> off & kick you so you'll feel
> it. like i ain't even gonna get
> angry. i'm just gonna let one
> fly. fix you good
>
> > better watch it
> > The Law

40 Dylan made fun of the woman in this song, and her fashions, by envisioning the things she loves, not her person: "...in your fog, your amphetamine, and your pearls" (verse 2).

41 On page 14 he said, "got too drunk last night"; but much later (pages 94-97) he seemed to be praying, calling God, "boss," and complaining about the doctors, nurses, and patients around him.

42 Pickering, *Dylan: A Commemoration*, 41.

43 Dylan, "Flunking the Propaganda Course," *Tarantula* 89-91. There is only prose, and no word-stream, in this chapter. A letter signed "plastic man" is attached at the end.

44 Goodchilde 55.

45 "The Drunken Boat" is printed in the appendix, beginning on page 235, and it is briefly discussed in chapter 8.

46 St. Louis is the Mississippi River port where the "confidence man" boarded the riverboat heading south, in Herman Melville's novel, *The Confidence Man*. It is a city visited by barges, like the one in Rimbaud's "The Drunken Boat." Dylan was born near the headwaters of the Mississippi River, in a county named, St. Louis.

47 *Broadside* #38, January 20, 1964, 5.

48 Dante called the *Inferno, Purgatorio*, and *Paradiso*, "canticles" *(cantichi)*, and he called the sections into which they are divided, "songs" *(canti)*.

49 C.S. Lewis, *English Literature in the 16th Century, Excluding Drama* (Oxford: Oxford U P,1954) 318.

50 The following two works by Rilke and Jarry would prove the point: "The Tale of the Hands of God," by Rainer Maria Rilke, may be found in *Stories of God*, translated by M.D. Herter Norton and Nora Purtscher Wydenbruck. (NewYork: Norton, 1932); "The Passion considered as an Uphill Bicycle Race" by Alfred Jarry, is included in *Selected Works of Alfred Jarry*, edited by Roger Shattuck and Simon Watson Taylor (NewYork: Grove, 1965).

51 Dylan mentions Marcel by name in the song, "Everything is Broken." For Marcel's ideas about *"le monde cassé,"* see Gabriel Marcel, *Mystery of Being 1: Reflection and Mystery* (Chicago: Gateway, 1960), beginning especially on page 26.

52 A musical adaptation of *Tarantula* by Darrel Larson, was staged at the Powerhouse Theatre in Santa Monica, California, in August 1974.

Chapter 5

Sad-Eyed Ladies

Dylan's storm songs made him uniquely effective as a voice of dissent in the 1960s; but some of Dylan's songs about women, and even some of his passing remarks about women, influenced the generation of love, too–because love shone more brightly in Dylan's portraits of women he loved than anywhere else in his oeuvre. To show what I mean I will briefly examine four songs from the era of the peace movement: "Tomorrow is a Long Time" (August 1962), "Oxford Town" (October 1962), "North Country Blues" (September 1963), and "Sad-Eyed Lady of the Lowlands" (December 1966).

Dylan wrote "Tomorrow Is a Long Time" when Suze Rotolo was taken away from him to live in Italy, after they had been lovers and roommates for almost a year. Dylan said that he wrote the song for Miss Rotolo the first time he played it,[1] and apparently it was about her; but in light of Dylan's subsequent compositions it can also be interpreted as being divine praise in allegorical form. One subtle detail that inclines me to think that this love song may be religious allegory is Dylan's use of the figures, "endless highway" and "crooked trail," in the opening lines of the first verse, because Dante used this sort of image in the first lines of the *Divine Comedy* to describe his situation. ("In the middle of the path of my life / I woke up in a dark wood...") The image of the road has been used countless numbers of times, of course, by countless numbers of poets–including Woody Guthrie and Robert Johnson, and the beat novelist, Jack Kerouac[2]; but Dante's example would have been more precious to Dylan in August 1962 than any of these, because Dylan had chosen to imitate Dante by prophesying when he wrote "Blowin' in the Wind" four months earlier. Furthermore, in September 1962 he would prophesy again, in "A Hard Rain's A-Gonna Fall," making several veiled allusions to Dante.[3]

"Tomorrow Is a Long Time" indicates quite explicitly that the singer once slept in the embrace of his lady–actually, the refrain celebrates this thought so insistently it almost drowns other thoughts the song produces.

This makes "Tomorrow Is a Long Time" different from anything Dante wrote (much as the fact that in the *New Life* and the *Divine Comedy* Dante ostensibly praised a woman who had died makes Dante's work different from Dylan's); but Dylan created a truly exquisite effect, that might be thought worthy of Dante, by speaking of his longing to hear the *sound* of his beloved's heartbeat, and to *rest* beside her.

The second verse is entirely made of hyperbole describing the effects of separation from this woman. The first figure, "I can't see my reflection in the waters," is the subtlest of four conceits. It may be taken to mean that the singer is weeping, and that his tears are blinding him and disturbing the surface of the "waters," or it may be taken to mean that the sun has stopped shining, or that rain is disturbing his "reflection"; but it may also refer to an event mystics ponder–the separation of "*Ein Sof*" and the "*Shekhinah*," whose original relationship is believed to be suggested in the first verse of the Bible:

> In the beginning God created the heavens and the earth. And the earth was formless and empty, darkness was over the surface of the deep, and the Spirit of God hovered over the waters.

Dylan's description of the symptoms of heartbreak in verse 2 is vaguely reminiscent of symptoms Dante described in the first half of the *New Life*–symptoms which occurred when he found himself in Beatrice's presence; but Dante's description of his affliction is comical, whereas "Tomorrow Is a Long Time" effects pathos. (Two prose passages from the *New Life*, narrating how Dante came apart when Beatrice was near, are printed in the appendix beginning on page 214. The first passage, from chapter 2 of the *New Life*, describes the first time he saw Beatrice, when she had just turned eight and he was almost nine; the second passage, from chapter 14 of the *New Life*, describes his breakdown the day he saw Beatrice at her wedding feast.)

Dylan's greater debt to Dante might be that Dante showed him that things he might say about his misery would not constitute praise of the woman he loved, and that his complaint, in itself, could not be truly beautiful. Dante said that he was taught this lesson by women; and telling the story he produced a lovely simile that likens the sound of women's voices and their sighs to rainfall mixed with snow. (This passage from chapter 18 is printed in the appendix beginning on page 215.) It may be that Dante's example inspired Dylan to produce the sublime praise in verse 3 of "Tomorrow is a Long Time," for Dante compared Beatrice to Christ in several passages in the *New Life*. (Two examples are printed in the appendix, on pages 216 to 218. He was about 19 years old when he wrote the first one, which is a canzone, "Ladies Who Have an Understanding of Love," and he was about 25 years old when he wrote the second, which is the prose passage from chapter 24 of the *New Life*.) Everything Dylan said in the first two verses of "Tomorrow is a Long Time" concerns pain and darkness; but in this third verse he spoke about his true love, and everything he said concerned beauty and light. He spoke of beauty as an abstraction, but he illustrated his thoughts by referring to what is genuinely substantial; and by the time he said the word, "beauty," for the *third* time, he had reminded his listener of the great outdoors and the expanse of the heavens, to prepare the listener for what he had to say about his true love's "eyes." (Dante's most remarkable praise of Beatrice's eyes may be found in the *Paradise*; but he did not liken Beatrice to Christ anywhere in the *Comedy*.)

Dylan's grand, redoubling hyperbole, and the familiar-sounding colloquialism, "...nothing...can touch the beauty...in her eyes," convey an impression of sincerity and certainty; but as water that is perfectly clear is often deeper than it appears to be, the harmoniously-balanced arrangement of Dylan's words make it difficult to fathom, or differentiate, all the ideas they contain. A "river" looks silvery when light is reflected on its surface, and the sky is filled with light at "sunrise," so the listener may be sure that the beauty Dylan was speaking of is some sort of light; and since the name he used to identify this woman is "my own true love," the listener may know that the beauty in her eyes was the light of love. Beyond this it would seem that Dylan remembered that he saw *himself* in the light of love, when he looked into the eyes of the woman he loved.

"Oxford Town" (October 1962) reports about specific incidents of racial violence and murder, that had just taken place at the time of writing, in the town of Oxford, Mississippi, in relationship to James Meredith's effort to enroll at the University of Mississippi[4]; but in verse 4 Dylan seemed to offer a glimpse into his private life, as he told what was happening in Oxford.

Dylan may have been thinking of Suze Rotolo when he sang the words, "my gal," because Miss Rotolo did participate in political demonstrations on behalf of human rights causes. Both Scaduto and Shelton say that she worked as a volunteer for the Congress of Racial Equality, and Bob Spitz, another of Dylan's biographers, adds that she picketed Woolworth's in Manhattan, in 1961, to protest Woolworth's segregated-counter-service policy[5]; but they also say that her mother and stepfather took her to Italy from June 1962 until January 1963.[6] That move kept her out of radical political circles and away from Dylan at the time this song was written; furthermore, Miss Rotolo did not have a "son."

Mention of a child is one of the most unusual features of this song. Woody Guthrie's songs or Berthold Brecht's plays might have influenced Dylan to put a child into his story, and Brecht in particular might have influenced him to hint that a woman with a child might be brave and principled[7]; but American pop songs of the early '60s did not portray women with children. None of the information Dylan provided about what was happening in Mississippi is the usual fare offered by American pop songs, of course—especially not Dylan's testimony about racism, violence and murder, which is the essential content of the song.

This brief sketch involving a man, woman, and child, forms an unexpected counterpoint, because it is about love. Unspoken within it it contains the idea that Dylan's friend cared enough about James Meredith's cause, and about the issue of school desegregation, to participate in a political demonstration far from her home, where she knew that opposition might be violent. It contains the idea that Dylan loved her and her child, and that he cared enough about what was happening in Mississippi to travel there, too. Although the anecdote is fictional, it indicates that Dylan identified with people who were part of the peace movement, and that he cared about the abuse they suffered. It expresses love most subtly in that it makes reference to Meredith and the murder victims first, then to "personal" experience. It does not mention the tear gas attack until it mentions the woman and her son, and then it does not say they were hurt–although they would have suffered acutely from direct exposure to tear gas (especially the child).

Dylan may have been thinking of Suze Rotolo, when he wrote "Tomorrow Is a Long time" and "Oxford Town," but "North Country Blues" (September 1963) portrays an aging woman from a mining town in Minnesota. This song is absolutely unique among Dylan's compositions because it is a woman's story, and Dylan told it as if it were his own. Woody Guthrie wrote a song called, "Hard, Ain't It Hard," in which a woman speaks bitterly about her unfaithful lover.[8] Dylan certainly knew that song–it was one of Guthrie's most successful pieces. Dylan also knew "The House of the Rising Sun," a traditional song in which a woman testifies about her life as a prostitute.[9] (He recorded "House of the Rising Sun" in 1961, and it was included on his first album.) Dylan also knew and performed "Dink's Song," another composition of uncertain origin in which the singer's role is that of a woman.[10] Any of these songs could have inspired Dylan to make up a song in which the lyrics indicate that a woman is singing; but "North Country Blues" was not modeled on "Hard, Ain't It Hard" or "House of the Rising Sun," because both those songs are complaints–it is more like "Dink's Song," because it is a portrait of a humble and composed human being. The circumstances of this woman's life have been exceedingly harsh; but she indicates that she has had friends, a husband, and children, she does not complain, and she does not speak about running away, although her father, brother, and husband have deserted her, and she predicts that her children will leave, too.

Dylan "knew his song well" in this case, because his parents moved to the mining town this song seems to concern when he was about five years old.[11] Hibbing, Minnesota, was torn apart in a peculiar way, beginning in 1918, when the town's leaders allowed mining interests to destroy some of Hibbing's principle streets and intersections, in order to dig a enormous pit in the middle of town. Some of Hibbing's buildings were successfully moved to a new location; but year by year the pit was enlarged, and more of the town's center was lost. Another shock hit in the mid-50s, when mining companies began to close their operations in Hibbing. "North Country Blues" would not be classified as a "blues" on the basis of its musical tonalities, rhythm, or verse structure; and it is not a complaint, as blues usually are. It is a blues because it concerns industry and capitalism, and the lives of miners and their families.

No one seems to have identified the woman portrayed in this song, although Scaduto and Shelton, and others who have written about Dylan, eagerly identify women they would have us believe were close to Dylan in his youth. This song suggests that Dylan visited the homes of miners and listened to their conversations. He may have learned something about his craft, and about humility, from "Mrs. John Thomas," the woman he portrayed in this song.

"North Country Blues" is Dylan's most successful piece of regional art. He filled each verse with images that recreate the specific environment he held in his mind's eye; and he took advantage of the potentiality of verse to create a sense of the present, and of the future, in a work that is principally focused on the past. To be precise, he combined vivid impressionistic detail (for example, "when the red iron pits ran plenty") with direct recounting of biographical detail (such as, "my mother took sick / And I was brought up by my brother"). Fluidity, heat, the color "red," babies, and the seasons of spring and summer, are associated with the past; stiffness, ice, cold, old men, cardboard, and winter, are associated with the present and the future.

The narrative is punctuated by numerous references to time, to segments of time, and to rapid or slow passage of time. Among them are two descriptions of unhappiness that speak of time spent looking out a window. The first is in verse 4: "A long winter's wait / From the window I watched." A longer one extends from verse 8 into verse 9:

> ...the sad silent song
> Made the hours twice as long
> As I waited for the sun to go sinkin'.

I lived by the window
As he talked to himself
The silence of tongues it was building...

The looking-out-the-window-motif appears in several songs Dylan wrote in the '60s.[12] He used it in his descriptions of hell in "Desolation Row" and "Visions of Johanna," where he suggested that the damned will be confined in derelict buildings; but here he included detail about silence and sadness, and the slowness of time spent looking out a window, to awaken sympathy for someone who has lived the life of a homemaker. Whereas Dylan mocked and censured other women for taking pride in possessions, and for seeking security in houses, he seemed to suggest that this patient woman, who is a victim of industrial society, and who is physically confined, is innocent, is superior to her circumstances, and is spiritually *free*.

Dylan pretended to talk to another woman-inside-a-house in "Sad-Eyed Lady of the Lowlands," which was one of the last songs he composed before his retirement.[13] "Sad-Eyed Lady of the Lowlands" is surrealistic, and more difficult to interpret than "North County Blues," "Tomorrow is a Long time," or "Oxford Town"; but it contains numerous clues that help the listener to envision a specific event. The question asked in the refrain, in particular, defines a dramatic situation: the singer is trying to talk to the "lady." He is outside and she is inside, and he is gently calling to her:

My warehouse eyes, my Arabian drums,
Should I leave them by your gate?
Or, sad-eyed lady, should I wait?

"It's All Over Now, Baby Blue" may have been a kind of model for "Sad-Eyed Lady of the Lowlands," because in that song, too, the lady seems to be inside, and the singer seems to be outside. It would have been a negative model, though, because the singer of "It's All Over Now, Baby Blue" tells "Baby Blue" that her days of comfort and freedom are over; whereas, the singer of this song tells the "Sad-Eyed Lady" that she is saved, that he has brought her gifts, and that he loves her.

In a song called "Sara" (1975) Dylan said he wrote "Sad-Eyed Lady of the Lowlands" for his wife, and some of the lines of the song undoubtedly make explicit reference to Sara Dylan[14]; but Dylan also made reference to other people and to himself, in the things he said about this lady–as he did in *Tarantula* in passages that praise aretha. The criticle point of resemblance is this: Dylan invested his portrait of the Sad-Eyed Lady, and his portrait of aretha, with ideas about the nature of God.

The essential model for Dylan's praise of his lady, in this instance, would seem to have been the Song of Songs. Jesus's parables that refer to weddings, wedding guests, and wedding garments, and John the Baptist's reference to Jesus as the "bridegroom," were probably important inspirational sources, too[15] (and probably so was the *Zohar*[16]); but Solomon's Song seems to have influenced the rhetorical character of "Sad-Eyed Lady of the Lowlands" more than any other text, and the idea that Solomon's portrayal of the rapture of a man and a woman who are in love is an allegory concerning the creation, fall, and redemption of the world, had a direct impact on Dylan's poetic enterprise–here, in "Tomorrow is a Long Time," and elsewhere. The principle clue to this interpretation of "Sad-Eyed Lady of the Lowlands" is the word "gate," and the dramatic situation Dylan created by saying, in effect, that the lady is *inside* and the singer is *outside*; because in the Song of Songs the lover repeatedly appears at the gate, and calls to the beloved. (Two passages from the Song of Songs in which the Lover appears "outside" are printed in the appendix, on page 223. The first is Song of Songs 2:8-13, and the second is Song of Songs 5:2-5.)

Every word of "Sad-Eyed Lady of the Lowlands" is addressed to the lady, and every verse says the same kinds of things: the singer names and praises the lady's virtues; he regrets the conduct and motives of her enemies; and he asks her the question that forms the refrain. The way the singer names specific features of his lady, one-by-one, is comparable to the way the lover names the beauties of the beloved in the Song of Songs (as in the passage beginning with the words, "How beautiful your sandaled feet, O prince's daughter," from Song of Songs chapter 7:1-9, which is printed in the appendix, on page 224); but in the Song of Songs it is the beloved, herself, who says that she has been abused by her "mother's sons" (Song of Songs 1:6) and by the "watchmen of the walls" (Song of Songs 5:7). (These

verses are printed in the appendix, on pages 224 and 225.)   Another difference is that the lover does not pose a question in the Song of Songs like the
question the singer asks in the refrain of "Sad-Eyed Lady of the Lowlands."

The most conspicuous difference between "Sad-Eyed Lady of the
Lowlands" and the Song of Songs would be that eroticism is not featured in
"Sad-Eyed Lady of the Lowlands," and neither is detail envisioning volup-
tuous landscapes and the splendor of a great king's court; however, the vivid
enigmatic detail Dylan packed into his praise of the lady, and into his
recriminations against her enemies, make "Sad-Eyed Lady of the Lowlands"
Dylan's most surreal song, and make it as faithful to Solomon's original in its
surrealism as anything ever written in imitation of the Song of Songs. I am
thinking, for example, of St. John of the Cross's magnificent *Spiritual
Canticle,* which imitates Solomon's poem very closely. (This poem is printed in prose translation in the appendix, beginning on page 220.[17])

Solomon's narrative is highly chaotic and full of contradiction; and
most important, Solomon's enigmatic references to seemingly unrelated
events in the present and the past suggest that he was speaking about what
was hidden in the future. Solomon referred to himself by name, to his
armies, his chariot, his queens and concubines, his crown, and his ascendan-
cy to the throne; but he also seemed to refer to the lives of others, without
naming them, including, perhaps, Adam and Eve, Abraham and Sarah, Jacob
and Rachel, Ruth and Boaz, and David and Bathsheba.[18] (Song of Songs
6:8-14, which exemplifies the rapid changes and surreal effects of the Song
of Songs, is printed in the appendix on page 225.)

The first line of the first verse of "Sad-Eyed Lady of the Lowlands"
would prove the point about Dylan's surreal and anachronistic praise of his
lady: "With your mercury mouth in the missionary times." It was not the
color or shape of the lady's lips, or the sweetness of her smile, that he
praised—in fact, his words do not prompt the listener to visualize a woman.
The singer seems to be speaking of something the lady did (or *does*)—something involving preaching or speaking, since her "mouth" is the feature he
praises, since the name, "Mercury," was given by the Greeks to a figure they
called the "messenger" of the gods, and since "missionaries" preach. Perhaps

Dylan wanted to suggest that this lady spoke the truth, and was quick to do so.

In the third verse he called her mouth, "your cowboy mouth." This comparison also guides his listener to think of a kind of work; but the work of cowboys does not usually involve eloquence or preaching—in fact, while they are working cowboys rarely speak to other people. At first glance then, this phrase, "cowboy mouth," may seem to contradict the phrase, "mercury mouth." Presumably, though, Dylan used the word, "cowboy," as a modern equivalent for "shepherd," the most familiar epithet for the Messiah in David's and Jesus's prophecies.[19] That was what he did, in my opinion, when he called the Messiah, "cowboy angel," in "Gates of Eden" and *Tarantula*.[20] The work of the good cowboy would involve speaking (and singing)—ideally, in fact, it would be the same work as that of a missionary.

Some of the things Dylan said about the lady's enemies help to establish that his praise was not made to fit his wife, or any mortal woman:

Who among them...could bury you?
Who among them...could carry you? (v. 1)

The kings of Tyrus with their convict list
Are waiting for their geranium kiss...
But who among them really wants just to kiss you? (v. 3)

The farmers and the businessmen they all did decide
To show you the dead angels that they used to hide
Why did they pick you to sympathize with their side?
How could they ever mistake you? (v. 4)

Who among them...could destroy you? (v. 5)

Above all, though, it is the terms Dylan chose to praise the lady that show that he was praising God as well as a woman. In the first stanza, for example, the opening couplet combines praise of disparate elements, so that what is tangible and familiar becomes evocative and mystical. "Your eyes like smoke," may mean that Sara Dylan's eyes are the color of smoke; but it may also be a reference to the idea that God went before the people of Israel in the wilderness, by appearing to them as a pillar of smoke (or cloud) by day, and as a pillar of fire by night (Exodus 13: 21,2). "Your voice like chimes," may mean that Sara Dylan's voice is musical and clear; but it may be an allusion to an idea expressed in "Chimes of Freedom"—that the thunder accompanying the apocalyptic storm will resound like "bells" "tolling." (In verse 2 of that song he called thunder, "wedding bells," and "the bells of the lightning.") "Your prayers like rhymes," and, "Your silver cross," may refer to Jesus's prayers and Jesus's cross, or to Sara Dylan's prayers and a cross she wears.

The most sensuous passage of the song is the couplet in verse 2, which makes reference to the lady's "silhouette" and her "eyes." It suggests that Dylan gathered comfort from being near the lady at nightfall, and that he loved to gaze into her eyes; but it envisions the woman by speaking of light, and as in "Tomorrow is a Long Time," instead of describing a woman's form, it leads the listener to think of the sky and the beauty of God's creation.

Only verse 5 refers to the storm. It hints that the "sea" is rising, and that an "alarm" has sounded; but the singer's gaze is not fixed on the storm. It rests on the figure of the lady, who seems to stand above the sea. Mary the Mother of Jesus can be recognized in Dylan's lady, because Mary is traditionally pictured with the sea at her feet and baby Jesus in her arms[21]; but Dylan's use of the words, "phony" and "hoodlum," suggests that the lady he is talking about lives in the twentieth century, rather than in the remote past. The virtue he seemed to see in the lady is that she has heard the alarm, she believes the evidence her eyes and ears give her, and she has responded by lifting the child up into her arms. Maybe Dylan remembered Jesus's prophecy about Judgement Day—"How dreadful it will be in those days for pregnant women and nursing mothers!"[22]—and he raised this lady above the sea to suggest that the love she expresses redeems her.

Dylan may have had some sort of revelation about this lady, years before he began to compose the words and melody of this song—or, it seems to me, that conclusion may be drawn from another song written later, called, "When I Paint My Masterpiece" (March 1971).[23] In this song Dylan hinted about a visit to Rome and a visit to Brussels—which is to say, "The Lowlands." He made explicit reference to architecture, Church history, and painting; and he hinted about hiding, or being saved. In the chorus he complained about someone, and about a broken promise.

Dylan visited Italy in December 1962. Scaduto says he went to Perugia to see Suze Rotolo, and that Miss Rotolo had already left before Dylan arrived there.[24] Shelton specifies that Dylan visited Rome.[25] Neither of them mentions a visit to Brussels–nor does Spitz. Dylan's references to the sights in Rome and Brussels, in "When I Paint My Masterpiece," and what he said about having a "date" with "Botticelli's niece" (which may have been his way of designating Miss Rotolo[26]) seem to be a combination of fact and fiction–like the things he said in "Oxford Town" about himself, his gal, and his gal's son.

Dylan described Rome as being "full of rubble," "cold," and "dark." He suggested that it was haunted when he talked about seeing his "double," about hearing "ancient footsteps," about facing "lions inside the Colisseum," and about meeting Botticelli's niece. On the other hand, he described Brussels as being bright, lively, and welcoming. The negative things he said about Rome were enigmatic, and so were the positive things he said about Brussels–especially the line, "Everyone was there to greet me when I stepped inside"; therefore, it is necessary to form some sort of conjecture in order to interpret this song.

My guess would be that Dylan visited Brussels, and perhaps the Flemish towns of Bruges and Ghent, in December 1962, after he went to Italy, and there he became acquainted with a set of miniature paintings from the middle ages illustrating the stations of the cross. Among them he found one composition to be especially piercing in its effect–one depicting Mary standing near the body of her son after it was freed from the cross, with John beside her, supporting her. In the composition I am thinking of, Mary is bending over to press her cheek against her son's cheek in a final caress, and both faces are seen side-by-side–his expressionless, and hers disfigured by grief.[27]

Dylan only mentioned the hubbub of the city of Brussels, not the fine arts museum or any churches; but several references he made in "When I Paint My Masterpiece" point to an appreciation of art and art history. He said that he visited the "Colisseum" and the "Spanish Stairs" in Rome, he indicated that he knew Botticelli among Italian masters, he said he traveled "with the picture of a tall oak tree by my side,"[28] and after every verse he talked about "painting" his "masterpiece." If Dylan spent time sightseeing in Rome and other cities (Shelton and Scaduto say he spent two weeks sightseeing as he drove across the country with friends in February 1964,[29] and he is shown sightseeing in Europe in *Don't Look Back* and in *Eat the Document*), presumably when he visited Brussels he would also have visited points of interest there–including art museums and churches. And if he cared about painting and Italian masters like Botticelli, presumably he would have taken time to see the works of Belgian, Dutch, and Flemish masters.

Miniatures, such as the one I describe above, invite the viewer to come very close, whereas figures in Botticelli's paintings can be seen from a distance of 10 feet or more. Dylan may have approached the sombre painting I am speaking of without having carefully examined anything like it before. Peering into this composition, and seeing the wretched look of sorrow on Mary's face, he may have been deeply moved. The misery and frailty of this Mary may have touched him in ways serene representations of the "Queen of Heaven" could not. He may have felt love for Mary for the first time in his life; and he may have been instructed by this painting concerning the song that would, perhaps, crown his prophetic work as his supreme masterpiece.

Here is another guess: when Dylan said that he dodged lions and wasted time in the Colisseum, and when he said he traveled from Rome to the North, he may have been speaking about events in religious history, as well as about events in his life during the 1960s. He may have been mocking the ineffectuality of the ancient Romans in their efforts to annihilate devout Jews and Christians. Perhaps he wished to imply that the Roman Church has persecuted innocent people, through violent and corrupt bishops, cardinals, and popes (as, for example, in the destruction of the nation of Provence, as in the Spanish Inquisition, and as in the complicity of some official leaders of the Church in the persecution of the people of many nations and religions during purges and pogroms of recent centuries–even, and especially, in our own century.) Perhaps he wished to remember that the gentility that characterized the conduct of members of the early Church has sometimes been found among the people of the Low Countries.[30] He did not say so, of course, but the name, "Sad-Eyed Lady of the Lowlands," may be a hint to the effect that the relationship the people of this region have to the sea influences their conduct benignly. When he said that he "came inside," in "When I Paint My Masterpiece," he may have been hinting that Jews were treated gently by Christians in the Low Countries–and, maybe, that he had become a Christian, or that he was able to imagine being Christian.

I have compared Dylan's portrait of the lady in "Sad-Eyed Lady of the Lowlands" to his portrait of aretha more than once, and I have said that I think that Dylan was speaking about God when he used these epithets. But I would like to conclude my remarks about "Sad-Eyed Lady of the Lowlands" by saying that Dylan envisioned the lady in this song from a different perspective, compared to the perspective he held when he spoke about aretha. In *Tarantula* he seemed to say that aretha is alone, and that she is the sea *and* the deluge about which he had prophesied; furthermore, he envisioned aretha from far away. In "Sad-Eyed Lady of the Lowlands" he did not suggest that the lady is the sea. He suggested that she has often been near him, that she has a child, and, finally, in the last verse of the song, that she has come outside, and stands beside him.

"Sad-Eyed Lady of the Lowlands" was finished and recorded during the period in which Dylan finished the draft of *Tarantula* that was submitted to his publishers; but both works may have been vaguely conceptualized in 1962 or 1963–that is to say, Dylan may have begun to formulate a plan years ahead of time, to write this "book" and this love song, and to suggest, through veil upon veil of imagry, that God will redeem the world with love like that of a bridegroom for his bride.

I left something out in chapter 3, where I discuss Dylan's relationship to the peace movement, that needs to be said here: the men and women of the peace movement were the first generation to feel the impact of the "birth control pill" in their adolescence. To be precise, in 1960, for the first time in the U.S.A., oral contraceptives were approved for sale (by physicians, that is, *not* through pharmacies), in 1961 the G.D. Searle Company began to manufacture "Enavid," and by 1962 widespread availability of "the pill" had become a significant factor in the climate of the times.[31]

Most political historians do not mention the pill, or the role physicans played by distributing the pill, either to private patients, or to patients in women's clinics that were founded in the '60s. The silence of historians on this subject may be proof that Americans remain divided and confused about the subject of extramarital sex, and about the morality of the use of devices that inhibit procreation. But the most revolutionary feature of the advent of the pill was the sudden empowerment it gave men and women to speak about sex. The pill became the criticle factor in the world's "sexual revolution," for a while, precisely because it was named, and its function was described, as it was sold to women. However, while the medical community in the U.S.A. began, in 1961, to encourage women to think about sex, talk about sex, and experiment with sex, physicians could not say anything about *love* –nor could pharmaceutical companies.

According to some of the reports and some of the images through which we remember the '60s, "free love" was the most attractive, and most explosive, issue on the peace movement's agenda. To compensate in part for my neglect, up to this point, of the subject of sexuality and politics, I would note that in 1968, at the Nanterre campus of the University of Paris, the issue of sexually-segregated dormitories became *the* incendiary issue.[32] The details of what happened at Nanterre are not really important to this essay, however, because the issue of segregated dormitories had been resolved relatively peacefully all across the U.S. before 1968, and Dylan had already been in retirement for two years before the barricades of student revolutionaries went up in Paris. Furthermore, Dylan did not express his opinion on matters like dormitory rules. He was perceived as being "sexually liberated" (in one song he angrily told grown-ups that they were "limited in sex" and warned them not to push "fake morals"[33]); but his authority flowed from the fact that his songs promoted love in the form of compassion and tenderness. Dylan helped his generation find their way in a confusing time, because he put love first, not sex–love of God, that is, not love of women. He kept his balance; and his example helped others keep balance, too.

Notes

1 Dylan recorded "Tomorrow Is a Long Time" in Minnesota, with the help of his friend, Tony Glover, on August 11, 1962. Krogsgaard 11.

2 A composition that speaks of the "road," from Guthrie's repertoire, might be, "I Been Doin' Some Hard Travelin'," from Johnson's repertoire, "Hellhound On My Trail," and from Kerouac's, *On the Road.*

3 Dante's influence on "Hard Rain" is discussed above, in chapter 2, on pages 15 and 26.

4 Meredith's act had a decisive impact on history, because it caused an uproar that presumably forced President Kennedy to call out the National Guard.

5 Scaduto 111-113, and Shelton 144-147. Bob Spitz, *Dylan: A Biography* (New York: McGraw Hill, 1989) 151. I will have reason to mention Spitz's work again in chapter 6.

6 Mrs. Rotolo was a widow when Dylan met her in the summer of 1961. She remarried a year later; and after that Dylan's relationship with her daughter was terminated. Scaduto and Shelton both say that the man who became Suze's and Carla's stepfather was a teacher at a college in New Jersey (Scaduto 123, Shelton 145, 6). Shelton also says that a professor at Rutgers, which is in New Jersey, told him Dylan bought "Blowin' in the Wind" (Shelton 184).

7 The phrase, "Me, an my gal, an' my gal's son," sounds Guthriesque. It brings "Talkin' Dust Blues" to mind, in which Guthrie portrayed a family who migrated to California during the dust bowl era. Dylan came to New York hoping to meet Guthrie. His interest in Brecht seems to have begun in New York, under Suze and Carla Rotolo's influence, when the sisters worked on a production called *Brecht on Brecht* (see Scaduto 104, and Shelton 152). *The Good Woman of Setzuan* may be the best example of Brecht's positive portrayals of women. The protagonist becomes successful in business when she assumes a man's clothing and a man's name. She is the mother of a young son, she is unmarried, and she must earn money for food and shelter.

8 "Hard, Ain't It Hard" seems to be the only song Guthrie wrote that suggests that a woman is singing.

9 Shelton reports that Dylan learned "House of the Rising Sun" from David Van Ronk. Shelton 121.

10 "Dink's Song" was recorded by John A. Lomax in 1904. Dylan learned it from Cynthia Gooding. Shelton 119. (Harry Weber, who teaches at the University of Missouri, told me that he introduced this song to Gooding, and that he also introduced Dylan to her.)

11 Dylan was born in Duluth, Minnesota.

12 Dylan portrayed himself looking out a window, in "It Takes A Lot to Laugh/It Takes a Train to Cry" (May 1965).

13 Apparently "Sad-Eyed Lady of the Lowlands" was recorded one time only, and has never been sung by Dylan on stage.

14 "Sara" reviews details of Mr. and Mrs. Dylan's life that mean nothing to the public; but verse 4 includes information that leaps out from the rest because it concerns Dylan's work:

> Stayin' up for days in the Chelsea Hotel
> Writin' "Sad-Eyed Lady of the Lowlands" for you.

15 According to St. Matthew, Jesus told a story about a wedding feast, and a story about a bridegroom, that began like this:

> The kingdom of heaven is like a king who prepared a wedding banquet for his son. He sent his servants to those who had been invited to the banquet to tell them to come; but they refused to come....(Matthew 22:2,3)

> At that time the kingdom of heaven will be like ten virgins who took their lamps and went out to meet the bridegroom. Five of them were foolish and five were wise....(Matthew 25:1,2)

According to St. John, before he was arrested John the Baptist spoke these words:

> The bride belongs to the bridegroom. The friend who attends the bridegroom waits and listens for him, and his heart is full of joy when he hears the bridegroom's voice. That joy is mine, and it is now complete. He must become greater, and I must become less.... (John 3:29,30)

16 The following remarks about the *Zohar* are drawn from Gershom Scholem's essay, "Shekhinah: The Feminine Element in Divinity":

> The sexual imagery of the Song of Songs is treated (in the *Zohar*) altogether differently than it is in the old allegories of God's relationship with Israel. Even a comparison of the *Zohar* with the earliest Kabbalistic commentary of the Song of Songs, that written by R. Ezra of Gerona a mere fifty or sixty years earlier and with which the author of the *Zohar* was acquainted, reveals the great difference in the use of erotic imagry. It was the author of the *Zohar* who read the entire text of the Song of Songs of as a nuptial hymn of the Godhead itself. In the *Zohar*, III, 214b, the stages of Union (*yihuda*) are portrayed as stages of sexual coupling (*zivuga*), in a highly naturalistic interpretation of the Song of Songs 2: 6. Many other biblical verses are likewise interpreted as hymns to the holy marriage (*tushbahta de zivuga*).

It is hardly by chance that the very first lines of the *Zohar* begin with the explicit sexual symbolism of the pollination of the rose—a symbol for the Shekhinah frequently used by the *Zohar*. This symbolism continues throughout the entire book....(the chief speaker of the book) ends with an unusually solemn but no less daring homily about Zion, the Holy of Holies, the place in which the oneness of all things in God is born; he calls Zion the womb of the Shekhinah, in which God procreates the blessing that spreads to the world.

Gershom Scholem, *On the Mystical Shape of the Godhead* (New York: Schocken, 1991) 184,5.

17 The prose translation of San Juan's poem is drawn from *Renaissance and Baroque Poetry of Spain. With English prose translations,* edited by Elias L. Rivers (New York: Scribners, 1966) 130-138.

18 The biblical narratives concerning Adam and Eve, Abraham and Sarah, Jacob and Rachel, Boaz and Ruth, and David and Bathsheba, begin with the following verses:

> So God created man in his own image
> in the image of God he created him
> male and female he created them. (Genesis 1:26)

> The Lord had said to Abram, "Leave your country, your people and your father's household and go to the land I will show you." (Genesis 12:1)

> While he was still talking...Rachel came with her father's sheep, for she was a shepherdess. (Genesis 29:9)

> So (Ruth) went out and began to glean in the fields behind the harvesters. As it turned out, she found herself working in a field that belonged to Boaz. (Ruth 2:3)

> In the spring, at the time when kings go off to war...David remained in Jerusalem." (2 Samuel 11:1)

19 The 23rd Psalm begins, "The Lord is my shepherd." And Jesus said, "The man who enters by the gate is the shepherd of his sheep." Jesus's description of "the good shepherd" is recorded in John 10: 1-18. He repeated and elaborated the idea that he calls his sheep, and they know his *voice*.

20 Verse 1 of "Gates of Eden" says, "Upon four-legged forest clouds the cowboy angel rides"; and the title of the fortieth chapter of *Tarantula* is "Cowboy Angel Blues."

21 Christian theologians teach that the following passage refers to Jesus, when it speaks of the woman's "offspring":

> I will put enmity between you and the woman, and between your off-

spring and hers; he will crush your head, and you will strike his heel. (Genesis 3:15)

Numerous sculptors and painters have shown Mary standing on Satan's head. Mary is also depicted with the sea at her feet. This idea is rendered in one poem that is discussed here, in chapter 8—"The Drunken Boat," by Arthur Rimbaud (reprinted in the appendix, beginning on page 235.) Mary is usually depicted in a robe the color of the sea.

22 Matthew 24:19

> Then let those who are in Judea flee to the mountains. Let no one on the roof of the house go down to take anything out of the house. Let no one in the field go back to get his cloak. How dreadful it will be in those days for pregnant women and nursing mothers.

23 "When I Paint My Masterpiece" was included on *Bob Dylan's Greatest Hits, Volume II* (November 1971). It was originally released on The Band's album, *Cahoots*, Kapp Records (1971).

24 Scaduto 129.

25 Shelton 368.

26 Scaduto refers to Suze Rotolo as a "Botticelli woman." Scaduto 90.

27 This miniature was exhibited in Brussels in fall 1975, in the municipal fines arts museum. The exhibition listing did not name the artist, but it attributed the painting to the 14th century.

28 The printed text of this song, in *Bob Dylan: Lyrics, 1962-1985*, does not include the line, "With the picture of a tall oak tree by my side." It is replaced by, "On a plane ride so bumpy I almost died." (The "picture of the tall oak tree" might be Odetta, who performed in Holland in 1961, and may have wished to visit there again in 1962, in Dylan's company.)

29 Scaduto 164-172, and Shelton 270-283.

30 An example of the gentility of the people of the Low Countries may be found in the annals of World War II. They successfully resisted Hitler and the Nazis by helping people who were pursued by the Third Reich. They hid their neighbors from the gestapo when their land was occupied by the Germans; and they acted in what seems to have been nearly perfect unanimity.

31 A.D.G. Gunn, *Oral Contraception in Perspective* (Park Ridge, New Jersey: Parthenon, 1987) 40-43.

32 David Caute, *The Year of the Barricades*, 86-88.

33 Verse 13 of "It's Alright, Ma (I'm Only Bleeding)" says:

> Old lady judges watch people in pairs
> Limited in sex they dare
> To push false morals, insult and stare

Chapter 6

Portrait of the Artist

The works that are discussed in the preceding chapters are a rather narrow sampling of Bob Dylan's oeuvre–insufficient, really, to show that Dylan made himself the essential protagonist of his work. The uniqueness of Dylan's accomplishment in self-portraiture is difficult to illustrate, because the first person is used by every poet at one time or another; but it would seem that only one other poet of the West directly portrayed himself in a significant body of verse, in a manner truly comparable to the way Dylan did in the '60s–and that would be Dante Alighieri. The principle likeness between Dante's self-portrait and Dylan's would be that both artists portrayed themselves as God-fearing, and the lowest-ordered likeness would be that some of the stories they told about themselves are fictional. They certainly did not write autobiography, per se, because they introduced facts only intermittently, and they effaced the truth about themselves as they pretended to portray themselves.

Dylan went farther than Dante in recreating his identity, because he changed his name and hinted that he was Christian, even though his family had nurtured him in Judaism; whereas, Dante did not change his name, and when he intimated that he was Christian it was in keeping with the fact that he had been baptised and schooled in Christianity. But some of Dante's ancestors may well have been Jewish.[1] I raise this point because, in both Dante's case and Dylan's, the decision to hint about Christianity would be the expression of the artist's personality and the feature of his self-portrait most worthy of deliberate study, since both poets expressed a radical point of view that set them at odds with the establishment.

Dylan probably became superficially acquainted with Dante's verse his junior or senior year in highschool, and he may have attempted to read Dante even earlier, if he learned that his mother's name, "Beatrice," was the name given to the woman Dante praised[2]; however, it is unlikely that anyone in Minnesota, or anything Dylan read before he came to New York, would have suggested to him that some of Dante's ancestors may have been Jewish. No trace of Dante's influence appeared in Dylan's work until 1962, but then it appeared in more than one composition. In "A Hard Rain's A-Gonna Fall" (September 1962) Dylan subtly suggested that he had read Dante, and that he was going to imitate Dante in his verse[3]; but a few months earlier, in "Blowin' in the Wind" (April 1962) and "Tomorrow Is a Long Time" (August 1962), Dylan *showed* that he understood Dante, and that he knew very well how to imitate him—in "Blowin' in the Wind" he told a riddle to prophesy about the end of the world and the will of God, and in "Tomorrow Is a Long Time" he praised a woman in terms that could be interpreted allegorically as divine praise.

These three songs were composed during the period in which Suze Rotolo was separated from Dylan and taken to live in Italy. To be specific, "Blowin' in the Wind" was written a few weeks before Miss Rotolo's departure, "Tomorrow Is a Long Time" was written a few weeks after her departure, and "A Hard Rain's A-Gonna Fall" was written three months after the young lovers' separation began. Since Scaduto says that this young Italian-American woman influenced Dylan's reading,[4] and since Shelton says that she and Dylan read verse together, and that Dylan bought books of verse for her,[5] it is reasonable to assume that Miss Rotolo read Dante with Dylan, and talked about Dante with Dylan, and that she recognized Dante's influence in these songs. Beyond that it may also be reasonable to think that she read the *Zohar* with Dylan, and introduced him to the Sephardic Jewish community of New York City.

Suze Rotolo's religious background is not mentioned by Dylan's biographers, nor do they say where she was born or why her parents came to the U.S. I am not sure any of these elements are of real concern; but Scaduto and Shelton both indicate that Suze and Carla Rotolo's deceased father was a political activist.[6] They do not say where he died or how he died—Shelton merely says, while speaking of Mrs. Rotolo, that her husband had "recently" died,[7] and he quotes Dylan as saying, "(Suze's) father and mother were associated with unions."[8] Scaduto repeats a flatterer's remark about Mrs. Rotolo's appearance that is offensive ("She was one of those rare Italian women who keep their face and figure into middle age"[9]), but he does not report about her political activism, or about her deceased husband's political activism, candidly, nor does he properly explain the impact her acquaintance, and her daughters' acquaintance, had on Dylan.

Bob Spitz reports that Suze Rotolo was fourteen years old when her father died[10]; but, like Scaduto and Shelton, he reports nothing about Mr. Rotolo's place of birth, the nature of his political activism, or the circumstances of his death. However, Spitz furnishes criticle information about Suze Rotolo and her relationship with Dylan when he specifies that she had had "radical left-wing upbringing," and that her mother edited a "left-wing" Italian paper.[11]

I have no inside information about Suze Rotolo's father; but I find it suspicious that Shelton, Scaduto, and Spitz, who tend to gossip, do not name this man, or report coherently about him. If his death was related to his political activities, or if he was a member of the Resistance in Italy during the fascist era, his story and the plight of his widow and children would have provided Dylan touching evidence about what might be required of a political activist and freedom fighter.

It is unlikely that Dylan could have heard the story of the Italian Resistance in any detail before coming to New York City; but in Greenwich Village he had an excellent opportunity to learn about it in detail, because of his friendship with the Rotolo's. And in February 1962, when Sophia Loren won an *Oscar* for her starring role in *Two Women*[12] (the first and only time the *Oscar* for "best actress" has been awarded to a non-American), *someone* could have told Dylan that the author of the novel, *Two Women*, Alberto Moravia, was of Jewish descent, that he had to hide from the fascists, and that he was the cousin of two particulary distinguished martyrs of fascism, Carlo and Nello Roselli.[13] If Mary Rotolo was an Italian native who lived in Italy during Mussolini's regime, and if she edited a liberal Italian paper, the Roselli's story would certainly have been known to her. Mary Rotolo may have known the widows and the children of the Roselli's personally, since the Roselli's took refuge in the U.S., and lived in Manhattan in the 1940s and '50s.

Years after Dylan wrote "Blowin' in the Wind," "Tomorrow is a Long Time," and "A Hard Rain's A-Gonna Fall," he composed a song called,

"Tangled Up In Blue" (1974), which hinted that a woman introduced him to Dante; but he did not name Suze Rotolo, and he did not seem to be speaking of her—or of anyone his biographers identify. Actually, Dylan may have been speaking of more than one woman in this song; but when he said, "She was working in a topless place," I wonder if he meant to say that the woman he was thinking of worked where people do not cover their heads—as tradition requires devout Jewish men and women to do, and I wonder if he was speaking of Suze Rotolo's mother, who Shelton says took Dylan in and cared for him when he was sick in 1961.[14] Here are the lines of the song that seem to refer to Dante:

> Then she opened up a book of poems
> And handed it to me
> Written by an Italian poet
> From the thirteenth century.
> And every one of those words rang true
> And glowed like burnin' coal
> Pourin' off of every page
> Like it was written in my soul from me to you,
> Tangled up in blue.

Dylan pretended to talk about his past in "Tangled Up In Blue," but he reported details that were not intended to satisfy the curiosity of his admirers. His reference to Dante stands out because it concerns his work, and because it is the most passionate praise for a writer of verse Dylan has expressed in his art[15]; however, Dylan's way of identifying Dante by saying that he was "an Italian poet from the thirteenth century," rather than by naming him, enabled him to hint that there was another poet in the 13th century whose "words rang true"—which may be an oblique reference to the author of the Zohar, who was a Spanish poet of the thirteenth century.[16]

Dylan made no explicit reference to the Zohar, to its author, or to its ideas, in the songs and written verse he published between 1961 and 1967; and he made no explicit reference to modern Jewish experience—except in one verse of "With God On Our Side" (December 1962), which referred to the murder of "six million" (verse 5). On the other hand, Dylan named Jesus as the authority behind his words in "Masters of War" (December 1962), he meditated on Jesus's crucifixion in "Long Ago, Far Away" (December 1962), and he referred to one of Jesus's desciples and to one of Jesus's stories in "I'd Hate To Be You On That Dreadful Day" (June 1962). He indicated religiosity that might be attributed to someone who believes in God and in the coming of the Messiah–but not necessarily in Jesus–when he compared the enemies of the peace movement to "Pharoah's tribe" and to "Goliath," in "When the Ship Comes In" (August 1963), and when he made reference to the Messiah without naming Jesus in "Train A-Travelin" (October 1962); however, there is nothing in either of these songs that would explicitly contradict the idea that Dylan might be Christian.

Dylan referred to himself as a "Jew" in an interview with Stephen Pickering in 1974,[17] and he was photographed in Jerusalem in 1985, on the occasion of his son's *bar mitzvah*, wearing the philacteries, prayer shawl, and *yarmulka* of Jewish tradition[18] (see page 135); but between 1961 and 1967 he seems to have avoided doing or saying anything in public that would have indicated that he wished to be identified as Jewish. An exception would be that he laughingly improvised one verse of the "*Hava Nagilah*" during a recording session for Columbia Records in April 1962.[19] In April 1965, when a reporter for the *Jewish-Chronicle* of London asked him, "Are you Jewish?" Dylan answered, "No, but some of my best friends are. You better interview Tito Burns, the manager for the tour, because I know he's Jewish."[20] The aggressiveness and specificity of this response are matched by the rectitude of its logic–as can be seen when these words are compared to Groucho Marx's parry to the question, "Do you belong to a country club?": "No," Marx replied, "I wouldn't belong to any club that would have me as a member."[21] Both men responded with irony, mocking the language and thought patterns of racists; but Marx emphacized his *deficiency* as a candidate for membership in a country club to hint that he was Jewish, whereas Dylan emphacized that the manager of his tour was Jewish to indicate that he *lacked nothing*.

If Dylan had been asked, "Are you Christian?" he might have mocked that question, too; but in May 1966, just before he retired, he had his portrait made with an irregularly-shaped metal cross in his hands[22] (this portrait

is reproduced on page 137). This cross is bulky and misshapen, like Dylan's drawing of a guitar that was published in *Writings and Drawings* in 1971[23]—in fact, I suspect that Dylan sketched it, and had it cast in bronze to his specifications. But the design of the cross is not so important as what the cross said in Dylan's hands.

By the end of May 1966 Dylan had become more of a cause celebre than ever before—because he insisted on playing with a rock and roll band, because he refused to sing any of the songs he had written in 1961, 1962, and 1963, *and* because he produced a song, "Rainy Day Women #12 & 35" (November 1965), that was banned on many radio stations in the U.S., and nationwide in England and Australia, when it was released as a single.[24] The offending line, "Everybody must get stoned," was the last line of every verse. The censors did not care to debate what it meant; and if they recognized that it alludes to the Bible story concerning Jesus and a mob that was about to stone a woman for committing adultery, that may have been what irked them most.[25] Jesus reminded the woman's accusers of their *own* sins, to convince them to put down the stones they had intended to use. Dylan testified about what it was like to be accused, and made light of it; but he was also warning young people that the establishment was intent on silencing and punishing them—and perhaps killing some of them.

In late May 1966 Dylan took his final bow and left the stage for a long rest; but "Rainy Day Women" continued to circulate, and in a sense it became the theme song of the counterculture. "Rainy Day Women #12 & 35" does not teach the range of sublime ideas "Blowin' in the Wind" teaches; but it is a great example of prophecy, because it became a "happening." To those who imagined that it only concerns drugs, it endorsed the use of stupifying substances. To those who looked for understanding in it, the phrases, "when you're trying to be so good," "when you're trying to go home," "when you're walkin' to the door," "when you are young and able," "when you're playing your guitar," etc., indicated that the song concerns Dylan—and that he had *not* changed. The "rainy day women" he sang about could have been promiscuous women; but more likely he was thinking of the woman he had married, of himself, of his friends, and of God.

I have concluded my discussion of Dylan's works from the days of the peace movement with "Rainy Day Women #12 & 35," because it helps me make one last point about Dylan's character and self-portrait—which is, that all this work of Dylan's, as a youthful composer, writer, and performer, suggests that he was brilliant, literate, self-disciplined, balanced, and successful, but the anecdotes in which he directly portrayed himself create the impression that he was ordinary, fearful, and likely to stumble and fall. In both regards, consciously or unconsciously, he imitated Dante.

I do not mean to say that Dante did not see visions of God and angels in heaven, or that Dylan did not see a vision of a global flood and rescue by ship; nor do I mean to say that the confession of Christianity implicit in Dante's work, or Dylan's, is feigned. I mean that they humbled themselves in their art by design, and that they both knew instinctively, and by careful study of Scripture and secular literature, how to move the hearts and minds of their listeners. They worked as artists, not as scholars or clergymen—fabricating freely, and taking advantage of artistic license, as any artist might, to advance an enriched and radical species of Christianity that influenced the course of history. Furthermore, the most revolutionary component of the faith to which Dante witnessed, and of the faith to which Dylan witnessed, in late adolescence and early adulthood, was its feminism. Neither Dante nor Dylan professed that God is female as well as male, but they both sowed the seeds of ideas that contradict the tendency of Judaism and Christianity to speak of God as male.

In Dylan's case consistant grooming in Jewish observance and tradition, beginning in early childhood, would partly account for the unique character of his Christianity; but it would not fully account for the mystical feminism in his work. That component of his thought, or faith, may have been awakened when he began reading the *New Life* and the *Zohar* with someone, or with several people, he met in 1961. I am convinced that Dylan made a commitment having to do with prophecy and politics, and maybe marrige, too, that year—his first year in New York City. Acquaintance with the Rotolo's may have shown him that he might be required to pay with his life, if he chose to get involved with political protest; and discovery of the

Hasidic and the Sephardic Jewish communities within the universe of New York City may have awakened in him a new understanding, and a more profound respect, for the diversity of Jewish experience. My guess would be that he wanted to marry Suze Rotolo, and that he confided to her, and to her sister and mother as well, that he was going to enter the movement, that he was going to compose a messianic apocalypse, and that he was going to retire early.

Dante did not indicate that he had studied Hebrew, or that he had made the acquaintance of Jews in Florence or anywhere else. As an adult he was widely traveled and exceedingly learned; but he wrote *nothing* about the repression of the Jewish community before the establishment of the Inquisition, or under the Inquisition. But Dante worked in exceedingly turbulent times, under murderously repressive circumstances; he *could not* comment specifically, or candidly, about the displacement and suffering of the Jews in Italy or anywhere else—not at the beginning of his career, when he wrote the verse and then the prose of the *New Life*, or later, after he was banished from Florence. Nevertheless, it is not unreasonable to wonder if Dante's Christian feminism was formulated under the influence of Jewish, as well as Christian, mystics—actually, nothing could be more reasonable than to assume that the kabbalistic writings that circulated in Provence, and which certainly influenced the author of the *Zohar*, would also have influenced Dante.[26]

Like Dylan, Dante portrayed himself as a kind of ideal Christian—one who admitted fear, but who seemed to desire to act in righteousness, and to proclaim the Day of the Lord. The visionary experiences Dante attributed to himself are different from Dylan's, and the issues he addressed are different from the issues Dylan addressed; but both Dante and Dylan continually interjected reference to themselves, and to real people and events, in order to influence the historical moment and establish a historical record. This runs counter to the norm and sets them apart from most poets. But Dante and Dylan expressed points of view in their early works that might be shared by *any* person of conscience; and as grown-ups they would turn their efforts toward establishing that their Christianity is fundamental.

Notes

1 Dante's father and mother were ostensibly Christian, and one of his ancestors, by the name of Cacciaguida, was a knight who fought in the Holy Land in the Second Crusade; still, the name Alighieri may have sounded Jewish to Florentine ears. I draw support for this idea from W. Boyd Carpenter, who made this remark about Beatrice: "...she is the symbol now of Theology, now of Florence, but always the *Shekhinah* of (Dante's) days and nights." W. Boyd Carpenter, *The Spiritual Message of Dante* (Cambridge, Massachusetts: Harvard UP, 1914) 68.

2 "Beatrice Stone" was Dylan's mother's maiden name. Shelton quotes one of the poems Dylan wrote for his mother when he would have been about ten years old. Shelton says the poem has *twelve* 4-line stanzas, and that the last line reads: "Hello, young lady! Happy Mother's Day!" Shelton 26. (He also reports that Dylan's maternal grandparents helped care for him as a child when his father was gravely ill, and that the Zimmerman's moved to Hibbing to be near the Stone's at that time.)

3 "Hard Rain" is discussed in chapter 2, on pages 15 and 26.

4 Scaduto says Suze Rotolo heightened Dylan's "growing awareness of the poetry of Rimbaud, Villiers, Villon, Robert Graves, Yevtushenko, and Brecht—especially Brecht." Scaduto 111.

5 "Bob read Suze's European and American poetry books, and bought her more, which they read together." Shelton 149.

6 Scaduto 112, Shelton 144.

7 Shelton 145.

8 Shelton 146.

9 Scaduto 102,3.

10 Spitz 152.

11 Spitz 151, 153.

12 *Two Women* (1961) does not explicitly portray Jewish experience. In a sense, it is an anti-war film. It tells a story that emphacizes one incident—the gang-rape of a woman and her adolescent daughter by men in uniform.

13 Alberto Moravia, author of the novel, *Two Women* (New York: Farrar and Strauss, 1958), traveled widely in the 1930s, but he hid in Italy during the final years of Mussolini's regime. His cousins, Carlo Roselli, a physician, and an outspoken, and exceptionally astute, critic of Mussolini's regime (he edited an opposition paper, *La liberta*, in Florence), and Nello Roselli, a historian, were murdered by the fascists in June 1937, in Paris. The movie, *Last Tango in Paris* (1972), directed by Bernardo Bertolucci, casts Marlon Brando as one of the mercenaries involved in that atrocity.

Moravia's novel, *The Conformist*, also concerns the Roselli murders–and Bertolucci made a film based on *The Conformist*, too (1970).

14 Shelton 146.

15 In the '60s Dylan responded to inquiries about himself and his work when he published verse in print. He praised Guthrie, Ginsberg, Bruce, Burroughs, Rimbaud, and Brecht, in writing; but in his songs he was, and is, more inclined to be vague about himself and the influence of others.

16 The authorship of the *Zohar* is debated; but the foremost authority on the subject, Gershom Scholem, argues convincingly that Moses de Leon wrote it, and that he wrote it between 1260 and 1280. The *Zohar* circulated secretly, and anonymously, piece by piece, in Aramaic–not in Spanish, Latin, or Hebrew.

17 Pickering, *Bob Dylan Approximately: A Portrait of a Jewish Poet in Search of God* (New York: David McKay, 1975). This quotation appears in the first sentence of the introduction.

18 This photo was taken by Zavi Cohen, September 20, 1983 (AP Wide World Photos).

19 Dylan's rendition of "*Hava Nagilah*" is "blue," because Dylan spoils the song's ryhthm. "*Hava Nagilah*" invites everyone to dance to express the joy of going up to Zion. Perhaps Dylan was playfully indicating that he didn't feel like dancing–or that he felt some ambivalence about political Zionism.

20 Shelton 334.

21 Groucho used this line on the radio in the '50s.

22 Jonatha Cott gives credit to Michael Gross for this photo, but he is mistaken. Cott 129. John Bauldie correctly credits Jerrold Schatzberg. Bauldie published this photo on the cover of Colbert S. Cartwright's book, *The Bible in the Lyrics of Bob Dylan* (Lancashire: Wanted Man, 1993).

23 Dylan's guitar-drawing also appears on the title page of *Lyrics*.

24 Paul Cable indicates that two singles of "Rainy Day Women" were released in 1966, one with "Pledging My Time" on the flip side, another with "Like a Rolling Stone." Paul Cable, *Bob Dylan: His Unreleased Recordings* (New York: Schirmer, 1978) 145.

25 John 8: 2-12:

> The teachers of the law and the Pharisees brought in a woman caught in adultery. They made her stand before the group and said to Jesus, "Teacher this woman was caught in the act of adultery. In the Law Moses commanded us to stone such a woman. Now what do you say?" They were using this question as a trap, in order to have a basis for accusing him.
> But Jesus bent down and started to write on the ground with his finger.

When they kept on questioning him, he straightened up and said to them, "If any one of you is without sin, let him be the first to throw a stone at her." Again he stooped down and wrote on the ground.

At this, those who heard began to go away one at a time, the older ones first, until only Jesus was left, with the woman still standing there. Jesus straightened up and asked her, "Woman, where are they? Has no one condemned you?"

"No one, sir," she said.

"Then neither do I condemn you," Jesus declared. "Go now and leave your life of sin."

26 Dante made repeated reference to Provence, and the language and poetry of Provence, in the prose of the *New Life*, in *The Banquet*, in *On Vernacular Eloquence* and in the *Comedy*. He wanted his readers to remember Provence, and to seek the truth about the mass murders that were perpetrated there in the name of Christ. The issues that would have interested him most may have been that, in Provence, Christians and Arabs sat down with Jews to translate and interpret Scripture, and in Provence, the book upon which kabbalistic writers focused their meditations was the Song of Songs.

Chapter 7

They Begin With A Riddle

"To Every Chosen Soul and Gentle Heart," by Dante Alighieri, and "Blowin' in the Wind," by Bob Dylan, are the works that first brought fame to their authors. Dante was seventeen years old when he wrote his sonnet, and Dylan was twenty when he wrote his song; but several traits that characterize each man's subsequent poetry were fully effective in these early works–among them a tendency to communicate enigmatically.

These poems are "formal riddles"–which is to say, they are the kind of enigmata that name the listener and invite the listener to answer. Dante's poem does this at the outset with ingratiating words and in an expansive manner. Dylan named his listener in the refrain of his song, describing the answer he wanted his listener to find, and repeating himself. Which is to say, both poets spent words generously in the address and invitation parts of their riddles; but both poets used very few words, and withheld criticle information, in their enigmata proper.

When Dante's poem is translated to English, and Dylan's song is reduced to print, the most obvious differences between the two works disappear; however, one distinct difference between them remains: Dante's poem tells a chronologically-ordered story, whereas Dylan's asks a series of questions. Dante began his story in a manner that would become characteristic of him in the *Comedy*, by making reference to the stars, in order to note the hour when a miraculous event occurred, before he said what happened. This enigmatic reference to the stars introduced Dante's readers to the mystical chronology that would subsequently provide order and beauty to the entire *New Life* and *Divine Comedy*. This riddle-within-a-riddle refers to the number "three," when it says the hours "tripled"; and it refers simultaneously to the number "nine," because the time of night when three hours have passed would be nine o'clock. This information may suggest to a superstitious reader that a dreadful event is about to be described, because according to numerology "nine" is associated with death[1]; but Dante emphasized the number "three," here and later, because he was speaking about the Trinity and eternal life.

The mystery Dante would later proclaim as a "miracle" is summed up in the *third* line of the anecdote: "Love appeared to me!" There is more to the riddle—in fact, the most sensational details are to come; but these words communicate the essence of Dante's oracle. In other works he would say that seeing Beatrice was like seeing Love—especially when she greeted him and smiled[2]—and in the last lines of the *Divine Comedy* he would say that in paradise he saw the face of Love in glory[3]; but here, at the outset, when he said he saw Love, he did not say he was dreaming, or that he was looking at Beatrice, or that he was in heaven.

As it was characteristic of Dante to speak of the stars and record precise details about their movements to indicate the passage of time, it was also characteristic of him to make reference to himself by speaking of his feelings as he told his story, and to suggest that he did not understand what was happening to him. At the opening of the *Divine Comedy* he said "fear" came back to him when he thought about the forest where he "woke up"; and in this first sonnet, immediately after he said that Love appeared to him, he spoke of the "horror" he felt when he remembered seeing Love. This establishes that he spoke as the witness of the event he was about to describe, and as the protagonist of his story. It also moderates the tempo of the sonnet, because this reference to himself forms a break between the summary sentence, "Love appeared to me," and the anecdote he was about to tell in full.[4]

There are several words in this sonnet that are difficult to translate because they have mystical associations as well as ordinary meaning—like the word, "*presa*," which can refer to being physically captured or spiritually chosen, and "*salute*," which can refer to corporeal health or to eternal salvation.[5] In the clause, "whose essence I am horrified to remember," the word, "remember," in both Italian and English, means, "to recall," and, "to give form to"; so the clause may be interpreted to mean that Dante felt horror when he thought about his dream, or that he felt horror because he was hinting that he seen God. The first interpretation seems plausible; but the second interpretation is surely the correct interpretation, because it is of a more sublime order, and it rings true in relationship to the rest of what Dante wrote.

Dante's riddle proper is told in the last six lines of the sonnet, in two sentences that guide the reader to imagine a man's figure. Dante's readers were familiar with verse that speaks of God as "Love"[6]; but there was no precedent, in Italian, to guide the reader to see that Dante wanted to say that Jesus had appeared to him in a vision.

"To Every Chosen Soul and Gentle Heart" appears in the opening pages of the *New Life*, Dante's prose memoire that preserves and annotates the poetry he wrote in his youth in praise of Love and "Beatrice" (a name that might be interpreted as, "Lady of Blessings"). He said he wrote this poem to describe a vision he had seen when he was alone in his room, after Beatrice had greeted him for the first time. He also said that he circulated this riddle-sonnet, and that sonnets were written to him in reply by several poets.[7] He quoted the first line of one of these sonnets, and he said that no one understood his riddle correctly at the time; but in closing he said, "...now it is very clear to the simplest persons." This equivocal statement may be taken to mean that subsequent events helped people to interpret his poem correctly, or that people who read his poems will understand him; but the primary meaning would be that people who are "chosen" and "gentle" understand him intuitively.

Any man or woman in Florence, where the message "God is Love" had been taught by the Church for centuries, should have been able to interpret the riddle correctly, if she or he could see that Dante meant to say that he had seen a vision of *Jesus*. The vision literalizes several ideas: Love held Dante's heart in his hand, and he carried Beatrice in his arms, because they were among his "chosen souls and gentle hearts"; Love brought Beatrice to Dante, woke her, and fed Dante's heart to her, to say that God was acting in Dante's life, and Beatrice's life, to bring them together; and Love turned away "weeping," because Beatrice was going to die.

The most important clues to this line of interpretation are the names Dante gave to the central figure of his story–he called him "Lord" and "Love"; because "Lord" is the principle epithet used throughout The Bible to speak of God, and because the Gospel is summarized, "God is love." Another important clue would be the last word of the poem, "weeping," because in two biblical accounts Jesus is said to have wept—when he was told that Lazarus had died, and when he prophesied the destruction of Jerusalem.[8] But if the reader gathers from these vague hints that Dante was speaking of Jesus, the reader may also see that this poem prophesies the death of a young woman. That idea may have been more difficult for the original readers to grasp than it is for us, since they read Dante's sonnet without having any idea who wrote it, or what would follow. Then again, if an epidemic raged in Florence around the time this riddle first circulated, people may have found the riddle's meaning more readily.[9] Some of them may have wondered whether the woman it portrayed might be someone they knew; and more than one woman may have wondered if the lady in Dante's vision might be herself.

Dante named one of the sonnets that was written in reply to his riddle, in chapter 4 of the *New Life*, after he presented "To Every Chosen Soul."[10] Its maker, Guido Cavalcanti, failed to see that Dante knew his poetic material and objective very well, and that he purposely withheld information that would have made his meaning clear. Cavalcanti demonstrated his skill in poesy by using the same rhyme sounds Dante used in his poem (as convention required), and Cavalcanti called "Love" a "Lord," as Dante did; but he said that Love saved the lady by feeding Dante's heart to her when she was near death. That was not Dante's theme.

The second respondant, Cino da Pistoia, said that Love happily fed Dante's heart to the lady to fulfill Dante's desire, and that Love wept afterwards, because he felt sorry for the lady, who had been resting blissfully before, but now would have to feel "the pain of love." That was not Dante's theme, either.

The third respondant mocked Dante's poem very aggressively. His sonnet bears mention because it shows that sonnets were written for all sorts of exchanges, including crude displays, and that they were written with the general public in mind, not just intellectuals, as is sometimes suggested. The author, Dante da Maiano, did not attempt to interpret Dante's riddle. He called Dante Alighieri, "ignorant one," and told him to cure himself of his "raving" by "washing his genitals." The spitefulness of this response would seem to have been occasioned by something other than the words of "To Every Chosen Soul and Gentle Heart." For example, Dante da Maiano may have been jealous, if ladies all over Florence were talking about Dante Alighieri's riddle.

Insofar as Dante addressed intellectuals, his sonnet seems to have been particularly effective, because it has been discussed in print many times during the centuries that have elapsed since its composition. It is not Dante's best-known sonnet; but it is the most controversial one. Another has been anthologized more frequently—"So Gentle and So Honest Does my Lady Seem"[11] (which is printed in the appendix on page 218). Some scholars praise the way Dante arranged and annotated the poetry preserved in the *New Life* to make the reader search for the meaning of his first riddle. An example would be Barbara Nolan's discussion of the relationship of "To Every Chosen Soul and Chosen Heart" to the rest of the poetry and prose of the *New Life*, in a book entitled, *The Gothic Visionary Perspective*.[12] Other scholars seem to be offended that the interpretation Dante offered in the *New Life* for his riddle might be taken seriously, preferring to believe that this work is profoundly flawed, and that Dante did not mean to say what his other poems and his prose tell us he meant to say. For example, Kennelm Foster and Patrick Boyde, the authors of a text entitled *Dante's Lyric Poetry*, argue that the prophetic interpretation of Dante's first sonnet may have been forced upon it after the fact.[13] They say the Christian interpretation depends on details which appear only in the prose[14]; then they conclude:

> The date of composition was almost certainly close to that stated in the prose, but the meaning of the vision may well have been different from that implied in the *New Life*. We shall never know what moved Dante to write it, or what interpretation he originally intended. In fact, it is highly probable that there never was a "correct solution," that like (other sonnets) it was never more than a piece of self-advertisement designed to secure recognition in Florentine literary circles.[15]

Foster and Boyde refuse to consider that Dante may have held in mind, from the outset, that concept concerning his salvation and his poetic purpose which influenced all his early poetry, the prose of the *New Life*, and the *Divine Comedy*. It is not clear why they resist the idea that "To Every Chosen Soul" renders Dante's theme concerning Beatrice and her death in microcosm; but the way they translate the poem, and the manner in which they present it, seem to be determined by their desire to obscure the emergence of the prophetic interpretation for readers of English.

Dante da Maiano, who attempted to mock Dante Alighieri in the first sonnet he wrote to him, indicated in a sonnet he wrote subsequently that he regretted his initial response to the great poet[16]; but the boast he made in his first poem for Dante included words to the effect that he would "never" change his opinion about Dante's sonnet.[17] Those words indicate stubbornness not unlike that of critics who read the entire *New Life* and *Divine Comedy*, and still refuse to admit that Dante may have meant to say that he saw a vision of Jesus, in that awe-filled poem he wrote when he was seventeen.

So far as I can determine, no one who has written about Dante's sonnet has attempted to compare it to other riddles—other than to riddle-sonnets written by Italian poets of Dante's day. Furthermore, it seems that before now no one who has written about enigmata has included "To Every Chosen Soul" among their examples.[18] This may be because its relationship to the subsequent works of its author, and its claim to historical verity, make it such an odd example of the genre that no one ever thought to compare it to other riddles. But Bob Dylan's song, "Blowin' in the Wind," offers a second example of the kind of riddle Dante posed in "To Every Chosen Soul"—that is, both of these riddles concern a visionary perception, or experience, that is recalled in the artist's subsequent work, both of them concern the nature and will of God, and both of them contain a social imperative that was exceedingly divisive.

"Blowin' in the Wind" begins with a question that might touch anyone, but that would be especially poignant for young men of Dylan's age: "How many roads must a man walk down before you call him a man?" It suggests that some people are not treated respectfully; and it depends for its logic on the familiar comparison of life to a "road." Dante's use of this figure in the first line of the *Divine Comedy* ("In the middle of the road of this life...") may well have influenced Dylan to talk about a man walking down a road to speak of an individual's experience of life; but the figure appears in oriental as well as western art, and it was favored by Jesus, who called himself "the way."[19]   One poem that may have influenced Dylan's formulation of this question is a written poem that does not contain the image of the road at all: Robert Burns's "Is There For Honest Poverty" (printed in the appendix, beginning on page 239[20]). Various ideas emerge from Dylan's first question; but I think a two-part interpretation of his words is necessary—such as, "everyone wants to be valued and respected," and "some people are arbitrarily denied respect."

The questions Dylan asked in "Blowin' in the Wind" may be called, "rhetorical questions," because they teach ideas and persuade the listener; but the term, "rhetorical," is not altogether fitting, because his questions, especially this first one, raise the possibility that Dylan felt overwhelmed by what was weighing on his mind. As was true of Dante, when Dylan insisted on his deficiency in treating his subject he increased the dramatic potential of his work, because humility would be appropriate to the recipient of an oracle.

Dylan's next question, "How many seas must the white dove sail before she sleeps in the sand?" might bring to mind the Bible story of the Flood, which says that Noah released a dove from the ark to search for land while water covered the earth[21]; and as I have already suggested in chapter 2, "White Dove" might be the name of the *ship* Dylan sings about, that will carry people to heaven.

The third question, "How many times must the cannonballs fly before they're forever banned?" is explicit in meaning, not metaphorical. It communicates the idea that war keeps recurring; and it presents the terms of an imperative: "The manufacture of weapons must be banned." Two more questions in "Blowin' in the Wind" expressly present the terms of a social imperative—one in each remaining stanza.

"How many years can a mountain exist before it is washed to the sea?" may be interpreted in this way: "Certain temporal phenonmena seem impervious to change"; and "Over time one element acts on another to effect change." There is no statement of moral imperative in this question; but in consideration of the content of the preceding verse, the listener might interpret Dylan's words like this: "We should struggle to bring an end to warfare, and to the manufacture of weapons, even if our efforts seem to be futile!"

The next question, "How many years can some people exist before they're allowed to be free?" is explicit. It communicates the idea that "some people" have been denied freedom for "many years"; and it partially presents the terms of an imperative: "Everybody should be allowed to be free!"

The last question in verse 2, "How many times can a man turn his head and pretend that he just doesn't see?" would seem to mean that evidence of suffering is all around us, and that some people avoid and deny the evidence of suffering they see with their own eyes. The unexpressed imperative might be phrased: "We should respond to the evidence of suffering we see in order to alleviate it!"

Like verses 1 and 2, the last verse begins with a question that uses figurative language in such a way as to make the idea the poet wished to express vague and difficult to understand. This question, "How many times must a man look up before he can see the sky?" introduced listeners to Dylan's viewpoint about prisons and the miscarriage of justice (which subsequently was elaborated more clearly in "The Walls of Red Wing," "Percy's Song," "I Shall Be Released," "George Jackson" and "Hurricane"). In this treatment of the subject Dylan suggested two things: "Everyone is blessed who can look up and see the sky"; and, "Some people are held captive where they cannot see the sky." He may have been thinking of confinement in houses, stores, offices, schools, and factories, rather than in prisons; but if we seek an imperative in his words, the most obvious would be: "We should abolish prisons, and stop the practice of incarceration!"

In each verse of "Blowin' in the Wind" the first question is vague, but the second and third questions are more explicit and prosaic. The question, "How many ears must one man have before he can hear people cry?" might be interpreted: "Pain is expressed by people who are suffering"; and,

"Human outcries of pain are willfully ignored by some people who could help those who are suffering." The imperative this question yields might be expressed like this: "We should listen for evidence of suffering to comfort people who are in pain!"

The ninth and final question, "How many deaths will it take 'till he knows that too many people have died?" is explicit; but the pronoun "he," which seems to refer to the man who turns his head and the man who cannot hear people cry, allows this question to communicate two ideas: "Some people do not recognize that killing is wrong," and the imperative: "Killing must be stopped!"

As the sense of Dante's riddle depends on the identification of "Love," and the thought that the lady in the vision will die, the sense of Dylan's riddle depends on the interpretation of the refrain—especially the word, "answer"—and the thought that the world will be destroyed on the last day. And as was true of Dante's sonnet, Dylan's song tests simple credence, because it suggests that he had been given special knowledge of God's plan for the redemption of the souls and gentle hearts of his chosen ones. The whole song overflows with meaning when the listener understands that Dylan used the expression "the answer" to speak of God.

Any man, woman, or child in Dylan's homeland, where Christianity is preached on radio and TV, as well as in churches, may at least have offered an opinion about the meaning of these questions, and the refrain, if he or she could imagine that the poet was speaking of God when he said something is "in the wind." This idea is the wisdom in Dylan's nine childlike questions, since Christianity and Judaism teach that God will appear on Judgment Day. But to be absolutely precise, Dylan did not say, "God appeared to me"; his words suggest that he had a perception of God through his sense of *sound*, for his reference is to the invisible wind—that is, in effect he said, "God spoke to me," or "I have heard God's voice."

George Montiero discusses Dylan's apocalyptic songs and their impact on "minds that were closed to all forms of literature," in a provocative, and generally accurate article, entitled, "Dylan in the Sixties."[22] Montiero makes an important point when he relates Dylan's apocalyptic work to that of a number of American writers, beginning with Herman Melville[23]; but Montiero states that it is his objective to describe metamorphoses in Dylan and Dylan's ideas, and he does not seem to recognize that "Blowin' in the Wind" is Dylan's first, and most influential, apocalyptic song.

Here one argument concerning Dante's riddle, to which I alluded before, has bearing–his detractors' argument, that Dante found his divine theme at some indefinite point in time *after* he wrote "To Every Chosen Soul and Gentle Heart." In both Dante's case and Dylan's scholars express skepticism about the vision of God that became manifest in riddles the poets composed in adolescence. In both cases the masterpiece that made the artist famous is sometimes dismissed as an insignificant youthful effort. But when these two poems are compared carefully to one another, in light of the idea that the youthful poets who made them wished to praise God, the truth shines through: they are sublime art works, in themselves, and each of them anticipates a historically-significant body of work.

The poetic riddle usually describes an object or phenomenon, and one word is required to answer it; furthermore, the object hidden in a riddle is supposed to be something familiar to everyone to whom the riddle is addressed. Listeners must know about the hidden "thing" and its characteristics, in order for the riddle to work as an entertainment and teaching device. Dante's and Dylan's riddles do not concern a thing–they describe "the ineffable"; but they work because the prevailing ideational system in thirteenth century Italy *and* in twentieth century America claims to know God and to name "him."

It is not simply felicitous or fortuitous that Dante and Dylan both wrote riddles. The genre is uniquely suited to prophecy–that is, it is a potent means for teaching religious principles, and for instilling a sense of initiation in people who experience it. Riddles are implements, they cannot be made accidentally; they *work,* or they are not riddles. These two riddles hold essential religious ideas: Dante's poem contains ideas concerning human sexuality and eternal life; and Dylan's poem contains ideas concerning human cruelty and divine judgement. They require us to think abstractly, and to consult wisdom within ourselves and around us, as we may, and thereby they "quicken" the churches, synagogues, seminaries, and schools that are expected to teach ideas about human fate.

Dylan may have been influenced by "To Every Chosen Soul and Gentle Heart" when he wrote his riddle-song, "Blowin' in the Wind"; but Dante's poem was not Dylan's formal model. I think it is likely that Dylan discovered Dante's riddle and understood it's place in Dante's work, and that he was influenced by it to write a riddle to serve his own situation. But while I assume that Dante's work influenced Dylan to see the role of the poet in society as he did, and that Dante's visionary mysticism influenced Dylan to be a visionary and a mystic, I would emphacize above all else that Dylan was directly and powerfully influenced by Biblical prophecy and narrative.[24] I would say the same about Dante. Both poets began to study sacred literature as children; both were taught a foreign language in order to read Scripture, and to learn songs, prayers, and habits of meditation.

There may have been several reasons, including subconscious ones, to explain why Dante and Dylan chose, in the first instance and characteristically thereafter, to compose poetry that operates enigmatically. The enigma is a poetic device—a duplicitous "container" of sorts—with power that is mysterious. I will examine several more poetic riddles in chapter 8; for now I would point out that riddles were among the first things people made, because language cannot work without intuition, and because intuition, which operates by design in the riddle, can be strengthened through riddling.

Riddles are held taboo in primitive societies because they imitate processes of vital importance; that is, they are only told in season. Riddles are thought to make things "come out," because *sense* comes out of a riddle; so in magic societies riddles are told after seeds are planted, after fishermen cast their nets, after women begin childbirth, and after a death, while the body of the deceased waits for interment (so that plants will grow out of the earth, so that fish will be drawn out of the sea, so that the infant will descend out of the mother, and so that the soul will pass from its body). Riddles are also told at wedding feasts, because conception is thought to be facilitated by riddling—that is, by the live exchange of riddles. And above all, rainfall is believed to be occasioned by this sport.

It is unlikely that Dante or Dylan thought about the use of riddles for imitative magic when they composed their riddle-poems. They were probably more interested in the possibility that they would be thought to be imitating Biblical prophecy, because the ubiquitous riddle, sometimes despised as a corny kind of "joke," and relegated to children, is one of the means the ancient prophets of Israel, and Jesus, used to change men's hearts.

In "To Every Chosen Soul and Gentle Heart" and "Blowin' in the Wind," Dante and Dylan recreated the ancient spectacle we might call "riddle theater," in which participants can come to understanding, and confirm understanding, *in unison*. This theatre is produced whenever one person challenges another person, or group of people, to answer an enigma. Any number of people may participate, as contestants or as witnesses. If they understand one another, a group's sense of oneness can be reaffirmed, and faith in communication can be reborn, through riddles; so the riddle itself is as important, in a way, as the mysteries it may be said to imitate.

Dante and Dylan composed enigmata of unusual dimensions in "To Every Chosen Soul and Gentle Heart" and "Blowin' in the Wind." As I see it, they framed their ideas so as to be understood by anyone who might come across their words, and they achieved an unusual measure of success in communicating with a general audience. In these poems they recreated the riddle-theater by challenging people to think about the Judeo-Christian idea of love; and they proved that many people deeply *enjoy* this variety of enigma.

Notes

1 "9" is associated with death, because it is equal to "0" in the reductionist computations of numerologists.

2 The sonnet in which Dante first praised Beatrice's smile may be found in chapter 26 of the *New Life*. It is entitled, "In her eyes my lady wears love" (*"Ne li occhi porta la mia donna amore"*). Here are the concluding three lines:

> What she seems when she smiles a little
> cannot be told or retained in the mind,
> such a new and gentle miracle it is.

3 In his final beatific vision Dante said he saw "our likeness," and then lost consciousness.

4 Dante told his story most deliberately: he always framed anecdotes by including elaborate digressions, replete with information he wanted to provide. Novices invariably protest that his digression are pointless, boring, and difficult; but, in fact, Dante never wasted a word.

5 A ciascun' alma presa e gentil core
> nel cui cospetto ven lo dir presente,
> in ciò che mi rescrivan suo parvente,
> salute in lor segnor, cioè Amore.
> Già eran quasi che atterzate l' ore
> del tempo che onne stella n' è lucente,
> quando m' apparve Amor subitamente,
> cui essenza membrar mi dà orrore.
> Allegro mi sembrava Amor tenendo
> meo core in mano, e ne le braccia avea
> madonna involta in un drappo dormendo.
> Poi la svegliava, d' esto core ardendo
> lei paventosa umilmente pascea:
> appresso gir lo ne vedea piangendo.

6 Guittone D'Arezzo and Guido Guinizelli, and others, wrote verse that anticipated Dante's praise of Beatrice, in that they suggested that a lady might be angelic; but only Dante described a vision of God, and wrote an extended narrative concerning God, the lady, and himself.

7 Three sonnets that were written to Dante in reply to his riddle may be found in Dante's collected works published by the Dante Society. "*Vedeste, al mio parere, onne valore*" by Guido Cavalcanti (page 57), "*Naturalmente chere ogni amadore,*" by Cino da Pistoia (page 58), and "Di ciò che stato sei dimandatore," by Dante da

Maiano (page 58).

8 Actually, there are two places that explicitly say that Jesus wept, and a third that suggests he wept without precisely saying so:

As he approached Jerusalem and saw the city he wept over it. (Luke 19:41)
When Jesus saw her crying, and the Jews who had come along with her also weeping, he was deeply moved in spirit and troubled. "Where have you laid him?" he asked. "Come and see, Lord," they replied. And Jesus wept. (John 11:35)
He took Peter and the two sons of Zebedee along with him and he began to be sorrowful and troubled. Then he said to them, "My soul is over-whelmed with sorrow to the point of death. Stay here and keep watch with me. Going a little further, he fell with his face to the ground and prayed. (Matthew 26:37-39)

9 J.F.C. Hecker, the 19th century epidemiologist quoted in chapter 3, reported that the oriental bubonic plague ravaged Italy sixteen times, between 1119 and 1340. He pieced together information about epidemics in various parts of Europe, and he expressed the opinion that some of the epidemics he described were related to natural cataclysms—such as earthquakes, hurricanes, and floods.

10 In English the title of Cavalcanti's sonnet would be, "In my opinion you beheld all virtue."

11 "So Gentle and So Honest" appears in chapter 26 of the New Life. Dante said that he wrote it after he spoke to those ladies whose voices and occasional sighs he compared to the sound of rainfall mixed with "lovely snow."

12 Barbara Nolan, The Gothic Visionary Perspective (Princeton: Princeton U P, 1977). The point in her discussion where Nolan shows that she understands about Dante's lady, and about Love, is on page 100: "Here, as many critics agree, Dante presents a prophecy not only of Beatrice's death, but also her translation of his love into heaven."

13 K. Foster and P. Boyde, Dante's Lyric Poetry, 2 volumes (Oxford: Oxford U P, 1967).

14 Foster and Boyde, Introduction to volume 1, 20.

15 Foster and Boyde, Introduction to volume 1, 21.

16 This sonnet ("Per pruove di saper com vale o quanto") is also published by the Dante Society in Dante's collected works, on page 67.

17 Here are the last three lines of da Maiano's sonnet:

Thus written, I render you my opinion;
nor will I ever change my interpretation.
And you should send your urine to a doctor!

18 Dante's youthful compositions included several "tenzoni," which were son-

nets that were addressed as a challenge to other poets, or as a response to someone else's challenge. They were posted for public view. Some of these sonnets named, or somehow designated, a particular person, as their intended reader. There was only one rule: a person who chose to respond to a sonnet had to imitate the rhyme scheme and meter of the sonnet he was answering (the "poets" were all men, because women were not allowed to write). Not all *tenzoni* were true riddles—indeed, very few were. Dante's *tenzoni* are preserved along with the *tenzoni* of his contemporaries, and scholars continually focus attention on relationships they see between these works.

19 John 14: 6, "I am the way, the truth, and the life...."

20 *The Poems of Robert Burns, Selected with an Introduction by Delancey Ferguson* (New York: Heritage, 1965) 174.

21 Genesis 8:8-12:

Then he sent out a dove to see if the water had receded from the surface of the ground. But the dove could find no place to set its feet because there was water over all the surface of the earth; so it returned to Noah in the ark. He reached out his hand and took the dove and brought it back to himself in the ark. He waited seven more days and again sent out the dove from the ark. When the dove returned to him in the evening, there in its beak was a freshly plucked olive leaf. Then Noah knew that the water had receded from the earth. He waited seven more days and sent the dove out again, but this time it did not return to him.

22 George Montiero, "Dylan in the Sixties," *South Atlantic Quarterly*, 73, 1974, 160-172.

23 Montiero is particularly interested in what he calls Dylan's "comic apocalyptic" songs:

...these apocalyptic songs constitute the most recent contribution to a manifestation of that American literary tradition defined by R. W.B. Lewis as stemming from Herman Melville's novel of disguises and metamorphoses, *The Confidence Man* (1857).... It is apparent to me that no *poet* has worked the comic apocalypse with as much success as the '*song poet*' Dylan has." (Montiero 168 and 169.)

24 The questions posed in "Blowin' in the Wind" might bring to mind Psalm 13, which begins:

How long, O Lord? Will you forget me forever?
How long will you hide your face from me?
How long must I wrestle with my thoughts
and every day have sorrow in my heart?
How long will my enemies triumph over me?

Chapter 8

Ethical Riddles

The sonnet that first brought Dante Alighieri fame is like the song that made Bob Dylan famous, in that both "To Every Chosen Soul and Gentle Heart" and "Blowin' in the Wind" ask their readers and listeners to interpret an enigma, and in that both riddles may be interpreted to mean that the poet had seen a vision of God. If this interpretation is chosen from the field of possibilities offered by the dialectics of the two poems, "To Every Chosen Soul" may be seen as a perfect microcosm of the verse Dante wrote subsequently, and "Blowin' in the Wind" may be seen as a microcosm of the verse Dylan has composed up to this time; however, the idea that either of these works may be interpreted in this way contradicts the judgement of some of the scholars who have written about Dante, and of some who have written about Dylan. In fact, it has frequently been argued that the confession of religiosity expressed in the later works of these artists contradicts the ideas expressed in their earliest works.[1]

The meaning of "To Every Chosen Soul," and the meaning of "Blowin' in the Wind," have been discussed in numerous books and articles, and each of these poems has been called an "enigma" repeatedly; but no one who has written about them has compared either of them to other riddles that teach ethics. "To Every Chosen Soul" has been compared to other riddle-sonnets written in Dante's day[2]; however, none of Dante's contemporaries pretended to prophesy, as Dante did, so very little can be learned from their enigmata about the way Dante's enigma works.

Most riddles concern objects, and may be answered by one word. "To Every Chosen Soul" and "Blowin' in the Wind" concern human fate, and cannot properly be answered by one word. Among riddles that concern life and death, perhaps the greater number project an atheistic world view. For example, the nursery-riddle, "Humpty Dumpty," which is taught to children as a description of an "egg," is also about death, and when it was first told it may have been understood to refer to a particular person.[3]

Another familiar riddle that concerns human fate is the riddle Sophocles attributed to the Sphinx, in *Oedipus*.[4] Although Oedipus thought he had interpreted the riddle correctly when he said it was a description of a "man," he failed to see that the riddle was a prophecy explicitly about *him*–that is, he did not know he would need a cane before he reached old age, or why he would need it. But Sophocles described Oedipus's encounter with the Sphinx in such a way as to suggest that Oedipus was given an extraordinary warning to stay out of Thebes, and he chose to ignore it.

These examples show that two processes are tested in enigma–logic and intuition. It is intuition that discovers the specific idea that may be called the "wisdom" of a given riddle, whereas logic is confounded by enigma and can only produce inadequate interpretations. Logic sorts the information in an enigma, logic determines that something is odd about this information, and logic draws inferences from an enigma's words; but logic cannot produce ideas.

"To Every Chosen Soul," "Blowin' in the Wind," "Humpty Dumpty," and the Oedipus-riddle, all comment on the human condition; but Dante's and Dylan's riddles are gracefully expressed, and they concern human relationships and the nature of love, whereas the two atheistic riddles are blunt and impersonal, and the vision of life they communicate excludes love. "Humpty Dumpty" places man in a kingdom with walls, where horses and men confer ineffectually, and where creatures move only to fall and break; and Sophocles' riddle sees man as a lonely *thing*, moving briefly and inexplicably through space. "Humpty Dumpty" and the Oedipus-riddle both contain wisdom, in the sense that "Humpty Dumpty" might help an adult to teach a child that a fall can hurt, and the Oedipus-riddle might be used to teach the idea that changes occur in our bodies as we get older; however, these facts are apparent, whereas "To Every Chosen Soul" and "Blowin' in the Wind" contain the idea that life is eternal, which is a mystery.

Aristotle discussed enigma very briefly in the *Rhetoric*, and in the *Poetics*, noting that riddles work through deceit, and that "surprise" is the effect that enigma employs to teach things[5]; but the brevity of his remarks, the fact that he did not describe, or mention, the context in which riddles might be exchanged, and the one example he cited–which describes a surgical procedure and an implement ("I saw one man use fire to glue bronze on another!": *phlebotomy*)–suggest that Aristotle despised enigma. Aristotle's riddle is a weak riddle, because it quite clearly describes a procedure in which one person does something to another person, with the use of implements and the application of heat; and it has a strictly limited range, because it is only accessible to those who share Aristotle's fascination with implements and surgery.

Aristotle may not have known about the use of riddles for imitative magic, or his loathing of magic may have heightened his disdain for riddles. The genre is misunderstood, however, if it is not seen that riddles are used for competition, and that they are sometimes posed and answered in front of witnesses, with something at stake for an individual, or for a group of people, in the outcome. Furthermore, enigmata have been used by every nation on earth to teach language and ideas. Aristotle may not have known that the prophets of Israel used riddles to prophesy,[6] and he could not know that Jesus would tell riddles, and would claim to have come into the world to fulfill the prophecies of Scripture[7]; but Aristotle should have seen that enigma is a potent poetic genre because it compels dialogue and confirms intuition.

Dante's and Dylan's first riddles stand out among examples of the genre, because their subject matter is sublime, and because they are exquisitely crafted. The obscurity of their makers did not spoil the potential of these works to surprise people; but in both cases discovery of the artist's true identity increases the fascination of his work, because unlike most riddlers Dante and Dylan pretended to speak about their own experience, and they appealed directly to their readers for attention and sympathy.

A poem which may properly be compared to Dante's and Dylan's riddles, insofar as it concerns man's fate and the nature of God, is the Old English poem, "The Dream of the Rood," which has been called, "the first and finest dream-revelation of the cosmic riddle to emerge from Western Europe."[8] ("The Dream of the Rood" is printed in the appendix, beginning on page 225.) The intent of the riddler in this instance, obviously, was not to teach through "deceit" and "surprise," so much as it was to tell the story of Jesus's crucifixion in an unusual and dramatic fashion–at length, rather than with absolute concision. Dante's and Dylan's riddles do not tell Jesus's story, but they are "revelations of the cosmic riddle" because their solutions depend on the idea of the Messiah; and they are particularly effective because Dante and Dylan did *not* speak about the remote past, and they did *not* say they were speaking about dreams. (In the prose of the *New Life*, written almost ten years after "To Every Chosen Soul and Gentle Heart," Dante said a "soft sleep" overcame him before he saw his vision of "Love"[9]; but his riddle does *not* say that he was sleeping or dreaming.)

The Exeter Book contains several poems that may be compared to Dante's and Dylan's riddles, because they reflect upon one another in such a way as to yield ideas about the creation and redemption of the world.[10] (Four of these Old English poems, "Wulf and Eadwacer," "The Wife's Lament," "The Husband's Message," and "Resignation," are printed in the appendix, beginning on page 229.) These poems are not always recognized as riddles; but they, and the other pieces of poetry preserved in The Exeter Book, work together in tandem to prophesy, much as Dylan's songs do–and Dante's verse, and the *Zohar's* stories. There is an important distinction to be made, though: unlike Dante and Dylan, who made themselves the protagonists of their poetry, the person who organized The Exeter Book, and the author of the *Zohar*, preferred to remain anonymous.[11]

Another literary riddle that might be said to concern man's fate, is "The Drunken Boat," which envisions a global flood.[12] ("The Drunken Boat" is printed in the appendix, beginning on page 235.) Arthur Rimbaud, the author, pretended to be a fragment of a wooden barge that rejoices in its atomization. The poem is not really about a "boat," though: it is about Rimbaud and his death wish. It preserves memories of a lonely childhood that might stir sympathy, but its misanthropic view of the world inhibits a sympathetic response–like the Oedipus-riddle and "Humpty Dumpty," which also seem to be about inanimate objects, it denies the idea that men and women are created in God's image.

Many literary works that are not usually called "riddles," are truly enigmatic. The sonnet, "The Virgin, Vivacious, Beautiful To-day," by Stephan Mallarmé, for example, resembles the man-riddle, the egg-riddle, and the boat-riddle, in that it pretends to describe an object–in this case, a "swan"; but it is really about Mallarmé himself, and his despair.[13] (Mallarmé's sonnet is printed in the appendix, on page 238.)

Moby Dick is more like Dante's and Dylan's poems, since it concerns ethics and may be said to be prophetic–if the white whale is understood to be "Leviathan," and a symbol of Christ.[14] But Melville did not indicate that he was portraying himself in *Moby Dick*, as Dante did in his work, and Dylan does in his; and he did not tell his readers that he expected them to "answer" or "write back." *Moby Dick* is too long for recitation; but its length, intricacy, and solemnity, make it one of the world's outstanding examples of a literary riddle. (A very brief passage from chapter 42 of *Moby Dick,* bearing a clue to the solution, is printed in the appendix, on page 238.)

One brief poetic work that might be compared to "To Every Chosen Soul" and "Blowin' in the Wind," because it was used for confrontational purposes, is "The Battle Hymn of the Republic" (printed in the appendix, beginning on page 239). This song is not a riddle; but it possesses the sort of dramaticity Dante and Dylan gave their works–as the first line proves: "My eyes have seen the glory of the coming of the Lord." Like "To Every Chosen Soul" and "Blowin' in the Wind," "The Battle Hymn of the Republic" enjoyed great popularity for several years.[15] Julia Ward Howe, the composer of the lyrics of this song, did not create a vast and complex body of verse, furthermore she borrowed the melody of a popular song for her composition; but her song is remembered, and is taught to children in American schools, because as it circulated it compelled people to pass judgment against slavery–much as "To Every Chosen Soul and Gentle Heart" compelled people to pass judgment against the social subjugation and intellectual repression of women, and "Blowin' in the Wind" compelled people to pass judgment against racism, militarism, and authoritarianism.

Dante said that many people tried to interpret his riddle, he quoted the first line of one sonnet that was sent to him in reply, and he said that no one understood his sonnet at the time. Then he said, "Now it is very clear to the simplest persons."[16] These words effectively rebuked the verse-makers who had written back to him; and they suggest that Dante's sonnet continued in circulation during the period of time that elapsed between its composition and the composition of the *New Life*–which was a period of eight or nine years. Dante's sonnet may have been read throughout Tuscany, throughout the entire Italian peninsula, and beyond Italy, in its season.

"Blowin' in the Wind" enjoyed a season of popularity that lasted for several years, too. Beginning in the spring of 1962, it was performed and recorded very frequently. Its popularity in America may have peaked before Dylan retired in 1966, but it continued to be a favorite, internationally, long after it ceased to be perceived as being radical–as may be seen by the fact that it became a top-selling hit, *again*, in 1968, when Stevie Wonder recorded it.[17]

Both Dante and Dylan first won fame through the success of their riddles; but Dante's personal fame was not equal to the fame of "To Every Chosen Soul and Gentle Heart," and Dylan's personal fame was not equal to the fame of "Blowin' in the Wind," until the artists demonstrated their capacity to fulfill the expectations these poems generate–namely, that they would have more to say about what they had seen that would be of interest to others. Before Dante completed the *New Life*, his personal fame was established far beyond his home town; and Dylan's fame had spread abroad, too, before he retired in 1966. Dante had repeatedly proven that he could produce sublime poetic effects, in the best means of communication available to poets at the time–that is, in Italian sonnets and *canzoni*; while Dylan used song forms related to dance music–especially rock and roll, which was the best means of communication available to a poet in the 1960s. Today Dante's fame rests primarily on the merit of the *Divine Comedy*, which he wrote in exile, more than a decade after the *New Life*; and someday Dylan's fame may rest of the merit of the work he performed and recorded after 1969–after he left Woodstock to avoid the crush of his followers.[18] But before that can happen, more people will have to forget the days of the peace movement.

Notes

1   Dylan made explicit confession of Christianity in the songs he began writing in 1978–sixteen years after he wrote "Blowin' in the Wind." Dante confessed Christianity in absolutely clear terms in the prose of the *New Life*, about ten years after he wrote "To Every Chosen Soul and Gentle Heart." Scholars who have disbelieved Dante include K. Foster and P. Boyde, whose skepticism is discussed in chapter 7. As for Dylan, disbelief is expressed in a book entitled, *Dylan–What Happened?: How and why did Bob Dylan become a born-again Christian?*, by Paul Williams (Glen Ellen, California: Entwhistle, 1979).

2   The primary source of evidence concerning the poetic competition in Florence, between Dante and other writers of verse, is an anthology called, *La giuntina* (Florence, 1527).

3   "Humpty Dumpty" goes like this:
Humpty Dumpty sat on the wall,
Humpty Dumpty had a great fall.
All the King's horses and all the King's men
Couldn't put Humpty Dumpty together again.

4   The Sphinx asked Oedipus: What goes on four legs in the morning, on two legs at noon, and on three legs in the evening?

5   Here is the relevant passage of the *Rhetoric*:
Again, the metaphors should not be far-fetched, but derived from cognate and homogenous subjects, giving a name to something which before was nameless, and manifesting their cognate character as soon as they are uttered. There is a metaphor of this kind in the popular enigma, "A man on a man gluing bronze by the aid of fire I discovered," for the particular process was nameless, but as both processes are kinds of application, the author of the enigma described the application of the "cupping-glass" as "gluing." It is generally possible in fact to derive good metapors from well-constructed enigmata, for as every metaphor conveys an enigma, it is clear that a metaphor derived from a good enigma is a good one... While metaphor is a very frequent instrument of clever sayings, another or an additional instrument is deception, as people are more clearly conscious of having learnt something from their sense of surprise at the way in which the sentence ends, and their soul seems to say, "Quite true, and I had missed the point." Again, the characteristic of clever apophthegms is that the speaker means more than he says, as e.g. the apophthegm of Stesichorus, that the cicalas will have to sing to themselves on the ground. This too is the reason of the pleasure afforded by clever riddles; they are instructive and metaphorical in their expression.

Aristotle, *The Rhetoric of Aristotle*, translated by J.E.C. Welldon (New York: Mac – Millan, 1886) 234, 5.

Here is the relevant passage of the *Poetics*:

> On the other hand the diction becomes distinguished and non-prosaic by the use of unfamiliar terms, i.e. strange words, metaphors, lengthened forms, and everything that deviates from the ordinary modes of speech. But a whole statement in such terms will either a riddle or a barbarism—a riddle, if made up of metaphors, a barbarism, if made up of strange words. The very nature of a riddle is this, to describe a fact in an impossible combination of words (which cannot be done with the real names for things, but can be with their metaphorical substitutes); e.g. "I saw a man glue brass on another with fire," and the like.

Aristotle, *Poetics,* translated by Ingram Bywater (New York: Modern Library, 1954) 253.

> 6 One example would be Ezekiel 29: 3-5:
>
> I am against you Pharoah, King of Egypt,
> you great monster, lying among your streams.
> You say, "The Nile is mine;
> I made it for myself."
> But I will put hooks in your jaws,
> And make the fish of your streams stick to your scales.
> I will pull you out from among your streams, leave you in the desert,
> With all the fish sticking to your scales.
> I will leave you in the desert,
> You and all the fish of your streams.
> You will fall on the open field
> And not be gathered or picked up.
> I will give you as food
> To the beasts of of the earth and the birds of the air.

7 Here is one of Jesus's riddles: "I am the bread of life." John 6: 35.

8 It is Craig Williamson who calls "The Dream of the Rood," "the first and finest dream revelation of the cosmic riddle to emerge in Western Europe." *A Feast of Creatures: Anglo-Saxon Riddle Songs*, Translated with Introduction, Notes and Commentary by Craig Williamson (Philadelphia: U of Pennsylvania P, 1982) 41. The authorship of "The Dream of the Rood" is uncertain. Stylistically and ideationally, it would seem to be the work of Cynewulf. It is convincingly attributed to the early 8th century. The translation I use is from *The Earliest English Poems, Translated and Introduced by Michel Alexander* (Harmondsworth, Middlesex and Baltimore, Maryland: Penquin, 1966).

9 "And thinking about her a light sleep overcame me, in which a marvelous

vision appeared to me…" Dante, *New Life*, chapter 2.

    10   James E. Anderson discusses the riddles of the Exeter Book, in, *Two Literary Riddles in the Exeter Book: Riddle 1 and The Easter Riddle* (Norman: Oklahoma U P, 1986). I use his translations of "Wulf and Eadwacer," "The Wife's Lament," "The Husband's Message," and "Resignation," and I am entirely indebted to him for insight into the religious significance of the poetry gathered in the Exeter Book. He speaks of the "logical progression in these poems, describing this progression as, "the Bride's compaint of abandonment on Good Friday, to the Bridegroom's return in the Eucharist on Easter" (Anderson xiv).

    11   Leofric, who was chosen by Edward the Confessor to be Bishop of Devon and Cornwall, and who was enthroned at Exeter by order of Pope Leo IX in 1050, is named as the likely compiler of the Exeter Book. Moses de Leon is mentioned in connection with the authorship of *Zohar* above, in Chapter 4.

    12   The translation of "Drunken Boat" that appears in the appendix is my own. I used Samuel Beckett's translation is my original manuscript, by permission, and I referred to Beckett as I prepared this piece.

    13   I use Grange Woolley's translation of Stéphane Mallarmé's, "The Virgin, Vivacious and Beautiful To-Day." Grange Woolley, *Stéphane Mallarmé 1842-1898: A commemorative presentation including translations from his prose and verse with commentaries.* (Madison, New Jersey: Drew University, 1942) 13.

    14   The following references to Leviathan are found in Job 41:"Can you pull in leviathan with a fishhook?" (verse 1); and "Behind him he leaves a glistening wake; one would think the deep had white hair" (verse 32).

    15   This song was sung by abolitionists during the years of the Civil War and after it. The following information about the composition of "The Battle Hymn of the Republic" appears in the *Book of World Famous Music*:

> The first printing of the words of "The Battle Hymn of the Republic" was in the January 14, 1862, issue of the New York *Daily Tribune*…It had been written in Washington D.C. in the early dawn of November 19, 1861…The first printings do not contain the "Glory Hallelujah" chorus, or indicate that the poem was intended to be sung to that melody…The first printing of the poem of the "Battle Hymn of the Republic" set to music was printed on April, 1862, by Oliver Ditson and Company, Boston… Mrs. Howe, famous as a reformer and social worker as well as poetess, was born in New York City in 1819, moved to Boston, and died in Middleton, R.I, in 1910.

James J. Feld, *Book of World-Famous Music* (New York: Dover, 1966) 130-2.

    16   Here is the passage, virtually complete:

> Thinking about what had happened to me, I proposed to make it known to many of those who were famous troubadours at that time. And since

I had already discovered the art of setting words to rhyme, I proposed to write a sonnet in which I would greet all Love's faithful ones; and begging them to judge my dream, I wrote to them what I had seen in my sleep. And then I began this sonnet which begins: "To Every Chosen Soul"... To this sonnet there was an answer from many, with varied interpretations; among whom, as a correspondent, was he whom I call the first among my friends. He wrote a sonnet beginning: "In my opinion you saw every value." This was more or less the beginning of a friendship between him and me, when he knew that I was the one who had sent him that. The true judgement of the so-called dream was not then perceived by anyone, but now it is prefectly clear to the simplest persons (Dante, *New Life*, chapter 3).

17 Shelton includes the following information concerning the success of "Blowin' in the Wind":

"Blowin' in the Wind" had a dual life as a pop standard and civil rights anthem. Within a year of the "Peter, Paul, and Mary" hit, nearly sixty other versions were recorded by the likes of Duke Ellington, Lena Horne, Marlene Dietrich, Spike Jones, Percy Faith, Trini Lopez, and Glen Campbell. Many more sang the song than those who recorded it."

18 Woodstock, New York, became a kind of mecca for "flower children" while Dylan lived there. The entrepeneurs who held the concert called, "Woodstock," in August 1969, made a profit from the crowds; but they were not encouraged to hope Dylan would participate. Dylan left Woodstock, instead.

Conclusion.

In 1282, when Dante began to circulate verse, women were officially denied the right to literacy; but unofficially many women were encouraged to learn to read Italian. Dante wrote for *them*. He said so repeatedly–for example, in the first line of his first canzone, "Ladies Who Have an Understanding of Love," and in the last three words of the *New Life*, where he called his readers, "my dear ladies." Dante knew that his contemporaries would understand that he was protesting official discrimination against women in his sonnets, ballads, and canzoni, and in the prose of the *New Life*. He could be certain that people around him would know that there were important ideas at stake–in particular, that women as well as men should be allowed to read, and that the Bible should be translated into every dialect–because these ideas were inflammatory, and to espouse and defend them could be dangerous.

Some of Dante's contemporaries in Italy would have recognized that Dante alluded, very subtly, to St. Francis and the story of St. Francis's sermon to the sparrows, in this concluding salutation of the *New Life*; for according to the written Latin and vernacular texts that circulated throughout the Italian peninsula in Dante's day, Francis once entered a meadow where he heard sparrows singing, and gathered the little birds around him by speaking to them gently, beginning with the words, "My sisters!" The sequence of the words attributed to Francis is distinctively marked in Italian; because it was reported that he said, "Sisters mine" ("*Sirocchie mie*"), following Latin usage–as any Italian might–rather than, "My sisters" ("*Mie sirocchie*"), which would be standard Italian. Dante made his Italian even more colorful, and sweeter, by saying, "*donne mie care*," which sounds, in Italian, something like, "dear ladies mine."

Dante evoked St. Francis in this final grace note to the *New Life*, even though he did not mention Francis's name anywhere in this little book, because St. Francis was a reformer who cared about the rights of women. I am not thinking of St. Francis as he is represented by us in quiet little statues, but of St. Francis the passionate, raggedy, mystic, who was not afraid of politics, and who loved the Church.

I should clarify that I use the word "Church," here, to speak of the community of living souls that might also be called "The Mystical House of Israel," of which Moses de Leon might be a member, as well as St. Francis. I do not mean the Church of Rome, or the Church of England, or the Baptist, Lutheran, Methodist, or Presbyterian Church; and I do not mean the modern nation of Israel, or the Jewish community of the diaspora. Another expression that would name this community might be "the peace movement." Dante and Dylan chose to teach ideas that belong inherently to this mystical body, and they *succeeded* brilliantly. That is the chief reason their works may be called prophetic. They did not create the ideas they advanced–far from it, they found these ideas already alive all around them, irresistable, embraceable, lovely, and worth fighting for–that is, holy and sufficient.

Notes

1 This point is blurred, or misunderstood, by some scholars. For example, Luigi Valli argues that when Dante wrote to women he actually was writing to men. Luigi Valli, *Il linguaggio segreto di Dante e dei "Fedeli d'amore"* (Rome: Bertoni, 1969) 63,4. The error of Valli's opinion is proven by the fact that he also says that he finds the *New Life* to be "largely incomprehensible" (Valli 15).

Contents of Appendix

Appendix

"Blowin' in the Wind"

How many roads must a man walk down
Before you call him a man?
Yes, 'n' how many seas must a white dove sail
Before she sleeps in the sand?
Yes, 'n' how many times must the cannon balls fly
Before they're forever banned?
The answer, my friend, is blowin' in the wind,
The answer is blowin' in the wind.

How many years can a mountain exist
Before it is washed to the sea?
Yes, 'n' how many years can some people exist
Before they're allowed to be free?
Yes, 'n' how many times can a man turn his head,
An' pretend that he just doesn't see?
The answer, my friend, is blowin' in the wind,
The answer is blowin' in the wind.

How many times must a man look up
Before he can see the sky?
Yes, 'n' how many ears must one man have
Before he can hear people cry?
Yes, 'n' how many deaths will it take till he knows
That too many people have died?
The answer, my friend, is blowin' in the wind,
The answer is blowin' in the wind.

"A Hard Rain's A-Gonna Fall"

Oh, where have you been, my blue-eyed son?
Oh, where have you been, my darling young one?
I've stumbled on the side of twelve misty mountains,
I've walked and I've crawled on six crooked highways,
I've stepped in the middle of seven sad forests,
I've been out in front of a dozen dead oceans,
I've been ten thousand miles in the mouth of a graveyard,
And it's a hard, and it's a hard, it's a hard, it's a hard

And it's a hard rain's a-gonna fall.

Oh, what did you see, my blue-eyed son?
Oh, what did you see, my darling young one?
I saw a newborn baby with wolves all around it,
I saw a highway of diamonds with nobody on it,
I saw a black branch with blood that kept drippin',
I saw a room full of men with their hammers a-bleedin',
I saw a white ladder all covered with water,
I saw ten thousand talkers whose tongues were all broken,
I saw guns and sharp swords in the hands of young children,
And it's a hard, and it's a hard, it's a hard, it's a hard
And it's a hard rain's a-gonna fall.

And, what did you hear, my blue-eyed son?
And, what did you hear, my darling young one?
I heard the sound of the thunder, it roared out a warnin',
Heard the roar of a wave that could drown the whole world,
Heard one hundred drummers whose hands were a-blazin',
Heard ten thousand whisperin' and nobody listenin',
Heard one person starve, I heard many people laughin',
Heard the song of a poet who died in the gutter,
Heard the sound of a clown who cried in the alley,
And it's a hard, and it's a hard, it's a hard, it's a hard
And it's a hard rain's a-gonna fall.

Oh, who did you meet, my blue-eyed son?
Who did you meet, my darling young one?
I met a young child beside a dead pony,
I met a white man who walked a black dog,
I met a young woman whose body was burning,
I met a young girl, she gave me a rainbow,
I met one man who was wounded in love,
I met another man who was wounded with hatred,
And it's a hard, and it's a hard, it's a hard, it's a hard
And it's a hard rain's a-gonna fall.

Oh, what'll you do now, my blue-eyed son?
Oh, what'll you do now, my darling young one?
I'm goin' back out 'fore the rain starts a-fallin',

I'll walk to the depths of the deepest black forest,
Where the people are many and their hands are all empty,
Where the pellets of poison are flooding their waters,
Where the home in the valley meets the damp dirty prison,
Where the executioner's face is always well hidden,
Where hunger is ugly, where souls are forgotten,
Where black is the color, where none is the number,
And I'll tell it and think it and speak it and breathe it,
And reflect it from the mountain so all souls can see it,
Then I'll stand on the ocean until I start sinkin',
But I'll know my song well before I start singin',
And it's a hard, and it's a hard, it's a hard, it's a hard
It's a hard rain's a-gonna fall.

"The Times They Are A-Changin'"

> Come gather 'round people
> Wherever you roam
> And admit that the waters
> Around you have grown
> And accept it that soon
> You'll be drenched to the bone.
> If your time to you
> Is worth savin'
> Then you better start swimmin'
> Or you'll sink like a stone
> For the times they are a-changin'.
>
> Come writers and critics
> Who prophesize with your pen
> And keep your eyes wide
> The chance won't come again
> And don't speak too soon
> For the wheel's still in spin
> And there's no tellin' who
> That it's namin'
> For the loser now
> Will be later to win
> For the times they are a-changin'.

Come senators, congressmen
Please heed the call
Don't stand in the doorway
Don't block up the hall
For he that gets hurt
Will be he who has stalled
There's a battle outside
And it's ragin'.
It'll soon shake your windows
And rattle your walls
For the times they are a-changin'.

Come mothers and fathers
Throughout the land
And don't criticize
What you don't understand
Your sons and your daughters
Are beyond your command
Your old road is
Rapidly agin'.
Please get out of the new one
If you can't lend your hand
For the times they are a-changin'.

The line it is drawn
The curse it is cast
The slow one now
Will later be fast
As the present now
Will later be past
The order is
Rapidly fadin'.
And the first one now
Will later be last
For the times they are a-changin'.

"When the Ship Comes In"

Oh the time will come up
When the winds will stop

And the breeze will cease to be breathin'
Like the stillness in the wind
'Fore the hurricane begins,
The hour when the ship comes in.

Oh the seas will split
And the ship will hit
And the sands on the shoreline will be shaking
Then the tide will sound
And the wind will pound
And the morning will be breaking.

Oh the fishes will laugh
As they swim out of the path
And the seagulls they'll be smiling
And the rocks on the sand
Will proudly stand,
The hour that the ship comes in.

And the words that are used
For to get the ship confused
Will not be understood as they're spoken
For the chains of the sea
Will have busted in the night
And be buried at the bottom of the ocean.

A song will lift
As the mainsail shifts
And the boat drifts on to the shoreline
And the sun will respect
Every face on the deck,
The hour that the ship comes in.

Then the sands will roll
Out a carpet of gold
For your weary toes to be a-touchin'.
And the ship's wise men
Will remind you once again
That the whole wide world is watchin'.

Oh the foes will rise

With the sleep still in their eyes
And they'll jerk from their beds and think they're dreamin'.
But they'll pinch themselves and squeal
And know that it's for real
The hour when the ship comes in.

Then they'll raise their hands,
Sayin', "We'll meet all your demands!"
But we'll shout from the bow, "Your days are numbered!"
And like Pharaoh's tribe,
They'll be drowned in the tide,
And like Goliath they'll be conquered.

"Chimes of Freedom"

Far between sundown's finish an' midnight's broken toll
We ducked inside the doorway, thunder crashing
As majestic bells of bolts struck shadows in the sounds
Seeming to be the chimes of freedom flashing
Flashing for the warriors whose strength is not to fight
Flashing for the refugees on the unarmed road of flight
An' for each an' ev'ry underdog soldier in the night
An' we gazed upon the chimes of freedom flashing.

In the city's melted furnace, unexpectedly we watched
With faces hidden while the walls were tightening
As the echo of the wedding bells before the blowin' rain
Dissolved into the bells of the lightening
Tolling for the rebel, tolling for the rake,
Tolling for the luckless, the abandoned an' foresaked
Tolling for the outcast, burnin' constantly at stake
An' we gazed upon the chimes of freedom flashing.

Through the mad mystic hammering of the wild ripping hail
The sky cracked its poems in naked wonder
That the clinging of the church bells blew far into the breeze
Leaving only bells of lightening and its thunder
Striking for the gentle, striking for the kind
Striking for the guardians and protectors of the mind
An' the unpawned painter behind beyond his rightful time

An' we gazed upon the chimes of freedom flashing.

Through the wild cathedral evening the rain unraveled tales
For the disrobed faceless forms of no position
Tolling for the tongues with no place to bring their thoughts
All down in taken-for-granted situations
Tolling for the deaf an' blind, tolling for the mute
Tolling for the mistreated, mateless mother, the mistitled prostitute
For the misdemeanor outlaw, chased an' cheated by pursuit
An' we gazed upon the chimes of freedom flashing.

Even though a cloud's white curtain in a far-off corner flashed
An' the hypnotic splattered mist was slowly lifting
Electric light still struck like arrows, fired but for the ones
Condemned to drift or else be kept from drifting
Tolling for the searching ones, on their speechless, seeking trail
For the lonesome-hearted lovers with too personal a tale
An' for each unharmful, gentle soul misplaced inside a jail
An' we gazed upon the chimes of freedom flashing.

Starry-eyed an' laughing as I recall when we were caught
Trapped by no track of hours for they hanged suspended
As we listened one last time an' we watched with one last look
Spellbound an' swallowed 'til the tolling ended
Tolling for the aching ones whose wounds cannot be nursed
For the countless confused, accused, misused, strung-out ones an' worse
An' for every hung-up person in the whole wide universe
An' we gazed upon the chimes of freedom flashing.

"Gates of Eden"

Of war and peace the truth just twists
Its curfew gull just glides
Upon four-legged forest clouds
The cowboy angel rides
With his candle lit into the sun
Though its glow is waxed in black
All except when 'neath the trees of Eden.

The lamppost stands with folded arms
Its iron claws attached

To curbs 'neath holes where babies wail
Though its shadow's metal badge
All and all can only fall
With a crashing but meaningless blow
No sound ever comes from the Gates of Eden.

The savage soldier sticks his head in sand
And then complains
Unto the shoeless hunter who's gone deaf
But still remains
Upon the beach where hound dogs bay
At ships with tattoed sails
Heading for the Gates of Eden.

Relationships of ownership
They whisper in the wings
To those condemned to act accordingly
And wait for succeeding kings
And I try to harmonize with songs
The lonesome sparrow sings
There are no kings inside the Gates of Eden.

The motorcycle black madonna
Two-wheeled gypsy queen
And her silver-studded phantom cause
The gray flannel dwarf to scream
As he weeps to wicked birds of prey
Who pick upon his bread crumb sins
And there are no sins inside the Gates of Eden.

The kingdoms of experience
In the precious wind they rot
While paupers change possessions
Each one wishing for what the other has got
And the princess and the prince
Discuss what's real and what is not
It doesn't matter inside the Gates of Eden.

The foreign sun, it squints upon
A bed that is never mine
As friends and other strangers

From their fates try to resign
Leaving men wholly, totally free
To do anything they wish to do but die
And there are no trials inside the Gates of Eden.

At dawn my lover comes to me
And tells me of her dreams
With no attempts to shovel a glimpse
Into the ditch of what each one means
At times I think there are no words
But these to tell what's true
And there are no truths outside the Gates of Eden.

"It's All Over Now, Baby Blue"

You must leave now, take what you need you think will last,
But whatever you wish to keep, you better grab it fast.
Yonder stands your orphan with his gun,
Crying like a fire in the sun.
Look out the saints are comin' through
And it's all over now, Baby Blue.

The highway is for gamblers, better use your sense.
Take what you have gathered from coincidence.
The empty-handed painter from your streets
Is drawing crazy patterns on your sheets.
This sky, too, is folding under you
And it's all over now, Baby Blue.

All your seasick sailors, they are rowing home
All your reindeer armies, are all going home.
The lover who just walked out your door
Has taken all his blankets from the floor.
The carpet, too, is moving under you.
And it's all over now, Baby Blue.

Leave your stepping stones behind, something calls for you.
Forget the dead you've left, they will not follow you.
The vagabond who's rapping at your door
Is standing in the clothes that you once wore.
Strike another match, go start anew

And it's all over now, Baby Blue.

"Desolation Row"

They're selling postcards of the hanging
They're painting the passports brown
The beauty parlor is filled with sailors
The circus is in town
Here comes the blind commissioner
They've got him in a trance
One hand is tied to the tight-rope walker
The other is in his pants
And the riot squad they're restless
They need somewhere to go
As Lady and I look out tonight
From Desolation Row.

Cinderella, she seems so easy
"It takes one to know one," she smiles
And puts her hands in her back pockets
Bette Davis style
And in comes Romeo, he's moaning
"You belong to me I believe"
And someone says, "You're in the wrong place, my friend
You better leave"
And the only sound that's left
After the ambulances go
Is Cinderella sweeping up
On Desolation Row.

Now the moon is almost hidden
The stars are beginning to hide
The fortunetelling lady
Has even taken all her things inside
All except for Cain and Abel
And the hunchback of Notre Dame
Everybody is making love
Or else expecting rain
And the Good Samaritan, he's dressing

He's getting ready for the show
He's going to the carnival tonight
On Desolation Row.

Now Ophelia she's neath the window
For her I feel so afraid
On her twenty-second birthday
She already is an old maid
To her death is quite romantic
She wears an iron vest
Her profession's her religion
Her sin is her lifelessness
And though her eyes are fixed upon
Noah's great rainbow
She spends her time peeking
Into Desolation Row.

Einstein, disguised as Robin Hood
With his memories in a trunk
Passed this way an hour ago
With his friend, a jealous monk
He looked so immaculately frightful
As he bummed a cigarette
Then he went off sniffing drainpipes
And reciting the alphabet
Now you would not think to look at him
But he was famous long ago
For playing the electric violin
On Desolation Row.

Dr. Filth, he keeps his world
Inside of a leather cup
But all his sexless patients
They're trying to blow it up
Now his nurse, some local loser
She's in charge of the cyanide hole
And she also keeps the cards that read
"Have Mercy on His Soul"
They all play on penny whistles
You can hear them blow

If you lean your head out far enough
From Desolation Row.

Across the street they've nailed the curtains
They're getting ready for the feast
The Phantom of the Opera
A perfect image of a priest
They're spoonfeeding Casanova
To get him to feel more assured
Then they'll kill him with self-confidence
After poisoning him with words
And the Phantom's shouting to skinny girls
"Get outta here! If you don't know,
Casanova is just being punished for going
to Desolation Row."

Praise be to Nero's Neptune
The Titanic sails at dawn
And everybody's shouting
"Which side are you on?"
And Ezra Pound and T.S. Eliot
Fighting in the captain's tower
While calypso singers laugh at them
And fisherman hold flowers
Between the windows of the sea
Where lovely mermaids flow
And nobody has to think too much
About Desolation Row.

Yes, I received your letter yesterday
(About the time the door knob broke)
When you asked how I was doing
Was that some kind of joke?
All these people that you mention
Yes, I know them, they're quite lame
I had to rearrange their faces
And give them all another name
Right now I can't read too good
Don't send me no more letters no
Not unless you mail them

From Desolation Row.

"Visions of Johanna"

Ain't it just like the night to play tricks
when you're tryin' to be so quiet?
We sit here stranded, though we're all doin' our best to deny it
And Louise holds a handful of rain, temptin' you to defy it
Lights flicker from the opposite loft
In this room the heat pipes just cough
The country music station plays soft
But there's nothing, really nothing to turn off
Just Louise and her lover so entwined
And these visions of Johanna that conquer my mind.

In the empty lot where the ladies play
blindman's bluff with the key-chain
And the all-night girls they whisper of escapades out on the "D" train
We can hear the night watchman click his flashlight
Ask himself if it's him or them that's really insane
Louise, she's all right, she's just near
She's delicate and seems like the mirror
But she just makes it all too concise and too clear
That Johanna's not here
The ghost of electricity howls in the bones of her face
Where these visions of Johanna have now taken my place.

Now, little boy lost, he takes himself so seriously
He brags of his misery, he likes to live dangerously
And when bringing her name up
He speaks of a farewell kiss to me
He's sure got a lotta gall to be so useless and all
Muttering small talk at the wall while I'm in the hall
How can I explain?
It's so hard to get on
And these visions of Johanna kept me up past the dawn.

Inside the museums, Infinity goes up on trial
Voices echo, "This is what salvation must be like after a while."
But Mona Lisa musta had the highway blues

You can tell by the way she smiles
See the primitive wallflower freeze
When the jelly-faced women all sneeze
Hear the one with the mustache say, "Jeeze I can't find my knees"
Oh, jewels and binoculars hang from the head of the mule
But these visions of Johanna make it all seem so cruel.

The peddler now speaks to the countess
who's pretending to care for him
Sayin', "Name me someone that's not a parasite
and I'll go out and say a prayer for him
But like Louise always says
"Ya can't look at much, can ya man?"
As she herself prepares for him
And Madonna, she still has not showed
We see this empty cage now corrode
Where her cape of the stage once had flowed
The fiddler, he now steps to the road
He writes, "Ev'rything's been returned that was owed."
On the back of the fish truck that loads
While my conscience explodes
The harmonicas play the skeleton keys in the rain
And these visions of Johanna are now all that remain.

"All Along the Watchtower"

"There must be some way out of here," said the joker to the thief,
"There's too much confusion, I can't get no relief.
Businessmen, they drink my wine, plowmen dig my earth,
None of them along the line know what any of it is worth."

"No reason to get excited," the thief, he kindly spoke,
"There are many here among us who feel that life is but a joke.
But you and I, we've been through that, and this is not our fate,
So let us not talk falsely now, the hour is getting late."

All along the watchtower, princes kept the view
While all the women came and went, barefoot servants, too.
Outside in the distance a wildcat did growl,
Two riders were approaching, the wind began to howl.

"Masters of War"

Come you masters of war
You that build all the guns
You that build the death planes
You that build the big bombs
You that hide behind walls
You that hide behind desks
I just want you to know
I can see through your masks.

You that never done nothin'
But build to destroy
You play with my world
Like it's your little toy
You put a gun in my hand
And you hide from my eyes
And you turn and run farther
When the fast bullets fly

Like Judas of old
You lie and deceive
A world war can be won
You want me to believe
But I see through your eyes
And I see through your brain
Like I see through the water
That runs down my drain.

You fasten the triggers
For the others to fire
Then you sit back and watch
When the death count gets higher.
You hide in your mansion
As young people's blood
Flows out of their bodies
And is buried in the mud.

You've thrown the worst fear
That can ever be hurled
Fear to bring children

Into the world
For threatening my baby
Unborn and unnamed
You ain't worth the blood
That runs in your veins.

How much do I know
To talk out of turn
You might say that I'm young
You might say I'm unlearned
But there's one thing I know
Though I'm younger than you
Even Jesus would never
Forgive what you do.

Let me ask you one question
Is your money that good
Will it buy you forgiveness
Do you think that it could
I think you will find
When your death takes its toll
All the money you made
Will never buy back you soul.

And I hope that you die
And your death'll come soon
I'll follow your casket
In the pale afternoon
And I'll watch while you're lowered
Down to your deathbed
And I'll stand o'er your grave
'Til I'm sure that you're dead.

"Mr. Tambourine Man"

Hey! Mr. Tambourine Man, play a song for me,
I'm not sleepy and there is no place I'm going to,
Hey! Mr. Tambourine Man, play a song for me,
In the jingle jangle morning I'll come followin' you.

Though I know that evenin's empire has returned into sand,

Vanished from my hand,
Left me blindly here to stand but still not sleeping.
My weariness amazes me, I'm branded on my feet,
I have no one to meet
And the ancient empty street's too dead for dreaming.

Hey! Mr. Tambourine Man, play a song for me,
I'm not sleepy and there is no place I'm going to,
Hey! Mr. Tambourine Man, play a song for me,
In the jingle jangle morning I'll come followin' you.

Take me on a trip upon your magic swirlin' ship,
My senses have been stripped, my hands can't feel to grip,
My toes' too numb to step, wait only for my boot heels to be wan-
    derin'
I'm ready to go anywhere, I'm ready for to fade
Into my own parade, cast your dancing spell my way,
I promise to go under it.

Hey! Mr. Tambourine Man, play a song for me,
I'm not sleepy and there is no place I'm going to,
Hey! Mr. Tambourine Man, play a song for me,
In the jingle jangle morning I'll come followin' you.

Though you might hear laughin' spinnin', swingin' madly across
    the sun,
It's not aimed at anyone, it's just escapin' on the run
And but for the sky there are no fences facin',
And if you hear vague traces of skippin' reels of rhyme
To your tambourine in time, it's just a ragged clown behind,
I wouldn't pay it any mind, it's just a shadow you're seein' that he's chasing.

Hey! Mr. Tambourine Man, play a song for me,
I'm not sleepy and there is no place I'm going to,
Hey! Mr. Tambourine Man, play a song for me,
In the jingle jangle morning I'll come followin' you.

Then take me disappearin' through the smoke rings of my mind,
Down the foggy ruins of time, far past the frozen leaves,
The haunted, frightened trees, out to the windy beach,
Far from the twisted reach of crazy sorrow.

Yeah, to dance beneath the diamond sky with one hand waving free,
Silhouetted by the sea, circled by the circus sands,
With all memory and fate driven deep beneath the waves,
Let me forget about today until tomorrow.

Hey! Mr. Tambourine Man, play a song for me,
I'm not sleepy and there is no place I'm going to,
Hey! Mr. Tambourine Man, play a song for me,
In the jingle jangle morning I'll come followin' you.

"Gypsy Lou"

If you getcha one girl, better get two
Case you run into Gypsy Lou
She's a ramblin' woman with a ramblin' mind
Always leavin' somebody behind.
Hey, 'round the bend
Gypsy Lou's gone again
Gypsy Lou's gone again.

Well, I seen the whole country through
Just to find Gypsy Lou
Seen it up, seen it down
Followin' Gypsy Lou around
Hey, 'round the bend
Gypsy Lou's gone again
Gypsy Lou's gone again

Well, I gotta stop and take some rest
My poor feet are second best
My poor feet are wearin' thin
Gypsy Lou's gone again.
Hey, gone again
Gypsy Lou's 'round the bend
Gypsy Lou's 'round the bend.

Well, seen her up in old Cheyenne
turned my head and away she ran
From Denver Town to Wichita
Last I heard she's in Arkansas.
Hey, 'round the bend

Gypsy Lou's gone again
Gypsy Lou's gone again.

Well, I tell what if you want to do
Tell you what, you'll wear out your shoes
If you want to wear out your shoes
Try and follow Gypsy Lou.
Hey, gone again
Gypsy Lou's 'round the bend
Gypsy Lou's 'round the bend.

Well, Gypsy Lou, I been told
Livin' down on Gallus Road
Gallus Road, Arlington
Moved away to Washington.
Hey, 'round the bend
Gypsy Lou's gone again
Gypsy Lou's gone again.

Well, I went down to Washington
Then she went to Oregon
I skipped the ground and hopped a train
She's back in Gallus Road again.
Hey, I can't win
Gypsy Lou's gone again
Gypsy Lou's gone again.

Well, the last I heard of Gypsy Lou
She's in a Memphis calaboose
She left one too many a boy behind
He committed suicide.
Hey, you can't win
Gypsy Lou's gone again
Gypsy Lou's gone again.

Dylan's Thomas Paine Award speech:

I haven't got any guitar, I can talk though. I want to thank you for the Tom Paine Award on behalf of everybody that went down to Cuba. First of all because they're all young and it's took me a long time to get young, and now I consider myself young. And I'm proud of it. I'm proud that I'm young. And I only wish that all you people who are sitting out here tonight weren't here and I could see all kinds of faces with hair on their head and everything like that, everything leading to youngness—"celebrating the anniversary when we overthrew the House Un-American Activities just yesterday"—because you people should be at the beach. You should be...swimming and...just relaxing in the time you have to relax. It is not an old people's world. It has nothing to do with old people. Old people, when their hair grows out, they should go out. And I look down to see the people that are governing me and making my rules—and they haven't got any hair on their head—I get very uptight about it. And they talk about Negroes, and they talk about black and white. And they talk about colors of red and blue and yellow. Man, then I just don't see any colors at all when I look out...I've never seen one history book that tells how anybody feels...And it don't help me one little bit to look back.

I wish sometimes I could have come in here in the 1930s like my first idol—used to have an idol, Woody Guthrie, who came in the 1930s. But it has sure changed in the time Woody's been here and the time I've been here. It's not that easy anymore. People seem to have more fears. There's no black and white, left and right, to me, anymore; there's only up and down—and down is very close to the ground. And I'm trying to go up without thinking about anything trivial such as politics. They have got nothing to do with it. I'm thinking about the general people and when they get hurt.

Now I want to accept this...Tom Paine Award, from the Emergency Civil Liberties Committee. I want to accept it in my name, and I'm not accepting it in any kind of group's name, any Negro group or any other kind of group...I was on the March on Washington up on the platform and I looked around at all the Negroes there and I didn't see any Negroes that looked like none of my friends. My friends don't wear suits. My friends don't have to wear any kind of thing to prove that they're respectable gentle people if they're my friends. And I'm not going to try to push anything over.

So I accept this award on behalf of Phillip Luce, who led the group to Cuba—which all people should go down to Cuba. I don't see why anybody can't go to Cuba. I don't see what's going to hurt by going anyplace. I don't see what's going to hurt anybody's eyes to see anything. On the other hand,

Phillip is a friend of mine who went to Cuba. I'll stand and to get uncompromisable about it, which I have to be to be honest. I just got to be, as I got to admit that the man who shot President Kennedy, Lee Oswald, I don't know exactly where–what he thought he was doing, but I got to admit honestly that I, too–I saw some of myself in him. I don't think it would have gone–I don't think it could go that far. But I got to stand up and say I saw things that he felt in me–not to go that far and shoot. (there was booing) You can boo, but booing's got nothing to do with it. It's a...I just...I've got to tell you, man, it's...Bill of Rights is free speech (the master of ceremonies told him his time was almost up)...and I just want to admit that I accept this Tom Paine Award on behalf of James Foreman of the Student Non-Violent Coordinating Committee and the people on behalf of who went to Cuba.

"Guns, the Falcon's Mouthbook and Gashcat Unpunished"

aretha/ crystal jukebox queen of hymn & him diffused in drunk transfusion wound would heed sweet soundwave crippled & cry salute to oh great particular el dorado reel & ye battered personal god but she cannot she the leader of whom when ye follow, she cannot she has no back she cannot...beneath black flowery railroad fans & fig leaf shades & dogs of all nite joes, grow like arches and cures the harmonica battalions of bitter cowards, bones & bygones while what steadier louder the moans & arms of funeral landlord with one passionate kiss rehearse from dusk & climbing into the bushes with some favorite enemy ripping the postage stamps & crazy mailmen & waving all rank & familiar ambition than that itself, is needed to know that mother is not a lady...aretha with no goals, eternally single & one step soft of heaven/ let it be understood that she owns this melody along with her emotional diplomats & her earth & her musical secrets

> the censor in a twelve wheel drive semi
> stopping in for donuts & pinching the
> waitress/ he likes his women raw & with
> syrup he has his mind set on becoming
> a famous soldier

manuscript nightmare of cut throat high & low & behold the prophesying blind allegiance to law fox, monthly cupid & the intoxicating ghosts of dogma...nay & may the boatmen in bathrobes be banished forever & anointed into the shelves of alive hell, the unimaginative sleep, repetition without change & fat sheriffs who watch for doom in the mattress...hallaluyah & bossman of the hobos cometh & ordaining the spiritual gypsy davy camp now being infiltrated by foreign dictator, the fink FBI & the interrogating unknown failures of peacetime as holy & silver & blessed with the texture of kaleidoscope & the sandal girl...to dream of dancing pillhead virgins & wandering apollo at the pipe organ/ unscientific ramblers & the pretty things lucky & lifting their lips & handing down looks & regards from the shoulders of adam & eve's minstrel peekaboo...passing on the chance to bludgeon the tough spirits & the deed holders into fishlike buffoons & yanking ye erratic purpose...surrendering to persuasion, the crime against people, that be ranked alongside murder & while doctors, teachers, bankers & sewer cleaners fight for their rights, they must now be horribly generous...& into the march now where tab hunter leads with his thunderbird/ pearl bailey stomps him against a buick & where poverty, a perfection of neptune's unused clients, plays hide & seek & escaping into the who goes there? & now's not the time to act silly, so wear your big boots & jump on the garbage clowns, the hourly rate & the enema men & where junior senators & goblins rip off tops of question marks & their wives make pies & go now & throw some pies in the face & ride the blinds & into aretha's religious thighs & movement find ye your nymph of no conscience & bombing out your young sensitive dignity just to see once & for all if there are holes & music in the universe & watch her tame the sea horse/ aretha, pegged by choir boys & other pearls of mamas as too gloomy a much of witchy & dont you know no happy songs

    the lawyer leading a pig on a leash
    stopping in for tea & eating the censor's
    donut by mistake/ he likes to
    lie about his age & takes his paranoia seriously

the hospital grave being advertised & given away in whims & journals the housewife sits on. finding herself financed, ruptured but never censored in & also never flushing herself/ she denies her corpse the courage to crawl—close his own door, the ability to die of bank robbery & now catches the heels of old stars making scary movies on her dirt & her face & not everybody can dig her now. she is private property...bazookas in the nest & weapons of ice & of weatherproof flinch & they twitter, make scars & kill babies among lady shame good looks & her constant foe, tom sawyer of the breakfast cereal cursing all females paying no attention to this toilet massacre to be hereafter called LONZO & must walk the streets of life forever with lazy people having nothing to do but fight over women...everybody knows by now that wars are caused by money & greed & charity organizations/ the housewife is not here. she is running for congress

    the senator dressed like an austrian
    sheep. stopping in for coffee & insulting
    the lawyer/ he is on a prune diet &
    secretly wishes he was bing crosby
    but would settle for being a close
    relative of edgar bergen

passing the sugar to iron man of the bottles who arrives with the grin & a heatlamp & he's pushing "who dunnit" buttons this year & he is a love monger at first sight...you have seen him sprout up from a dumb hill bully into a bunch of backslap & he's wise & he speaks to everyone as if they had just answered the door/ he dont like people that say he comes from the monkeys but nevertheless he is dull & he is destroyingly boring...while Allah the cook scrapes hunger from his floor & pounding it into the floating dishes with roaring & the rest of the meatheads praising each other's power & argue over acne & recite calendars & pointing to each other's garments & liquid & disperse into segments & die crazy deaths & bellowing farce mortal farm vomit & why for Jesus Christ be just another meathead? when all the tontos & heyboy lose their legs trying to frug while kemosabe & mr. palladin spend their off hours remaining separate but equal & anyway why not wait for laughter to straighten the works out meantime & WOWEE smash & the rage of it all when former lover cowboy hanging upside down & Suzy Q. the angel putting new dime into this adoption machine as out squirts a symbol squawking & freezing & crashing into the bowels of some hideous soap box & it's a rumble & iron man picking up his "who dunnit" buttons & giving them away free & trying to make friends & even tho youre belonging to no political party, youre now prepared, prepared to remember something about something

> the chief of police holding a bazooka
> with his name engraved on it. coming in
> drunk & putting the barrel into the face
> of the lawyer's pig. once a wife beater,
> he became a professional boxer
> a clubfoot/he would literally like to
> become an executioner. what he doesn't know
> is that the lawyer's pig has made friends
> with the senator

gambler's passion & his slave, the sparrow & he's ranting from a box of black platform & mesmerizing this ball of daredevils to stay in the morning & dont bust from the factories/ everyone expecting to be born with whom they love & theyre not & theyve been let down, theyve been lied to & now the organizers must bring the oxen in & dragging leaflets & gangreen enthusiasm, ratfinks & suicide tanks from the pay phones to the housing developments & it usually starts to rain for awhile...little boys cannot go out & play & new men in bulldozers come in every hour delivering groceries & care packages being sent from las vegas...& nephews of the coffee bean expert & other favorite sons & graduating with a pompadour & cum laude—praise be & a wailing farewell to releasing the hermit & beautifully ugly & fingering eternity come down and save your lambs & butchers & strike the rose with its rightful patsy odor...& gramps scarecrow's got the tiny little wren & see for yourself while saving him too/ look down oh Great Romantic, you who can predict from every position, you who know that everybody's not a Job or a Nero nor a J.C. Penny...look down & seize your gambler's passion, make high wire experts into heroes, presidents into con men. turn the eventual...but the hermits being not talking & lower class or insane or in prison...& they dont work in the factories anyway

> the good samaritan coming in with the
> words "round & round we go" tattooed on
> his cheek/ he tells the senator to stop
> insulting the lawyer/ he would like to
> be an entertainer & brags that he is
> one of the best strangers around, the
> pig jumps on him & starts eating his
> face

illiterate coins of two head wrestling with window washer who's been reincarnated from a garden hoe & after once being pushed around happily & casually hitting a rock once in a while is now bitter hung up on finding some inferior. he bites into the window ledge & by singing "what'll we do with the baby-o" to thirsty peasant girls wanting a drink from his pail, he is thinking he is some kind of success but he's getting his kicks telling one of the two headed coins that tom jefferson used to use him around the house when the bad stuff was growing...the lawrence welk people inside the window, theyre running the city planning division & they hibernate & feeding their summers by conversing with poor people's shadows & other ambulance drivers, & they dont even notice this window washer while the families who tell of the boogey men & theyre precious & they wear pictures of them playing golf & getting blacker & they wear oil in the window washer's union hall & these people consider themselves gourmets for not attending charlie starkweather's funeral ye gads the champagne being appropriate pagan & the buffalo, tho the restaurant owners are vague about it, is fast disappearing into violence/ soon there will be but one side of the coin & mohammed wherever he comes from, cursing & window washers falling & then no one will have any money...broad save the clean, the minorities & liberace's countryside.

> the truck driver coming in with a carpet
> sweeper under his eyes/ everybody says

"hi joe" & he says "joe the fellow that
owns this place. i'm just a scientist. i
aint got no name" the truck driver hates
anybody that carries a tennis racket/ he
drinks all the senator's coffee & proceeds
to put him in a headlock

first you snap your hair down & try to tie up the kicking voices on a table &
then the sales department people with names like Gus & Peg & Judy the
Wrench & Nadine with worms in her fruit & Bernice Bearface blowing her
brains on Butch & theyre all enthused over locker rooms & vegetables &
Muggs he goes to sleep on your neck talking shop & divorces & headline
causes & if you cant say get off my neck, you just answer him & wink & wait
for some morbid reply & the liberty bell ringing when you dont dare ask
yourself how do you feel for God's sake & what's one more face? & the difference between a lifetime of goons & holes, company pigs & beggars &
cancer critics learning yoga with raving petty gangsters in one act plays with
V-eight engines all being tossed in the river & combined in a stolen mirror...compared to the big day when you discover lord byron shooting craps in
the morgue with his pants off & he's eating a picture of jean paul belmondo
& he offers you a piece of green lightbulb & you realize that nobody's told
you about This & that life is not so simple after all...in fact that it's no more
than something to read & light cigarettes with...Lem the Clam tho, he really
gives a damn if dale really does get nailed slamming down the scotch & then
going outside with Maurice, who aint the Peoria Kid & dont look the same
as they do in Des Moines, Iowa & good old debbie, she comes along & both
her & dale, they start shacking up in the newspapers & jesus who can blame
'em? & Amen & oh lordy, & how the parades dont need your money baby...
it's the confetti & one george washington & Nadine who comes running &
says where's Gus? & she's salty about the bread he's been making off her
worms while dollars becoming pieces of paper...but people kill for paper &
anyway you cant buy a thrill with a dollar as long as pricetags, the end of the
means & only as big as your fist & they dangle from a pot of golden rainbow...
which attacks & which covers the saddles of noseless poets & wonder blazing
& somewhere over the rainbow & blinding my married lover into the ovation
maniacs/ cremating innocent child into scrapheap for vicious controversy &
screwball & who's to tell charlie to stop & not come back from garbage men
arent serious & they gonna get murdered tomorrow & next march 7th by the
same kids & their fathers & all the rest of these people that would make lead-

belly a pet...they will always kill garbage men & wiping the smells but this rainbow, she goes off behind a pillar & sometimes a tornado destroys the drugstores & floods bring polio & leaving Gus & Peg twisted in the volleyball net & Butch hiding in madison square garden...Bearface dead from a flying piece of grass! I.Q.–somewhere in the sixties & twentieth century & so sing aretha... sing mainstream into orbit! sing the cowbells home! sing misty ...sing for the barber & when youre found guilty of not owning a cavalry & not helping the dancer with laryngitis... misleading valentino's pirates to the indians or perhaps not lending a hand to the deaf pacifist in his sailor jail...it then must be time for you to rest & learn new songs...forgiving nothing for you have done nothing & make love to the noble scrubwoman

> what a drag it gets to be. writing
> for this chosen few. writing for any-
> one cpt you. you, daisy mae, who are
> not even of the masses...funny thing,
> tho, is that youre not even dead yet...
> i will nail my words to this paper,
> an fly them on to you. an forget about
> them...thank you for the time.
> youre kind.
>> love an kisses
>> your double
>> Silly Eyes (in airplane trouble)

"Oxford Town"

> Oxford Town, Oxford Town
> Ev'rybody's got their heads bowed down
> The sun don't shine above the ground
> Ain't a-goin' down to Oxford Town
>
> He went down to Oxford Town
> Guns and clubs followed him down
> All because his face was brown
> Better get away from Oxford Town
>
> Oxford Town around the bend
> He come to the door, an' he couldn't get in
> All because of the color of his skin
> What do you think about that, my friend?
>
> Me an' my gal, an' my gal's son
> We got met with a teargas bomb
> I don't even know why we come
> Goin' back where we come from
>
> Oxford Town in the afternoon
> Ev'rybody's singin' a sorrowful tune
> Two men died 'neath the Mississippi moon
> Somebody better investigate soon
>
> Oxford Town, Oxford Town
> Ev'rybody's got their heads bowed down
> The sun don't shine above the ground
> Ain't a-goin' down to Oxford Town

"Tomorrow Is a Long Time"

> If today was not an endless highway,
> If tonight was not a crooked trail,
> If tomorrow wasn't such a long time,
> Then lonesome would mean nothing to you at all.
> Yes, and only if my own true love was waitin',
> And if I could hear her heart a-softly poundin',
> Only if she was lyin' by me,
> Then I'd lie in my bed once again.
>
> I can't see my reflection in the waters,
> I can't speak the sounds that show no pain.

I can't hear the echo of my footsteps,
Or remember the sound of my own name.
Yes, and only if my own true love was waitin',
And if I could hear her heart a-softly poundin',
Yes, only if she was lyin' by me,
Then I'd lie in my bed once again.

There's beauty in the silver, singin' river,
There's beauty in the sunrise in the sky,
But none of these and nothing else can touch the beauty
That I remember in my true love's eyes.
Yes, and only if my own true love was waitin',
And if I could hear her heart a-softly poundin',
Only if she was lyin' by me,
Then I'd lie in my bed once again.

"North Country Blues"

Come gather 'round friends
And I'll tell you a tale
Of when the red iron pits ran plenty.
But the cardboard filled windows
And old men on the benches
Tell you now that the whole town is empty.

In the north end of town,
My own children are grown
But I was raised on the other.
In the wee hours of youth
My mother took sick
And I was brought up by my brother.

The iron ore poured
As the years passed the door,
The drag lines an' the shovels they was a-humming.
'Til one day my brother
Failed to come home
The same as my father before him.

Well, a long winter's wait
From the window I watched.
My friends they couldn't have been kinder.
And my schooling was cut

As I quit in the spring
To marry John Thomas, a miner.

Oh the years passed again
And the givin' was good,
With the lunchbucket filled every season.
What with three babies born
The work was cut down
To a half a day's shift with no reason.

Then the shaft was soon shut
And more work was cut.
And the fire in the air, it felt frozen.
'Til a man come to speak
And he said in one week
That number eleven was closin'.

They complain in the East
They are paying too high.
They say that your ore ain't worth diggin'.
That it's much cheaper down
In the South American towns
Where the miners work almost for nothing.

So the mining gates locked
And the red iron rotted
And the room smelled heavy from drinkin'
Where the sad, silent song
Made the hour twice as long
As I waited for the sun to go sinkin'.

I lived by the window
As he talked to himself
This silence of tongues it was buildin'.
Then one morning's wake,
The bed it was bare,
And I's left alone with three children.

The summer is gone,
The ground's turning cold,
The stores one by one they're a foldin'.
My children will go
As soon as they grow,
Well, there ain't nothing here now to hold them.

"Sad-Eyed Lady of the Lowlands"

With your mercury mouth in the missionary times,
And your eyes like smoke and your prayers like rhymes,
And your silver cross, and your voice like chimes,
Oh, who among them do they think could bury you?
With your pockets well protected at last,
And your streetcar visions which you place on the grass,
And your flesh like silk, and your face like glass,
Who among them do they think could carry you?
Sad-eyed lady of the lowlands,
Where the sad-eyed prophet says that no man comes,
My warehouse eyes, my Arabian drums,
Should I leave them by your gate,
Or, sad-eyed lady, should I wait?

With your sheets like metal and your belt like lace,
And your deck of cards missing the jack and the ace,
And your basement clothes and your hollow face,
Who among them can think he could outguess you?
With your silhouette when the sunlight dims
Into your eyes where the moonlight swims,
And your match-book songs and your gypsy hymns,
Who among them would try to impress you?
Sad-eyed lady of the lowlands,
Where the sad-eyed prophet says that no man comes,
My warehouse eyes, my Arabian drums,
Should I leave them by your gate,
Or, sad-eyed lady, should I wait?

The kings of Tyrus with their convict list
Are waiting in line for their geranium kiss,
And you wouldn't know it would happen like this,
But who among them really wants just to kiss you?
With your childhood flames on your midnight rug,
And your Spanish manners and your mother's drugs,
And your cowboy mouth and your curfew plugs,
Who among them do you think could resist you?
Sad-eyed lady of the lowlands,
Where the say-eyed prophet says that no man comes,
My warehouse eyes, my Arabian drums,
Should I leave them by your gate,

Or, sad-eyed lady should I wait?

Oh, the farmers and businessmen, they all did decide
To show you the dead angels that they used to hide,
But why did they pick you to sympathize with their side?
Oh, how could they ever mistake you?
They wished you'd accepted the blame for the farm,
But with the sea at your feet and the phony false alarm,
And with the child of the hoodlum wrapped up in your arms,
How could they ever, ever persuade you?
Sad-eyed lady of the lowlands,
Where the sad-eyed prophet says that no man comes,
My warehouse eyes, my Arabian drums,
Should I leave them by your gate,
Or, sad-eyed lady, should I wait?

With your sheet-metal memory of Cannery Row,
And your magazine-husband, who one day just had to go,
And your gentleness now, which you just can't help but show,
Who among them do you think would employ you?
Now you stand with your thief, you're on his parole
With your holy medallion, which your fingertips fold,
And your saintlike face, and your ghostlike soul
Oh, who among them do you think could destroy you?
Sad-eyed lady of the lowlands,
Where the sad-eyed prophet says that no man comes,
My warehouse eyes, my Arabian drums,
Should I leave them by your gate,
Or, sad-eyed lady, should I wait?

"When I Paint My Masterpiece"

Oh, the streets of Rome are filled with rubble,
Ancient footprints are everywhere.
You can almost think that you're seein' double
On a cold, dark night on the Spanish Stairs.
Got to hurry on back to my hotel room,
Where I got me a date with Botticelli's niece.
She promised that she'd be right there with me
When I paint my masterpiece.

Oh, the hours I've spent inside the Coliseum,
Dodging lions and wastin' time.

Those mighty kings of the jungle, I can hardly stand to see 'em
Yes, it sure has been a long, hard climb.
Train wheels runnin' through the back of my memory,
When I ran on the hilltop following a pack of wild geese.
Someday, everything is gonna be smooth like a rhapsody
When I paint my masterpiece.
Sailin' round the world in a dirty gondola.
Oh, to be back in the land of Coca-Cola!

I left Rome and landed in Brussels,
With a picture of a tall oak tree by my side.
Clergymen in uniform and young girls pullin' muscles,
Everyone was there to greet me when I stepped inside.
Newspapermen eating candy
Had to be held down by big police.
Someday, everything's gonna be diff'rent
When I paint my masterpiece.

"Tangled Up In Blue"

Early one mornin' the sun was shinin'
I was layin' in bed
Wond'rin' if she'd changed at all
If her hair was still red.
Her folks said our lives together
Sure was gonna be rough
They never did like Mama's homemade dress
Papa's bankbook wasn't big enough.
And I was standin' on the side of the road
Rain fallin' on my shoes
Heading out for the East Coast
Lord knows we paid some dues gettin' through,
Tangled up in blue.

She was married when we first met
Soon to be divorced
I helped her out of a jam, I guess,
But I used a little too much force.
We drove that car as far as we could
Abandoned it out West
Split up on the dock that night
Both agreein' it was best.

She turned around to look at me
As I was walkin' away
I heard her say over my shoulder,
"We'll meet again someday on the avenue,"
Tangled up in blue.

I had a job in the great north woods
Working as a cook for a spell
But I never did like it all that much
And one day the axe just fell.
So I drifted down to New Orleans
Where I happened to be employed
Workin' for a while on a fishin' boat
Outside of Delacroix.
But all the while I was alone
The past was close behind,
I seen a lot of women
But she never escaped my mind, and I just grew
Tangled up in blue.

She was workin' in a topless place
And I stopped in for a beer.
I just kept lookin' at the side of her face
In the spotlight so clear.
And later on as the crowd thinned out
I's just about to do the same,
She was standing there in back of my chair
Sayin' to me, "Don't I know your name?"
I muttered somethin' underneath my breath,
she studied the lines in my face.
I must admit I felt a little uneasy
When she bent down to tie the laces of my shoe,
Tangled up in blue.

She lit a burner on the stove and offered me a pipe
"I thought you'd never say hello," she said
"You look like the silent type."
Then she opened up a book of poems
And handed it to me
Written by an Italian poet
From the thirteenth century.
And every one of them words rang true

And glowed like burnin' coal
Pourin' off of every page
Like it was written in my soul from me to you,
Tangled up in blue.

I lived with them on Montague Street
In a basement down the stairs,
There was music in the cafes at night
And revolution in the air.
Then he started in to dealing with slaves
And something inside of him died.
She had to sell everything she owned
And froze up inside.
And when finally the bottom fell out
I became withdrawn,
The only thing I knew how to do
Was to keep on keepin' on like a bird that flew,
Tangled up in blue.

So now I'm goin' back again,
I got to get to her somehow.
All the people we used to know
They're an illusion to me now.
Some are mathematicians
Some are carpenters' wives.
Don't know how it all got started,
I don't know what they do with their lives.
But me, I'm still on the road
Headin' for another joint
We always did feel the same,
We just started from a different point of view.
Tangled up in blue.

"With God on Our Side"

Oh my name it is nothin'
My age is means less
The country I come from
Is called the Mdwest
I's taught and brought up there
The laws to abide
And that the land that I live in

Has God on its side.

Oh the history books tell it
They tell it so well
The cavalries charged
The Indians fell
The cavalries charged
The Indians died
Oh the country was young
With God on its side.

Oh the Spanish-American
War had its day
And the Civil War too
Was soon laid away
And the names of the heroes
I's made to memorize
With guns in their hands
And God on their side.

Oh the First World War, boys
It closed out its fate
The reason for fighting
I never got straight
But I learned to accept it
Accept it with pride
For you don't count the dead
When God's on your side.

When the Second World War
Came to an end
We forgave the Germans
And then they were friends
Though they murdered six million
In the ovens they fried
The German's now too
Have God on their side.

I've learned to hate Russians
All through my whole life
If another war starts
It's them we must fight
To hate them and fear them

To run and to hide
And accept it all bravely
With God on my side.

But now we got weapons
Of chemical dust
If fire them we're forced to
Then fire them we must
One push of the button
A shock the world wide
But you never ask questions
When God's on your side.

In many a dark hour
I've been thinkin' about this
That Jesus Christ
Was betrayed by a kiss
But I can't think for you
You'll have to decide
Whether Judas Iscariot
Had God on his side.

So now as I'm leavin'
I'm weary as Hell
The confusion I'm feelin'
Ain't no tongue can tell
The words fill my head
And fall to the floor
If God's on our side
He'll stop the next war.

"Long Ago, Far Away"

To preach of peace and brotherhood,
Oh, what might be the cost?
A man he did it long ago
And they hung him on a cross.
Long ago, far away;
These things don't happen
No more, nowadays.

The chains of slaves
They dragged the ground

With heads and hearts hung low.
But it was during Lincoln's time
And it was long ago.
Long ago, far away;
Things like that don't happen
No more, nowadays.

The guns they went off wild,
The whole world bled its blood.
Men's bodies floated on the edge
Of oceans made of mud.
Long ago, far away;
Those kind of things don't happen
No more, nowadays.

One man had much money,
One man had not enough to eat,
One man he lived just like a king,
The other man begged on the street.
Long ago, far away;
Things like that don't happen
No more, nowadays.

One man died of a knife so sharp,
One man died from the bullet of a gun,
One man died of a broken heart
To see the lynchin' of his son.
Long ago, far away;
Things like that don't happen
No more, nowadays.

Gladiators killed themselves,
It was during the Roman times.
People cheered with bloodshot grins
As eyes and minds went blind.
Long ago, far away;
Things like that don't happen
No more, nowadays.

And to talk of peace and brotherhood,
Oh, what might be the cost?
A man he did it long ago
And they hung him on a cross.

Long ago, far away;
Things like that don't happen
No more, nowadays, do they?

"I'd Hate to Be You on that Dreadful Day"

Well, your clock is gonna stop
At Saint Peter's gate.
Ya gonna ask him what time it is,
He's gonna say, "It's too late."
Hey, Hey! I'd sure hate to be you
On that dreadful day.

You're gonna start to sweat
And you ain't gonna stop.
You're gonna have a nightmare
And never wake up.
Hey, hey! I'd sure hate to be you
On that dreadful day.

You're gonna cry for pills
And your head's gonna be in a knot,
But the pills are gonna cost more
Than what you've got.
Hey, hey! I'd sure hate to you
On that dreadful day.

You're gonna have to walk naked,
Can't ride in no car.
You're gonna let ev'rybody see
Just what you are.
Hey, hey! I'd sure hate to be you
On that dreadful day.

You're gonna yell and scream,
"Don't anybody care?"
You're gonna hear out a voice say,
"Shoulda listened when you heard the word down there."
Hey, hey! I'd sure hate to be you
On that dreadful day.

"Train A-Travelin'"

> There's an iron train a-travelin' that's been a-rollin' through the years,
> With a firebox of hatred and a furnace full of fears.
> If you ever heard its sound or seen its blood-red broken frame,
> Then you heard me voice a-singin' and you know my name.
>
> Did you ever stop to wonder 'bout the hatred that it holds?
> Did you ever see its passengers, its crazy mixed-up souls?
> Did you ever start a-thinkin' that you gotta stop that train?
> Then you heard my voice a-singin' and you know my name.
>
> Do you ever get tired of the preachin' sounds of fear
> When they're hammered at your head and pounded in your ear?
> Have you ever asked about it and not been answered plain?
> Then you heard my voice a-singin' and you know my name.
>
> I'm a wonderin' if the leaders of the nations understand
> This murder-minded world that they're leavin' in my hands.
> Have you ever laid awake at night and wondered 'bout the same?
> Then you've heard my voice a-singin' and you know my name.
>
> Have you ever had it on your lips or said it in your head
> That the person standin' next to you just might be misled?
> Does the raving of the maniacs make your insides go insane?
> Then you've heard my voice a singin' and you know my name.
>
> Do the kill-crazy bandits and the haters get you down?
> Does the preachin' and the politics spin your head around?
> Does the burning of the buses give your heart a pain?
> Then you've heard my voice a-singin' and you know my name.

"Rainy Day Women #12 & 35"

> Well, they'll stone ya when you're trying to be so good,
> They'll stone ya just like they said they would.
> They'll stone ya when you're tryin' to go home.
> Then they'll stone ya when you're there all alone.
> But I would not feel so all alone,
> Everybody must get stoned.
>
> Well, they'll stone ya when you're walkin' down the street
> They'll stone ya when you're tryin' to keep your seat.
> They'll stone ya when you're walkin' on the floor.
> They'll stone ya when you're walkin' to the door.

But I would not feel so all alone.
Everybody must get stoned.

They'll stone ya when you're at the breakfast table.
They'll stone ya when you are young and able.
They'll stone ya when you're tryin' to make a buck.
They'll stone ya an' then they'll say, "Good luck."
Yeah, but I would not feel so all alone,
Everybody must get stoned.

Well, they'll stone you and say that it's the end.
Then they'll stone you and then they'll come back again.
They'll stone you when you're riding in our car.
They'll stone you when you're playing your guitar.
Yeah, but I would not feel so all alone,
Everybody must get stoned.

Well, they'll stone you when you're walkin' all alone.
They'll stone you when you are walkin' home.
They'll stone you and then say you are brave.
They'll stone you when you're set down in your grave.
But I would not feel so all alone,
Everybody must get stoned.

"To Every Chosen Soul and Gentle Heart"

> To every chosen soul and gentle heart
>> into whose presence this poem comes
>> that you might write your opinion back to me,
>> Greetings in your lord, who is Love.
>> The hours were already almost tripled
>> of that time when every star is shining
>> when love suddenly appeared to me
>> whose essence I am horrified to remember.
> Love seemed happy to me holding
>> my heart in his hand, and in his arms he had
>> my lady, wrapped in a cloth, sleeping.
>> Then he woke her, and of this burning heart,
>> frightened, she humbly ate:
>> then I saw him turn away weeping.

The New Life, chapter 2:

> She appeared dressed in the noblest color, humble and honest, blood red, bound at the waist and ornamented in a fashion that suited her very young age. At that point, I say truthfully, that the spirit of life that lives in the most secret chamber of my heart began to quake so powerfully, that it became horribly apparent in my slightest pulses; and quaking it said these words, "Here is a god stronger than I, who comes to rule me." At that point my soul's spirit, which lives in the high chamber where unto all my spirits of sensation carry their perceptions, began to marvel greatly, and speaking especially to the spirits of my face, it spoke these words, "Now your beatitude has appeared!" At that point my natural spirit, which lives in that place where our nourishment is consumed, began to weep, and weeping it said these words, "O misery, for I will frequently be impeded hereafter." From then on, I say that Love ruled my soul, which was then completely devoted to him, and he began to assume such control and such lordship over me through the virtue my imagination gave him, that it pleased me to do everything he wanted completely.

The New Life, chapter 14:

> ...it happened that this most gentle one came to a place where many ladies were gathered; I was brought to this place by a convivial friend, who thought he was doing me a great favor, in that he led me there, where so many women displayed their beauties. But, almost not know-

ing where I was directed, and trusting this person who had brought one of his friends to the extremity of life, I said to him, "Why have we come to these ladies?" Then he told me, "To make sure that they are treated well." And the truth is that they were gathered there in the company of a gentle woman who was married that morning; because following the custom of the above mentioned city, it was fitting that they keep her company on the occasion of her first seating at dinner in the home of her new spouse. So I, thinking of pleasing this friend, decided to remain at the service of the ladies in his company. And at the end of my decision I seemed to feel a noticeable tremor begin in my breast on the left side, and suddenly spread through all the parts of my body. Then I say that I slumped my body dramatically against a painted mural that went around this house; and fearing lest others should notice my trembling, I raised my eyes, and looking at the women, I saw among them most gentle Beatrice. Then were my spirits so destroyed through the power Love seized, seeing himself in such nearness to the very gentle lady, that none of them remained alive any more except the spirits of my face; and these still remained out of their instruments, because Love wanted to be in their very noble place to see the admirable lady. And it happened that I was other than at first, so much these spirits hurt me, which were loudly lamenting and were saying, "If this one did not blast us thus out of our place, we could be looking at the marvel of this woman just as others like us do." I say that many of these ladies, noting my transfiguration, began to marvel, and talking they made fun of me with this gentlest one; so my deceived friend of good faith took me by the hand, drew me out of the view of these ladies, and asked me what was wrong with me.

The New Life, chapter 18:

With it being that through my appearance many people had discovered the secret of my heart, certain ladies who were gathered together enjoying themselves in one another's company knew my heart well, because each of them had been present at many of my discomfitures; and I, passing near to them, as if guided by fate, was summoned by one of these gentle ladies. The lady who had called me was a lady of very gracious speech; so when I had come before them and had noted carefully that my most gentle lady was not with them, taking heart I greeted them, and asked what would please them. The ladies were many, and among them there were some who were laughing together. There were others who were watching me, awaiting what I might say.

One of them, turning her eyes toward me and calling me by name, said these words, "To what end do you love this lady of yours, since you cannot endure her presence? Tell us, for certainly the end of such love must be truly unique." And after she had said these words to me, not only she, but all the others began noticeably to wait for my response. Then I said these words to them: "My ladies, the end of my love once was the greeting of this lady, about whom perhaps you understand, and in that resided the blessedness which was the end of all my desires. But after it pleased her to deny it to me, my lord Love, in his mercy, placed all my blessedness in that which cannot let me down." Then these ladies began to talk among themselves; and just as sometimes we see water fall mixed with beautiful snow, so it seemed to me to hear their words mixed with sighs. And after they had talked among themselves, this lady who had first spoken to me, also told me these words: "We pray you that you say where this blessedness of yours resides." And I, answering her, said this: "In those words which praise my lady." Then she who was talking with me answered: "If you were telling the truth, these words that you have said describing your condition, have been fashioned with a different intention." Wherefore I, thinking about these words, almost shamefully took leave of them, and came away saying within myself, "Since such blessedness is in those words that praise my lady, why has other speech been mine?"

"Ladies Who Have An Understanding of Love"

    Ladies who have an understanding of love,
       I wish to speak with you about my lady,
       not because I expect to complete her praise,
       do I speak, but to unburden my mind.
       I say that, thinking of her goodness,
       Love so sweetly makes me listen to him,
       that if I did not then lose the flame,
       in speaking would make people fall in love.
       And I do not want to speak so highly,
       that because of boldness I become base;
       but I will treat of her gentle state
       delicately, in respect for her,
       with you, amorous ladies and girls,
       for it is not something to speak of with others.
    An angel cries out in the divine intellect
       and says, "Master, in the world a wonder

can be seen in action that proceeds
from a soul that shines all the way up here."
The heavens, which have no other defect
save having her, request her of their lord.
Only pity defends our side,
for God speaks who understands about my lady:
"My delights, suffer now in peace,
that your hope remains so long as pleases me
there were someone prepares himself to lose her,
who will say in hell, "O evil born,
I saw the hope of the blessed!"
My lady is desired in highest heaven:
now I would let you know about her virtue.
I say to whomever would seem a gentle lady:
Go with her; for when she goes along the way
Love casts a frost into base hearts,
so that their every thought freezes and dies.
And whoever would suffer by staying there to see her,
becomes something noble, or he dies.
And when she finds someone who is worthy
of seeing her, that man feels her virtue,
so that what she gives to him in greeting agrees with him,
and so humbles him, that he forgets every offense.
God has even granted him, for greater grace,
that he cannot end badly who has spoken to her.
Love says of her, "How can anything
mortal be so lovely and so pure?"
Then he looks at her, and within himself he swears
that God intended to make of her something new.
She has almost the color of pearl, and such a form as
it suits a woman to have, not beyond measure:
she is as much of good as nature can make;
beauty is proved by her example.
From her eyes, as she moves them,
spirits go out inflamed with love,
that wound the eyes of him who stares at her,
and they pass through, so that his heart finds each one:
you see her with Love painted on her face,
there, where no one can fix his gaze on her.
My song, I know that you will go around talking
to ladies continually, when I send you forth.

Now I admonish you, since I have raised you
to be the little daughter of Love, young and open,
that where you arrive, you will say in prayer:
"Teach me where to go, for I am sent
to that one in whose praises I am adorned."

New Life, chapter 24:

I saw a gentle lady come towards me who was famous for her beauty, and who had long been the lady of my best friend. And the name of this lady was Johanna, except that for the sake of her beauty, according to what others believe, the name "Primavera" was given to her; and so she was called. And looking after her I saw wonderful Beatrice coming. These women went close by me this way, the one after the other; and it seemed that Love spoke to me within my heart, and said, "That first one is called Primavera solely for this event today. For I moved the giver of the name to call her Primavera, that is, 'She will come first the day that Beatrice shows herself after the vision of her faithful one.' If you also wish to consider her first name, it means "She will come first" as well, since her name Johanna is from that John who preceded the true light, saying: "I am the voice calling in the wilderness, 'Prepare the way of the lord.'" It seemed to me that afterward he told me this, "Whoever would consider subtly would call Beatrice, Love, for the great resemblance she has to me."

"So Gentle and So Honest Does My Lady Seem"

So gentle and so honest does my lady
    seem, whenever she greets someone,
    that, trembling, every tongue falls mute,
    and eyes do not dare to look.
    She goes along, hearing herself praised,
    benignly dressed in humility;
    and she seems to be a thing come
    from heaven to earth to work a miracle.
She shows herself so pleasing to whoever sees her,
    that through his eyes she gives a sweetness to his heart,
    that one cannot understand who does not feel it:
    and it seems that from her lips moves
    a soft spirit full of love,
    that goes to the soul saying: Sigh!

"Creation of Man" (*Zohar*, I. 34 a)

> Rabbi Simeon then rose and spoke: In meditating, I have perceived that when God was about to create man, then above and below all creatures commenced to tremble. The course of the sixth day was unfolding when at last the divine decision was made. Then there blazed forth the source of all lights and opened up the gate of the East, from where light flows. The light which had been bestowed on it at the beginning, the South gave forth in full glory, and the South took hold upon the East. The East took hold on the North, and the North awakened and, opening forth, called loud to the West that he should come to him. Then the West traveled up into the North and came together with it, and after that the South took hold on the West and the North and the South surrounded the Garden, being its fences. Then the East drew near to the West, and the West was gladdened and it said, "Let us make man in our image, after our likeness" [Gen.I:26], to embrace like us the four quarters and the higher and the lower. Thereupon were East and West united, and produced man. Therefore have our sages said that man arose out from the site of the Temple.

> Moreover, we may regard the words "Let us make man" as conveying this: to the lower beings who derived from the side of the upper world God disclosed the secret of how to form the divine name Adam, in which is encompassed the upper and the lower, in the force of its three letters *alef*, *dalet*, and *mem* final. When the three letters had come down below, there was perceived in their form, complete, the name Adam, to comprehend male and female. The female was fastened to the side of the male, and God cast the male into a deep slumber, and he lay on the site of the Temple. God then cut the female from him and decked her as a bride and led her to him, as it is written, "And he took one of his sides, and closed up the place with flesh" [Gen. 2:21]. In the ancient books, I have seen it said that here the word "one" means "one woman," that is, the original Lilith, who lay with him and from him conceived. But up to that time, she was no help to him, as it is said, "but for Adam there was not found an help meet for him" [Gen. 2:20]. Adam, then, was the very last, for it was right that he should find the world complete when he made his appearance.

"No shrub of the field was yet in the earth" [Gen. 2:5].

> Rabbi Simeon went on to say: The allusion is to the magnificent trees which grew later, but as yet were minute. Adam and Eve, as we have said, were created side by side. Why not face to face? For the reason that heaven and earth were not yet in complete harmony, "the Lord God had not caused it to rain upon the earth" [Gen. 2:5]. When the lower union was rendered perfect, and Adam and Eve turned face to face, then was the

upper union perfected.

This we may know from the matter of the Tabernacle: for we have learned that together with it there was put up another tabernacle, nor was the upper one raised until the lower one was erected; and so it was in this case. Moreover, inasmuch as all above was not yet perfectly ordered, Adam and Eve were not created face to face. This is borne out by the order of the verses in the Scripture; first it is written, "For the Lord God had not caused it to rain upon the earth," and following, "there was not a man to till the ground" [ibid.], and it signifies that man was yet imperfect, for only when Eve was made perfect, was he then made perfect too. Further proof is that in the word *vayisgor* [and he closed], there occurs for the first time in this passage the leter *samekh*, which signifies "support," as much as to say that male and female they now supported the one the other. In like wise, do the lower world and the upper sustain each other. Not until the lower world was made perfect, was the other world also made perfect. When the lower world was made to support the upper, by being turned face to face with it, the world was then finished, for previously "the Lord God had not caused it to rain upon the earth."

Then, "There went up a mist from the earth" [Gen. 2:6], to make up for the lack, by "watering the whole face of the ground" [ibid.]; and the mist rising is the yearning of the female for the male. Yet another interpretation says that we take the word "not" from the first verse to use in the second with "mist," and this means that God failed to send rain because a mist had not gone up, for from below must come the impulse to move the power from above. Thus, to form the cloud, vapor ascends first from the earth. And likewise, the smoke of the sacrifice ascends, creating harmony above, and the uniting of all, and so the celestial sphere has completion in it. It is from below that the movement starts, and thereafter is all perfected. If the Community of Israel failed to initiate the impulse, the One above would also not move to go to her, and it is thus the yearning from below which brings about the completion above.

Spiritual Canticle

Bride: 1. Where have you hidden yourself, my love, and left me moaning: Like the stag you have fled, having wounded me; I came out, crying, after you, and you had gone away. 2. Shepherds, you who are going there to the hill for your flocks, if by any chance you see him whom I love most dearly, tell him that I am suffering, mourning, dying. 3. In search of my love I will cross those mountains and river banks; I will neither pick the flowers nor fear the beasts, and I will pass forts and frontiers. *She asks the creatures*:

4. Oh woods and thickets, planted by the hand of my beloved, oh green meadow bedecked with flowers, tell me whether he has passed near you! *The creatures reply:* 5. Shedding countless graces, he passed hastily through these thickets, and as he passed, looking at them, by the mere sight of him, left them clothed in beauty. *Bride:* 6. Alas, who can heal me! Yield yourself to me fully and truly now; don't send me any more messengers after today, for they cannot tell me what I want to know. 7. And all the wanderers keep telling me of your countless graces. And they all wound me more deeply, and I am left dying by something mysterious which they keep murmuring. 8. But how can you continue, my life, when you are living far away form your source of life and making for yourself suicidal arrows out of your own inner conceptions of the beloved? 9. Why, since you have wounded my heart, have you not healed it? And since you have stolen it from me, why have you abandoned it thus and not taken away what you have stolen? 10. Cool my madness, for no one can destroy it, and let my eyes see you, for you are their light, and for you alone I wish to have them. 11. Oh crystal spring, if only in your silvery face you would suddenly let take shape the eyes I long for, which I have engraved in my heart! 12. Take them away, beloved, for I am soaring! *Bridegroom:* Come back, dove, for the wounded stag shows himself on the hill, in the breeze of your flight, and cools himself. *Bride:* 13. My beloved, the mountains, the solitary wooded valleys, the distant isles, the sounding rivers, the whistling of the loving breezes; 14. the quiet night, near the break of dawn, the silent music, the sounding solitude, the supper of recreation and love; 15. our bed of flowers, woven of lion caves, stretched out upon purple, built of peace, surmounted by countless golden shields. 16. Following your footsteps the young maidens run wildly out to the road; at the touch of the spark and the taste of the spiced wine, there are waves of divine balm. 17. In my beloved's inner wine cellar I drank, and when I came out, all the way down the meadow I was no longer aware of anything, and I lost the sheep that I had been following before. 18. There he gave me his breast, there he taught me very pleasant knowledge, and I gave him myself indeed, holding nothing back, there I promised him to be his wife. 19. My soul and all my possessions have been used in his service; I no longer herd sheep or have any other job, for my only occupation now is love. 20. So now, if I'm not seen or found again in the pasture after today, you will say that I've let myself be lost; that being in love, I wandered and strayed, and I was won. 21. Of blossoms and emeralds, gathered on cool mornings, we shall make garlands, flowery with your love and woven together with one of my hairs: 22. with only that hair which you watched being wafted on my neck; you looked at it on my neck, and you became imprisoned in it, and you were

wounded by one of my eyes. 23. While you were looking at me, your eyes imprinted upon me your grace; that is why you loved me, and for that reason my eyes were worthy of adoring what they saw in you. 24. Don't despise me, for though you found me to be dark in color, you may well look at me now, after you have looked upon me, for you thereby left grace and beauty in me. 25. Catch the foxes for us, for our vineyard is in bloom, while we make a cluster of roses, and let no one appear upon the mountain. 26. Restrain yourself, deadly north wind; come, west wind, with memories of love, and breathe through my garden, and let its fragrance flow, and my beloved will graze among the flowers. *Bridegroom*: 27. The bride has entered into the pleasant garden we've desired, and she rests pleasantly, reclining her neck upon the beloved's sweet arms. 28. Under the apple tree, there you were first betrothed to me, there I gave you my hand, and you were redeemed where your mother was raped. 29. Swift birds, lions, deer, leaping harts, mountains, valleys, river banks, waters, airs, wakeful warmths and fears of the night. 30. By the pleasant harp and songs of the mermaids I beseech you to lay aside your wreaths and not to touch the wall, so that the bride may more soundly sleep. *Bride*: 31. Oh nymphs of Judea, so long as amber perfumes the flowers and rose bushes, stay in the dwellings on the edge of town, and do not try to reach our threshold. 32. Hide yourself, my darling, and look with your face upon the mountains, and keep our secret; but look upon the companions of her who travels through the distant isles. *Bridegroom*: 33. The little white dove has come back to the ark with the branch, and now the little turtledove has found her longed-for mate on the green riverbanks. 34. In solitude she lived, and in solitude she has laid her nest, and in solitude she is guided all alone by her lover, who was also wounded in solitude by love. *Bride* 35. Let us enjoy one another, beloved, and let us see ourselves in your beauty, going to the mountain or the hill where the pure water gushes up; let us go deeper into the thicket. 36. And then we will go away to the high rock caverns, which are well-hidden, and there we shall enter and taste the juice of pomegranates. 37. There you would show me that thing which my souls was seeking, and you would give me there my love, that thing which you gave me the other day: 38. the breathing of the air, the song of the sweet nightingale, the woods and its charm, in the quiet night of flame which destroys and causes no regrets; 39. for no one saw it, nor did Aminadab appear, and the siege was relaxed, and at the sight of the water the horsemen descended.

Song of Songs 2:8-13

> Listen! My lover!
>> Look! Here he comes,
> leaping across the mountains,
>> bounding over the hills.
> My lover is like a gazelle or a young stag.
>> Look! There he stands behind our wall,
> gazing through the windows,
>> peering through the lattice.
> My lover spoke and said to me,
>> "Arise, my darling,
>> my beautiful one, and come with me.
> See! The winter is past;
>> the rains are over and gone.
> Flowers appear on the earth;
>> the season of singing has come,
> the cooing of doves
>> is heard in our land.
> The fig tree forms its early fruit;
>> the blossoming vines spread their fragrance.
> Arise, come, my darling;
>> my beautiful one, come with me."

Song of Songs 5:2-5

> Listen! My lover is knocking;
> "Open to me, my sister, my darling,
>> my dove, my flawless one.
> My head is drenched with dew,
>> my hair with the dampness of the night."
> I have taken off my robe—
>> must I put it on again?
> I have washed my feet—
>> must I soil them again?
> My lover thrust his hand through the latch-opening;
>> my heart began to pound for him.
> I arose to open for my lover,
>> and my hands dripped myrrh,
>> on the handles of the lock.

Song of Songs 7:1-9

> How beautiful your sandaled feet,
> > O prince's daughter!
> Your graceful legs are like jewels,
> > the work of a craftsman's hands.
> Your naval is a rounded goblet
> > that never lacks blended wine.
> Your waist is a mound of wheat
> > encircled by lilies.
> Your breasts are like two fawns,
> > twins of a gazelle.
> Your neck is like an ivory tower.
> Your eyes are the pools of Heshbon
> > by the gate of Bath Rabbim.
> Your nose is like the tower of Lebanon
> > looking toward Damascus.
> Your head crowns you like Mount Carmel.
> Your hair is like royal tapestry;
> > the king is held captive by its tresses.
> How beautiful you are and how pleasing,
> > O love, with your delights!
> Your stature is like that of the palm,
> > and your breasts are like clusters of fruit.
> I said, "I will climb the palm tree;
> > I will take hold of its fruit."
> May your breasts be like the clusters of the vine,
> > the fragrance of your breath like apples,
> > your mouth like the best wine.

Song of Songs 1:6:

> Do not stare at me because I am dark,
> > Because I am darkened by the sun.
> My mother's sons were angry with me
> > And made me take care of the vineyards
> > my own vineyard I have neglected.

Songs of Songs 5:7:

> The watchmen found me
> > as they made their rounds in the city

They beat me, they bruised me;
    they took away my cloak,
    those watchmen of the walls!

Song of Songs 6:8-14
    (Lover)
    Sixty queens there may be
      and eighty concubines,
      and virgins beyond number;
    But my dove, my perfect one, is unique,
      the only daughter of the one who bore her.
    The maidens saw her and called her blessed;
      the queens and concubines praised her.
    Who is this that appears like the dawn,
      fair as the moon, bright as the sun,
      majestic as the stars in procession?
    I went down to the grove of nut trees
      to look at the new growth in the valley,
      to see if the vines had budded
      or the pomegranites were in bloom.
    Before I realized it,
      my desire set me among the royal chariots of my people.

    (Friends)
    Come back, come back, O Shulamite
    Come back, come back that we may gaze at you!

    (Lover)
    Why would you gaze on the Shulamite
    as on the dance of the Mahanaim?

"The Dream of the Rood"
    Hwaet!
    A dream came to me
      at deep midnight
    when humankind
      kept their beds
    —the dream of dreams!
      I shall declare it.

    It seemed I saw the Tree itself

borne on the air, light wound around it,
—a beam of brightest wood, a beacon clad
in overlapping gold, glancing gems
fair at its foot, and five stones
set in a crux flashed from the crosstree.

Around angels of God
        all gazed upon it.
since first fashioning fair.
        It was not a felon's gallows,
for holy ghosts behold it there,
and men of mould, and the whole Making shone for it
        —*signum* of victory!

        Stained and marred,
stricken with shame, I saw the glory-tree
shine out gaily, sheathed in yellow
decorous gold; and gemstones make
for their Maker's Tree a right mail-coat.

Yet through the masking gold I might perceive
what terrible sufferings were once sustained thereon:
it bled from the right side.
        Ruth in the heart.

Afraid I saw that unstill brightness
change raiment and colour
        —again clad in gold
or again slicked with sweat
        spangled with spilling blood.

Yet lying there a long while
I beheld, sorrowing, the Healer's Tree
till it seemed that I heard how it broke silence,
best of wood, and began to speak:

"Over that long remove my mind ranges
back to the holt where I was hewn down;
from my own stem I was struck away,
        dragged off by strong enemies,
wrought into a roadside scaffold.
        They made me a hoist for wrongdoers.

The soldiers on their shoulders bore me,

until on a hill-top they set me up;
many enemies made me fast there.
　　　　Then I saw, marching toward me,
mankind's brave King;
　　　　He came to climb upon me.

I dared not break or bend aside
against God's will, though the ground itself
shook at me feet. Fast I stood
who falling could have felled them all.

Almighty God ungirded Him,
　　　　eager to mount the gallows,
unafraid in the sight of many:
　　　　He would set free mankind.
I shook when His arms embraced me
　　　　but I durst not bow to ground,
stoop to Earth's surface.
　　　　Stand firm I must.

I was reared up, a rood.
　　　　I raised the great King,
liege lord of the heavens,
　　　　dared not lean from the true.
They drove me through with dark nails:
　　　　on me are the deep wounds manifest,
wide-mouthed hate-dents.
　　　　I durst not harm any of them.
How they mocked at us both!
　　　　I was all moist with blood
sprung from the Man's side
　　　　after He sent forth His soul.

Wry weirds a-many I underwent
upon that hill-top; saw the Lord of Hosts
stretched out stark. Darkness shrouded
the King's corse. Clouds wrapped
its clear shining. A shade went out
wan under cloud-pall. All creation wept,
keened the King's death. Christ was on the Cross.

But there quickly came from afar
earls of the One there. All that I beheld;

had grown weak with grief,
       yet with glad will bent then
meek to those men's hands,
       yielded Almighty God.

They lifted Him down from the leaden pain,
       left me, the commanders,
standing in a sweat of blood.

       I was all wounded with shafts.
They straightened out His strained limbs,
       stood at His body's head,
looked down on the Lord of Heaven
       -for a while He lay there resting-
set to contrive Him a tomb
       in the sight of the Tree of Death,
carved it of bright stone,
       laid in it the Bringer of victory,
spent from the great struggle.
       They began to speak the grief-song,
sad in the sinking light,
       then thought to set out homeward;
their hearts were sick to death,
       their most high Prince
they left to rest there with scant retinue.

Yet we three, weeping, a good while
stood in that place after the song had gone up
from the captains' throats. Cold grew the corse,
fair soul-house.
       They felled us all.
We crashed to ground, cruel Weird,
and they delved for us a deep pit.

The Lord's men learnt of it,
His friends found me...
It was they who girt me with gold and silver."

"Wulf and Eadwacer," "The Wife's Lament," "The Husband's Message"
and "Resignation," are from *Two Literary Riddles in the Exeter book*
Riddle 1 and The Easter Riddle, A Critical Edition with Full Translations,
James E. Anderson (Copyright © 1986 by the University of Oklahoma Pres

"Wulf and Eadwacer"

> For my people it's as if someone sent them a victim.
> They'll eat him up if he comes upon the pack.
> It's not like that for us.
> Wulf's on an island, I'm on another.
> That island's sealed off, encircled by fen.
> Men eager for blood are there on the island.
> They'll eat him up if he comes to the pack.
> Things are not like that for us.
> I dogged by design my Wulf's footsteps in exile.
> When the weather was rainy, and I, wailing one, sat,
> then this man bold in war mounted me with his shoulders.
> It was thus far my pleasure, that it still was my pain.
> Wulf, my Wulf, thoughts of you
> made me sick—your rare returnings
> and a mourning mind, not at all lack of meat.
> Do you hear, wealth watcher? Wulf's bearing off
> our poor whelp to the wood.
> One soon tears asunder what never was joined,
> our song together.

"The Wife's Lament"

> I'll recite this song of myself most sad,
> a tale of my own. Then I can tell
> what sorrows I've suffered since I grew up,
> new ones, and old ones, no more than right now.
> I know always the woe of my wanderings in exile.
> First my lord fled hence from the land,
> over the welling of waves; I had worry in darkness
> where my liege lord on land would be.
> So I left to go plead for my rightful place
> as patronless outcast, in my piteous need.
> Then the former man's kinsmen began to conspire
> with secret scheming so that they might divide us,
> so that farthest apart in the world we lived
> in utmost agony, and I ached with longing.
> My overlord told me to take up a home here.
> I had few loved ones in this plot of land,
> loyal defenders. This is why my mind is downcast.
> Then I had found the man fully matched to me

grim in his spirit, gloomy in mind,
concealing his mind, dwelling on murder
(but) peaceful in manner. Many's the time that we two promised
no cause would divide us except death alone,
no other thing. That's since turned around:
our love is now as if it never had been.
I have far and near my dearly
beloved's blood feud to bear.
I have been told to go live in a grove of the wood,
under an oak tree, in this earthen cave.
Old in this earth hall; I'm all worn out with longing.
Dim are the dales, the hills rising high,
cruel citadels crept over with briars,
a cheerless abode. Often indeed my husband's departure
has seized me here harshly. On earth there are helpmates,
loving ones living, keeping their couches,
while I pace alone in the midnight darkness,
under an oak tree, around and around these pits in the earth.
There I must sit out a long day of summer;
there I may beweep my wanderings in exile,
my many misfortunes. For I never can rest
from my misery of mind,
nor from all the longing that's seized me in this life.
A young man should always be stern in his mind,
hardened the thought of his heart. In this way he shall have
cheerful bearing and breast care besides,
a throng of ceaseless sorrows, be all his joy in the world
from himself alone, be he banned a long way
in a far-off kingdom. [Ah,] that my friend sits
beneath a stone cliff, iced over by storm
a friend weary in spirit, flooded round by water
in a dreary hall! This friend of mine suffers
great anguish of mind: too much he remembers
a happier house. Woe be unto him
who, compelled by longing, must wait for a loved one.

"The Husband's Message"
I was by the sand, near the seashore,
near the waves from the deep, dwelt
firm in my first home. Few there were

of humankind who would ever behold
my spot there in that solitude;
but each dawn the bright breaker
lapped me instead with its wet embrace. Little I thought
that early or late I ever should speak
without mouth over mead [bench]
traffic in words. A great wonder it is,
strange skill to his mind who knows not such things,
how the dagger's point and the dextral hand,
an earl's inner thought and the point together,
thus connected me closely with you, so that I'd
boldly announce for us both as one
a message in speech, so more children of men
should not tell it more widely, our dealing in words.
I want now to say aside to you
(.......) kind of tree, (? from what) kinship I grew.
(Yew) me (? men...) shall in another land
(? set..............) salt streams
(...........................)
I very often on a boat's (........) sought
where my liege lord me (.........)
over high seas. Now I've come hither
on a big ship's planks, and now you shall know
how you should think in your thoughts
of my lord's deep love. I dare to pledge
that there you shall find an honor-bound promise.
Hear! He who engraved this wood then ordered to ask you,
O ring-covered one, yourself recall
in your mind those commitments in words
that you two often uttered in earlier days,
while yet in the mead towns you both had the might
to watch your domain, live in one land,
further your friendship. A feud drove him away
from the glorious nation. Gladly now he himself has commanded
that you make ready to drive through the deeps
as soon as you've heard on the high cliff's head
the woeful cockoo's cry in the wood.
Do not suffer yourself to be kept from the voyage;
let no man living delay your going.
Go seek out the ocean, the seagull's home:
mount the seagoing ship, so that off to the South,

over the course of the main, you find your man.
There he, prince, is expecting you.
No wish in the world can (? be)
more on his mind, since he told me himself
when almight God should willingly grant
(? that you two) together may thenceforth (? mete out)
to true men and retainers (? your costly treasures),
riveted rings. He has enough
of hammered go(ld........)
...) a foreign folk have his home,
fair field(s.........
? of loyal) heroes, though here my (lord)
friend (..........)
driven by need, shoved his ship out,
and had to (? go alone) onto the (? lashing) of waves,
travel the floodpath, take flight in haste,
stir the sea streams. Now the man has
won out over woes; he lacks no delights,
neither horses nor jewels nor joys of mead,
nothing on earth of an earl's treasures,
if he may have, noble's daughter, enough of you.
Above the old vow of your common devotion
I (? hear) in a sum S,R together,
EA, W, and D declare with an oath
that by him who is living he would fulfill
the pledge of faith and the partner's promise
that you two often uttered in former days.

"Resignation"

May the almighty God own me,
the holy Lord help me! You shaped both heaven and earth
and all the wonders, my wondrous King,
that lie thereon, my Lord eternal,
great things, and manifold. To you, great God,
I consign my soul and my very own body,
and my words, and my work, wise Lord,
and all my limbs, Keeper of light,
and the manifold thoughts of my mind.
Show me a sign, Shepherd of stars,
where for my soul it were wisest

to mark the way of the Maker's will,
that for you I may flourish in all my affairs,
and increase, righteous King,
your ends in myself. Let not the arch-thief
strike from the shadow. Though I've served the Creator,
the King of glory, Lord for all kingdoms,
more feebly than was my first aim,
in your mercy forgive, God ever-living,
my bitter bad deeds. With my mind on atonement,
O Glory of kings, I come near, if I may.
Lend me, my Lord, some repose and insight
and patience and purpose to meet all things
that you will send me, sound King of truth,
to know me in trials. Now you know of me
many monstrous deeds; yet admit me,
O Judge, in your mercy, though I have done more
grievous wrongs than God forgave me.
Therefore I have need to obtain nonetheless,
some kindness of you, good heavenly King,
in my dwindling days, to see and desire
life hereafter, so that then gracious God
may give me there gladness eternal,
allow me to live, though I've purged my offenses
more slowly than meets the commands
of the holy Power of heaven. Hear me, for you had given me here
many   . I put my hope in you,
my fearful precautions, that fixed and firm
it may stand established. Lift up my spirit,
good King of souls, to the profit already prepared.
Now I hasten to you, Father of humankind,
away from this world, now that I come I'll
depart in a very short while. Welcome me, then,
Guide of all fates, into your glorious joy,
and let me pass, Lord of beloved ones,
preserve my soul. When too many foes
are given to hatreds, then I have help
from the Lord, though in my time I earned little
honor. But let angels yet take me
into your presence, preserving King,
O Measurer, for your mercy's sake, though I've done many
evils day by day. But never let devils

lead me, your limb, on the loathsome journey,
lest they might be pleased with their ancient plotting
by which they, the arrogant angels,
to themselves seemed better than Christ eternal.
In that belief they deluded themselves; thus they must long
endure exile, cursed creatures.
Stand by me and repel them whenever a storm may come
against my spirit; then spare
my soul, mighty Sovereign,
defend it, sustain it, Father of men,
(it is) busied with cares. Cure it, God of ages,
O Judge with strong might. My heart is stained
even now with sins, and for my soul I am
sometimes afraid, though for me you have furnished
many honors on this earth. To you be all thanks
for the goodness and kindness which you have given me.
No merits for this were in me [among.......]
yet from it all I will find strength
and be happy, and hope for myself,
adorn myself for the journey hence, and myself make haste
toward the pilgrimage I must depart on,
make my soul ready, and for my own good suffer it all
with a glad bearing, now that I'm girded
fast in my heart. The Lord surely levies against me
certain sins which I cannot myself,
clearly discover. I have provoked
God, champion of men, for which I was chastized
thus bitterly before the world, so that my works
were great before men, that I might undergo
a harsh martyrdom. I am not a just judge,
wise before multitudes; thus I speak these words
with a sorrowing heart, since there once came
hardships to me upon the earth. I bore it always,
year after year–thank God for it all!–
miseries of mind more than anything else,
fear among the folk; thus I am driven
poor from my homeland. Against this the lone pilgrim,
without joy of his people, can no longer last,
a patronless outcast: the Lord is angry with him.
Men of his following mourn,
and so each time assist him,

add to his agonies and he suffers it all,
the wounding words of men, and his heart is ever sad,
his mind downcast at dawn. Of myself most especially
I tell this sad tale, and speak of a journey,
saddened by longing, and think of the sea.
My   does not know with what I might buy a boat on the sea,
a ship on the main. I have not much gold,
nor, indeed, the friend who might foster me
for the voyage. Devoid now of means,
I cannot myself fulfill my desire.
The wood may flourish of itself, expect its fate,
shoot forth its branches; because of calumny I cannot
love in my heart anyone who is human,
no man in my homeland. Alas, my Lord,
my mighty Spokesman, how sick I am in my spirit,
How bitterly hurt! The cure comes from you
after this life. I cannot live
free of afflictions in this earth's light
by any means, miserable being;
when for myself I had shelter from strangers,
fitting kinsfolk, for me woe was always
the reward of loves such as I've lived.
As yet it's still best, when one cannot himself
foil his fate, that he suffer well.

"Drunken Boat"

> As I floated down impassive Rivers
> I no longer felt the tug of boatmen's ropes,
> Screaming redskins had made targets of them,
> Had nailed them naked to painted stakes.
>
> Carrier of Flemish grain and English cotton,
> I was unmindful of my cargo.
> When the Rivers had finished the noise of my boatmen
> They let me float along where I wished.
>
> Last winter upon the furious clapping of the waves,
> More deaf than the brain of a child
> I ran—and the uprooted peninsulas
> Did not suffer more triumphant chaos.
>
> The tempests blessed my maritime risings.

Lighter than a cork I danced ten nights on the billows
That are called the rolling, eternal, murderous tide,
And I did not miss the foolish eyes of lanterns.

Sweeter to me than sour apples to a child
The green water seeped into my hull of pine.
It washed the stains of blue wine and the vomitings
From me, scattering helm and grappling.

And since then I am bathed in the poem
Of that sea infused with stars and milky,
Devouring the blue-greens, where, floating paley
And enraptured, a sad drowned corpse sometimes descends.

Where suddenly staining the blueness, delirious
And slow rhythms under the glaring of day,
Stranger than alcohol, more vast than lyres,
The bitter rednesses of love ferment!

I know the heavens split with bolts, waterspouts,
Surfs, and currents; I know evening
And dawn exalted like a rising flock of doves,
And I have sometimes seen what man thought he saw.

I have seen the low sun tainted with mystic horrors,
Luminant with long violet coagulations;
Like actors in ancient dramas,
Far away the waves roll their dovecote shivers.

I have dreamed green night with startled snows,
Kisses climbing slowly to the eyes of the seas,
The risings of unheard saps,
And the yellow and blue call of singing phosphors.

For months entire, I have followed the surge,
Storming reefs, like stampeding herds,
Without imagining that Mary's luminous feet
Could curb the snout of the short-winded Oceans.

I have collided, you know, with unbelievable Floridas,
Tangling with blossoms the eyes of panthers, with skins
Of men the rainbows held like reigns
Upon the horizon of the seas, with glaucous herds.

I have seen the marshes ferment, enormous snare
Where a whole Leviathan rotted upon the reeds;

The collapse of waters in the midst of calms,
And the distances tumbling toward the abyss.

Glaciers, silver suns, pearly billows, hot-coal skies,
Hideous beachings at the bottom of dark gulfs
Where giant serpents devour roaches
Dropping from trees wrung with dark perfumes.

Sometimes, martyr weary of poles and zones,
The sea, whose sob made my rusts sweet,
Showed to me her shadow-flowers of gusty yellows,
And I was left then like a woman on her knees.

Peninsula afloat, upon my planks the quarrels
And the shams of the clamorous birds with blond eyes
And I drifted, until across my frail lines
The drowned descended to sleep upside down.

Now I, boat lost in the tresses of the coves,
Thrown by the hurricane into the birdless ether,
I, whose drunken carcass the Monitors and the Hanse sailing ships
Would not have fished out of the water,

Free, reeking, surmounted by violet mists,
I, who pierced the reddening partition-sky
That brings exquisite confection for good poets,
Sunshine lichen and azure snot,

Who ran scarred with electric moons,
Foolish bark, escorted by black sea horses,
When the July's made the ultramarine skies
Collapse by cudgel blows into burning craters.

I, who trembled hearing the rut of Behemoths
And dense maelstroms moaning in fifty places,
Eternal mesh of blue immobilities,
I miss the Europe of ancient parapets.

I have seen sidereal archipelagoes and islands,
Where the delirious skies are spread.
Is it on these bottomless nights that you sleep and depart
Million golden birds, O future Life?

True, yes, I have wept too much. The dawns are heartrending
Every moon is atrocious, and every sunny sky bitter.
Sour love has swollen me with intoxicating torpors.

Oh, that my keel would burst! Oh, that I might be joined to the sea!

If I desire European waters, it is the pond
Black and cold where towards perfumed twilights
A stooping child, full of sadness, releases
A boat, as fragile as a May butterfly.

I can no longer breast the wake
Of cotton carriers, bathed in your langours, o waves,
Nor penetrate the pride of banners and torches,
Nor swim beneath the horrid eyes of bridges.

"The Virgin, Vivacious and Beautiful Today"

The virgin, vivacious and beautiful today
    Shall it tear for us now with a drunken wing's blow,
    This hard lake forgotten which neath powdered snow
    Is haunted by flights which have ne'er flown away;
    A swan of the past remembers 'tis he
    Magnificent, but who is vanquished at last
    For not having known where to go when the blast
Of drear winter blows o'er the old white ennui.
    All his neck will then shake off the white agony,
    Inflicted by space on the bird who denied it,
    But not horror of earth where his plumage is caught.
    Fantom his brightness assigns to this spot,
    Disdainfully dreaming there does he sit,
    In cold bitter exile and proud apathy.

"The Whiteness of the Whale" (*Moby Dick*, chapter 42):

What the White Whale was to Ahab, has been hinted; what, at times, he was to me, as yet remains unsaid. Aside from those more obvious considerations touching Moby Dick, which could not but occasionally awaken in any man's soul some alarm, there was another thought, or rather vague, nameless horror concerning him, which at times by its intensity completely over-powered all the rest; and yet so mystical and well nigh ineffable was it, that I almost despair of putting it in a comprehensible form. It was the whiteness of the whale that above all things appalled me. But how can I hope to explain myself here; and yet, in some dim and random way, explain myself I must, else all these chapters might be naught...

"Battle Hymn of the Republic"

Mine eyes have seen the glory of the coming of the Lord,
He is trampling out the vintage where the grapes of wrath are stored,
He hath loos'd the fateful lightning of His terrible swift sword,
His truth is marching on!

Glory, glory hallelujah!
Glory, glory hallelujah
Glory, glory hallelujah!
His truth is marching on!

I have seen Him in the watch fires of a hundred circling camps;
They have builded Him an altar in the ev'ning dews and damps;
I can read His righteous sentence by the dim and flaring lamps,
His day is marching on.
(Chorus)

I have read a fiery gospel writ in burnish'd rows of steel:
"As ye deal with My contemners, so with you My grace shall deal";
Let the Hero born of woman crush the serpent with His heal,
Since God is marching on.
(Chorus)

He has sounded forth the trumpet that shall never call retreat;
He is sifting out the hearts of men before His judgement seat.
Oh, be swift, my soul, to answer Him! Be jubliant my feet!
Our God is marching on.
(Chorus)

In the beauty of the lillies Christ was born across the sea,
With a glory in His bosom that transfigures you and me;
As He died to make men holy let us die to make men free,
While God is marching on.
(Chorus)

"Is There for Honest Poverty"

Is there for honest Poverty
That hings his head, an' a' that;
The coward slave—we pass him by,
We dare be poor for a' that!

For a' that, an' a' that,
Our toils obscure, an' a' that,
The rank is but the guinea's stamp,
The man's the gowd for a' that.

What though on hamely fare we dine,
Wear hoddin grey, an' a' that?
Gie fools their silks, and knaves their wine,
A man's a man for a' that:
For a' that, an' a' that,
Their tinsel show, an' a' that;
The honest man, tho' e'er sae poor,
Is king o' men for a' that.

Ye see yon birkie ca'd "a lord,"
Wha' struts, an' stares, an' a' that;
Tho' hundreds worship at his word.
He's but a cuif for a' that:
For a' that, an' a' that,
His ribband, star, an' a' that;
The man o' independent mind,
He looks an' laughs at a' that.

A prince can mak a belted knight,
A marquis, duke, an' a that;
But an honest man's aboon his might,
Guid faith, he mauna fa' that!
For a' that, an' a' that,
Their dignities, an' a' that;
The pith o' sense, an' pride o' worth,
Are higher rank than a' that.

Than let us pray that come it may,
(As come it will for a' that),
That Sense and Worth o'er a' the earth,
Shall bear the gree, an' a' that.
For a' that, an' a' that,
It's comin yet for a' that,
That man to man, the world o'er,
Shall brothers be for a' that.

"To Dante"

That is your hardest riddle where you say
    that Love fed Beatrice your live heart.
    I find one clue that's offered through your art,
    where you call me, "won soul," as I would say.
    And so I dare to see my Lord's own form
    shining in your solitary room,
    carrying your lady in a swoon,
    wrapped up in red cloth and unadorned.
He wed you to her mystically (though she
    and you would never wed on earth) and sealed
    you in the love your verse would celebrate.
    When Jesus turned, and wept, and took your mate,
    He let you feel
    The horror from which faith would set you free.